AF470482

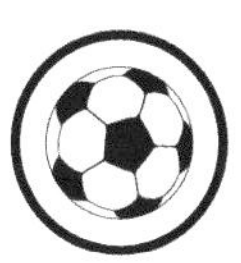

MITJA VELIKONJA

THE CHOSEN FEW

AESTHETICS AND IDEOLOGY IN FOOTBALL-FAN GRAFFITI AND STREET ART

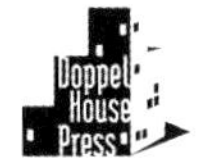

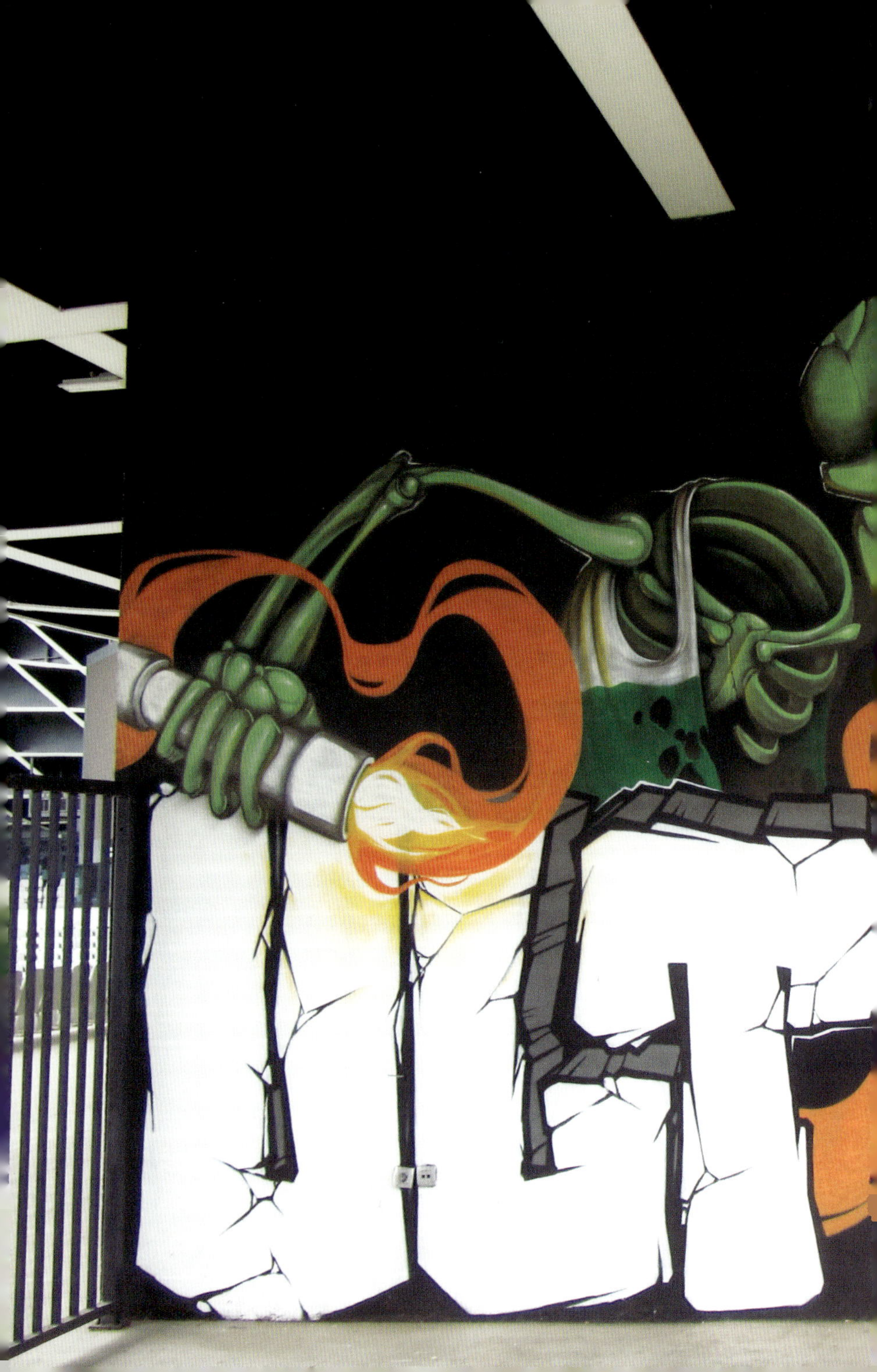

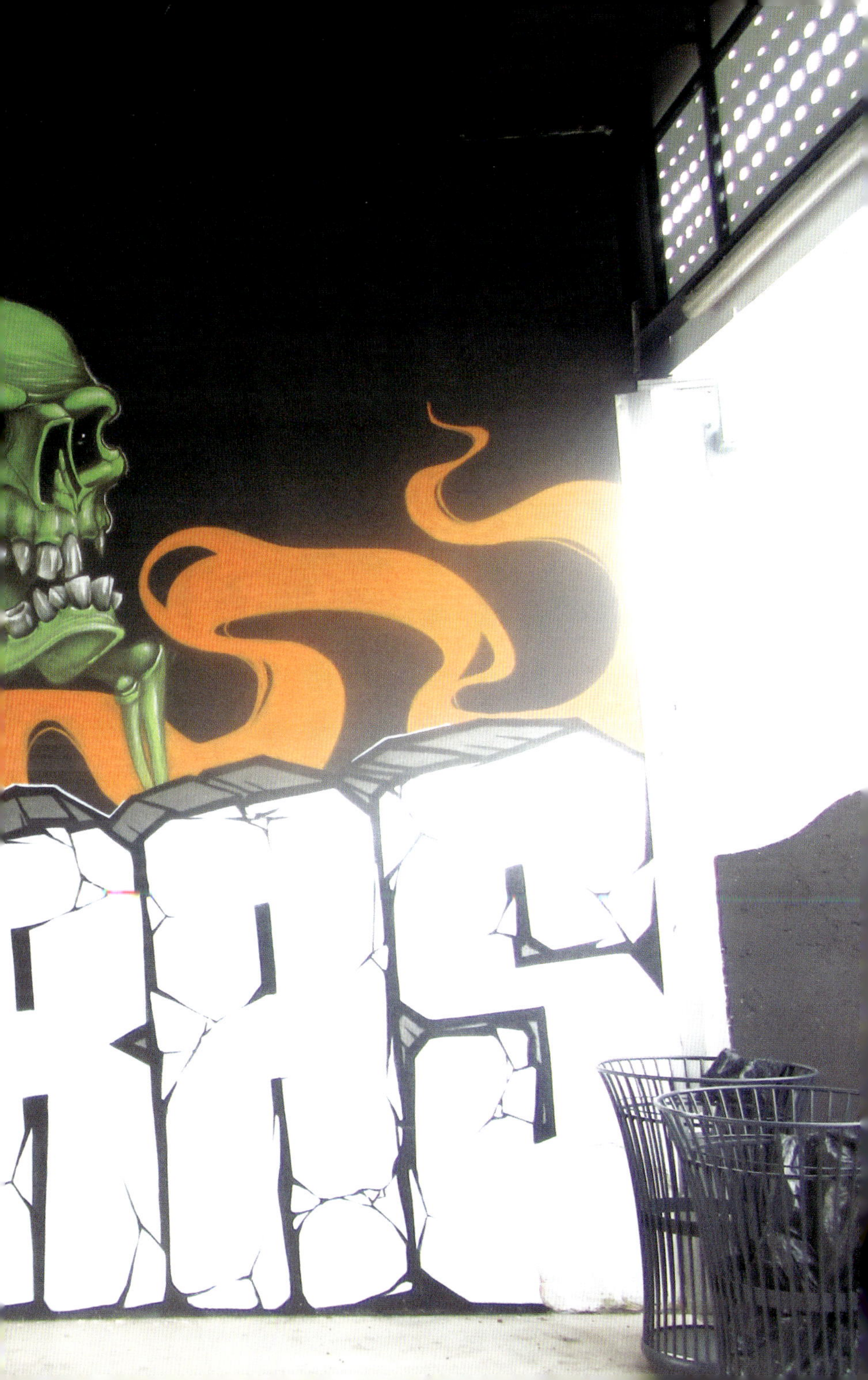

Mitja Velikonja
THE CHOSEN FEW: Aesthetics and Ideology in
Football-Fan Graffiti and Street Art

Significantly adapted and excerpted texts from
Chapters 10–11 and the Conclusion in
Post-Socialist Political Graffiti in the Balkans and Central Europe,
Edn. 1 by Mitja Velikonja, © 2019 Routledge UK.
Reproduced by permission of Taylor & Francis Group.

Book design: Tauras Stalnionis
Editor and typesetting: Carrie Paterson

Previous page: *Ultras*; by *Green Dragons*, fans of FC Olimpija
Ljubljana; mural; Ljubljana, Slovenia; 2019.

Following page left: *La resistente — ASD — Atleti socialisti*
(*Socialist sportsmen*); Italian left-leaning supporters of
amateur, self-organized local football (and sport in general);
sticker; Genova, Italy; 2020.

Following page right: *aachen* with altered Adidas logo over
the top of *Sotto cultura Ultras* (*Ultras subculture*); by unidentified ultras; stickers; Aachen, Germany; 2012.

Publisher's Cataloging-in-Publication data

Names: Velikonja, Mitja, author.
Title: The chosen few : aesthetics and ideology in football-fan graffiti and
street art / Mitja Velikonja.
Description: Includes bibliographical references. | Los Angeles, CA:
DoppelHouse Press, 2021.
Identifiers: LCCN: 2021938022 | ISBN: 9781954600027 (paperback) |
9781954600089 (ebook)
Subjects: LCSH Soccer fans--Graffiti. | Soccer fans--Europe. | Soccer
fans--Slovenia. | Soccer fans--United States. | Street art. | BISAC ART /
Graffiti & Street Art | SOCIAL SCIENCE / Anthropology / Cultural &
Social | SPORTS & RECREATION / Soccer | HISTORY / Europe / Eastern
Classification: LCC GT3912 .V45 2021 | DDC 751.7/3--dc23

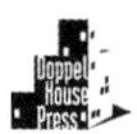

DoppelHouse Press | Los Angeles

Contents

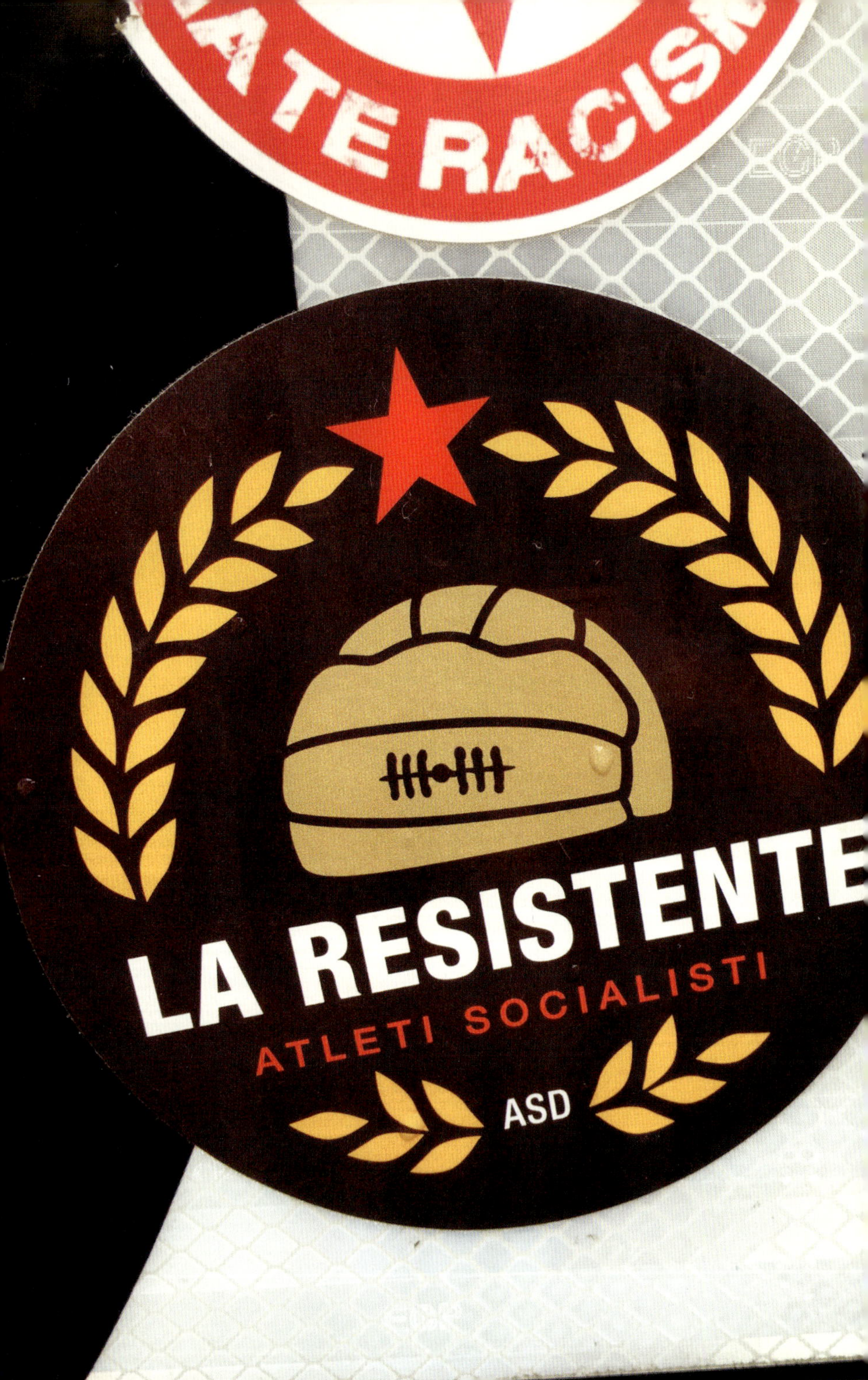
ATE RACISM
LA RESISTENTE
ATLETI SOCIALISTI
ASD

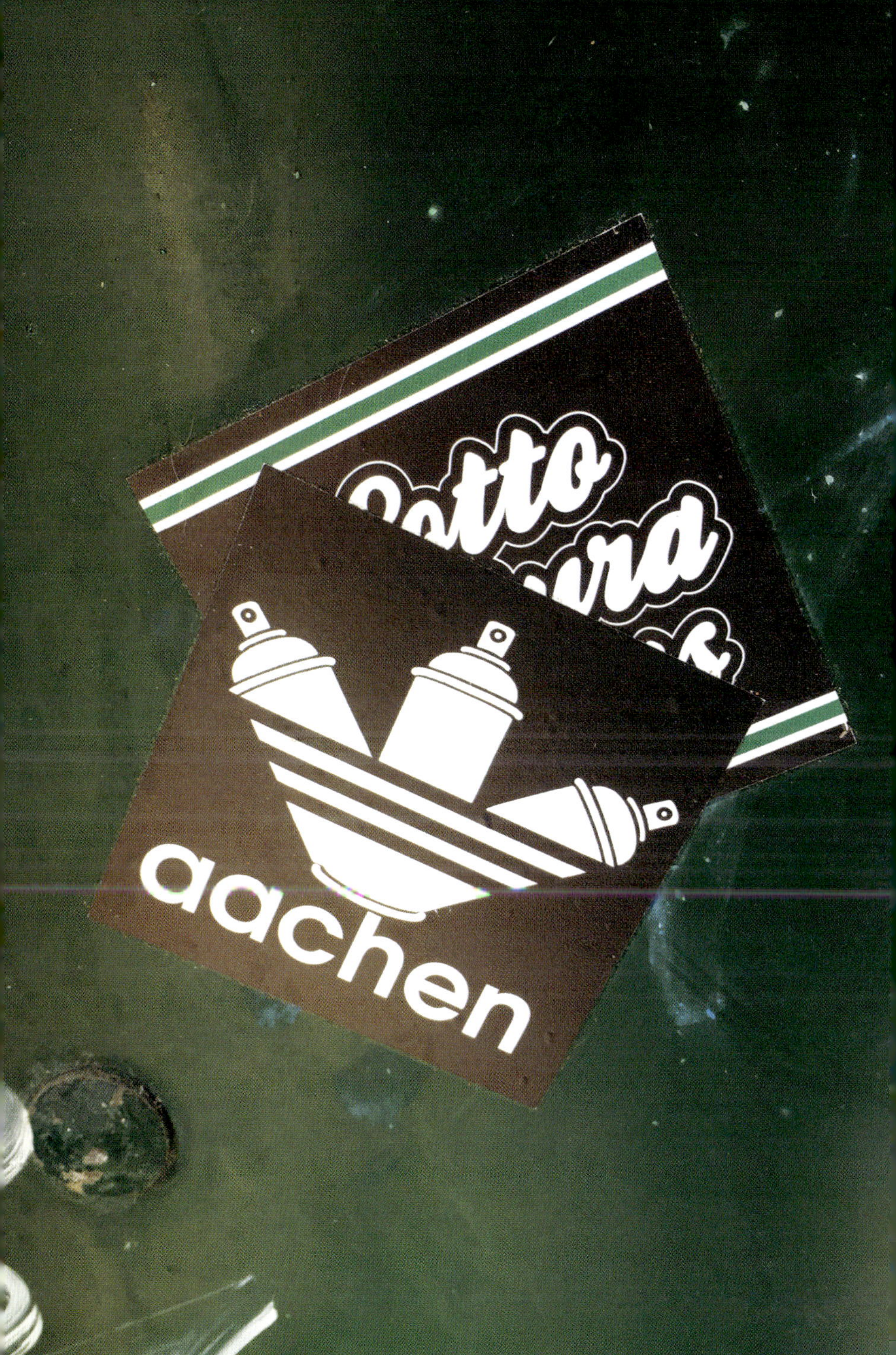
aachen

I. MAPPING FOOTBALL——-FAN GRAFFITI AND STREET ART

Wandering without a plan through the labyrinth of narrow streets of South Manhattan, armed with my camera and curiosity for the unconventional, I was struck by an image on the wall. Not particularly visually attractive, it was lost in the company of immensely more evocative graffiti, stickers, stencils, various inscriptions, these urban frescoes of contemporary metropolises. It said simply, in Italian, *Juve merda!* — referring to FC Juventus from Turin, one of the most popular Italian and most successful European clubs with an impressive number of trophies — *Juve, is shit!*

If I were anywhere in Europe, not only in Italy, I wouldn't have paid special attention to it. Coming from Slovenia, a small country between Central Europe, The Balkans and the Mediterranean, I'm used to such images. Walls on the *Old Continent* are literally covered with all kinds of football-fan graffiti, stickers, stencils, posters, inscriptions, graffiti-battles (cross-out wars) and murals. From the main roads to city centers, from self-declared ghettos to stadiums: football fans make it instantly and completely clear who's the boss here, who *rules* the city or town, which club is *ours*, who they like and who they hate. For them, it is of crucial importance whether you are *Milanista* or *Interista* (two FCs from Milan); *Romanista* or member of *Irriducibili* (rivals from Rome); *Grobar* or *Delija*;[1] *Het Legioen* (*The Legion*, fans of FC Feyenoord, Rotterdam) or *AFCA* (a hooligan club of FC Ajax, Amsterdam); fan of Istanbul's rivals Fenerbahçe, Beşiktaş or Galatasaray; fan of Wisła or of Cracovia — foes from the same city of Kraków, fighting what is known for the locals as *The Holy War* between them since the beginning of the 20th century.

But for anyone interested in urban subcultures, that particular New York Ultra graffiti is significant for two reasons: it is something that simply shouldn't be there. Football — *soccer*, to be completely clear in American English, is still something hopelessly (mostly) European and Latin American. Although it has become a global phenomenon, it is still the most preferred sport in these countries. In the United States, other sports like basketball, American football, ice-hockey and baseball are immensely more widespread and more popular.

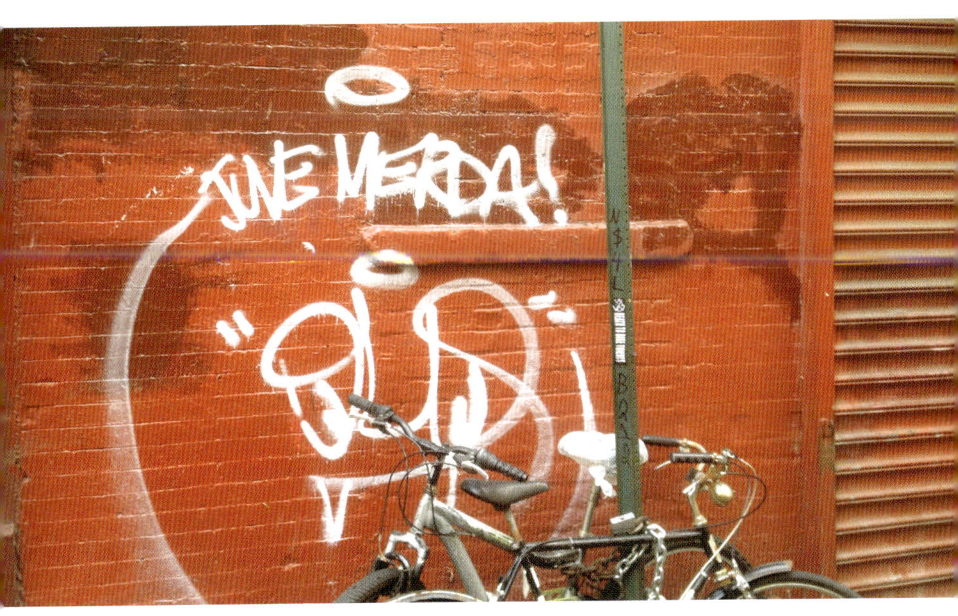

Juve Merda (*Juventus is shit*); ultra graffiti; New York, USA; 2018.

Soccer fans in the U.S.A.

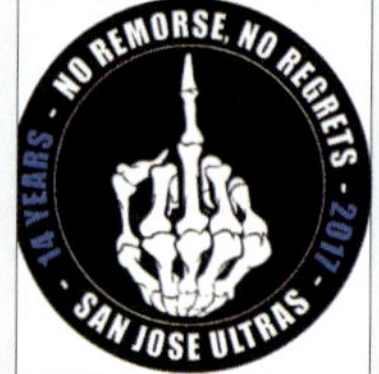

In the United States, soccer has been growing in popularity ever since Major League Soccer (MLS) was established for U.S. and Canadian soccer teams starting in 1993. In fact, soccer was, until recently, best recognized for its women's teams (in contrast to American football and baseball, which have no women's equivalent). The U.S. women's national team is the most successful in international women's soccer with a series of titles.

On the football club (FC) fan level, writer and reporter James Montague (2020) describes several novel specifics of the nine Ultras' groups that are united under the Los Angeles FC: women hold important positions in these groups; *capotifosi* (leaders of the fan groups) travel to Europe to study its football-fan culture; because of MLS policy, their (visual) messages are strictly apolitical; their honor codes forbid racist, sexist and misogynist chants; they support Gay Pride; they work with local street-artists; and they are closely connected to (Latin-American) immigrant cultures.

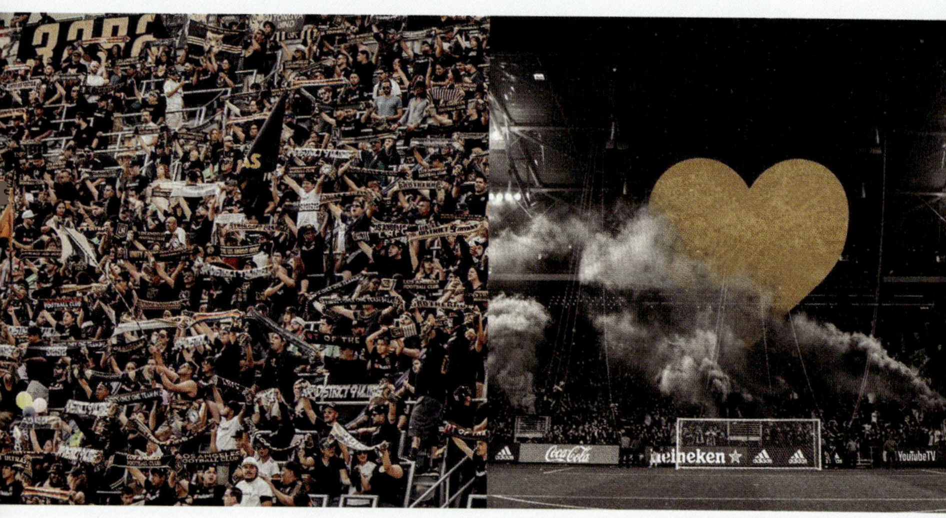

Above: *No Remorse, No Regrets*; sticker by *San Jose Ultras*, fans of San Jose Earthquakes; San Jose, CA, USA; 2017. Image via Instagram.

Below: LAFC 3252 ultra fan section in gold and black club colors with pride flags (left) and piro (right), 2019. Images via Instagram.

Even when it comes to "more American" sports, there's a striking difference between the European and American urbanscape: in the United States, there are practically no sport-related graffiti and street art, while in Europe, they are everywhere. Whether you like it or not, you are a constant witness to the fans' graffiti territorial marking. Secondly, although New York was and is one of the world's centers of graffiti and street-art culture, they are still considered vandalism and damage to public and private property, and their authors are persecuted. Paradoxically, one of the most original, most typical American contributions to the world of radical aesthetic is still criminalized — or, on the other hand, contradictatorily accepted into the artistic mainstream, meaning locked in galleries and art museums.

That's why I took this controversial example as the starting point of my short book that deals with one particular aspect of my broader and long-lasting interest in graffiti and street art. Over 20-plus years of systematic and intensive fieldwork, research, and comparative studies of visual ideologies of street art and graffiti, I have written and co-edited scientific and popular articles in journals at home and abroad; given public presentations and academic lectures in university courses in Slovenia and elsewhere, including Yale University, Columbia University and NYU; led workshops and seminars; guided graffiti tours for students and the wider public; and compiled my theoretical, methodological, historical and comparative approaches into a comprehensive analytical book with Routledge, *Post-Socialist Political Graffiti in the Balkans and Central Europe*, from which this book is partially excerpted and expanded upon.

I have compiled this book from my personal archive of around 25,000 photographs of graffiti and street art, taken from various countries on different continents. All these years, together with other political graffiti, I also have been taking photos of graffiti and street art by avid football fans or, to use insider jargon, a global-ized Italian word, *tifosi* (deriving from *tifo*, an Italian term for supporting a sports team). Their numbers rise to the thousands, examples originate from practically all corners of football-addicted Europe: from Russia to the British Islands, from Scandinavia and Germany to the Mediterranean — but mostly from my region, Central and Eastern Europe. Here, in the words of foot-ball journalist Robert O'Connor, "sports and politics are familiar bedfellows" (2021: xi).

Having performed a comparative, a historical and finally a semiotic analysis, examining the current fan graffiti as well as graffiti from the clubs' pasts, it is clear that above all, football-fan graffiti and street art always need to be contextualized in time and space. My photographs are amateur, not professional. When I say amateur, I mean not only something about their technical quality, but also amateur in the etymologic sense of the Latin word *amator*, a lover of such visual expressions. As a "blissful amateur" — to borrow Dubravka Ugrešić's term (2008: 43) — I am not proud of the technical imperfection of my shots, but I did try to capture all that piqued my interest.

So, I'm interested mostly in graffiti and street-art pieces made by football fans or *ultras* who — accord-ing to James Montague in his a fascinating comparative study of this global phenomenon, based on his exten-sive knowledge, first-hand experiences and interviews — "became one of the world's most populous youth subcultures" (2020: xv). To analyze and understand them, I used analytic repertoire unusual for studies of sports phenomena, combining visual cultural studies, art theory, critics of ideology and transitology.[2] This analysis leaves aside other public visualizations of these *weekend warriors* (choreographies or, in short, *choreo*, pyrotechnics or *pyro*, dress codes, tattoos, interior design of their places, web pages, FB profiles, blogs, magazines, etc.), non-visual representations (chants, club anthems, unofficial songs, cheering, their

[2] By transitology I mean interdis-ciplinary study of different interconnected processes of democratization and pluralization of societies once ruled by author-itarian regimes: in this particular case, those in post-socialist Europe.

slang, expressions, etc.), their pre-game rituals (the organized procession of fans to the stadium), their ways of organizing and their group dynamics.[3]

This study not only researches, but also problematizes football-fan discourse in general, as it is represented in different specific ways in their graffiti and street art. To get a credible insight and precise idea of what it looks like, this book deliberately includes some very disturbing and deeply offensive terms, phrases, images and symbols which are an inseparable part of it. Graphically, these words and statements, the ideological speech of this subculture, is always written in *italics* to be clearly separated from my analytic interpretations, which sharply confront them.

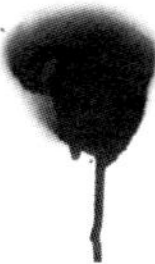

I understand graffiti and street art as specific, two- or three-dimensional illegal visual expressions conveying messages in connection with the public space in which they are created. They can be found in every public space: on walls, sidewalks, fences, bridges, underpasses, sports fields (especially basketball courts and skate parks), traffic signs, on and in public transport vehicles, public toilets, bus and train stations, park benches, waiting rooms and schools, trees, doors of electrical panels, etc.

More specifically, graffiti is a plural noun denoting two-dimensional multi- or monochromatic, figurative or abstract wall paintings done with the help of spray cans, felt-tip pens, markers, sprayers, various types of paints, shoe polish, chalk, etc. (see the next example of a *Green Dragons* of Olimpija Ljubljana's graffiti, featuring a masked character with green robe in a fighting posture). Street art developed later, in the last 25 or 30 years: as it is "a descendant of graffiti" (Crommelin 2016: 4),

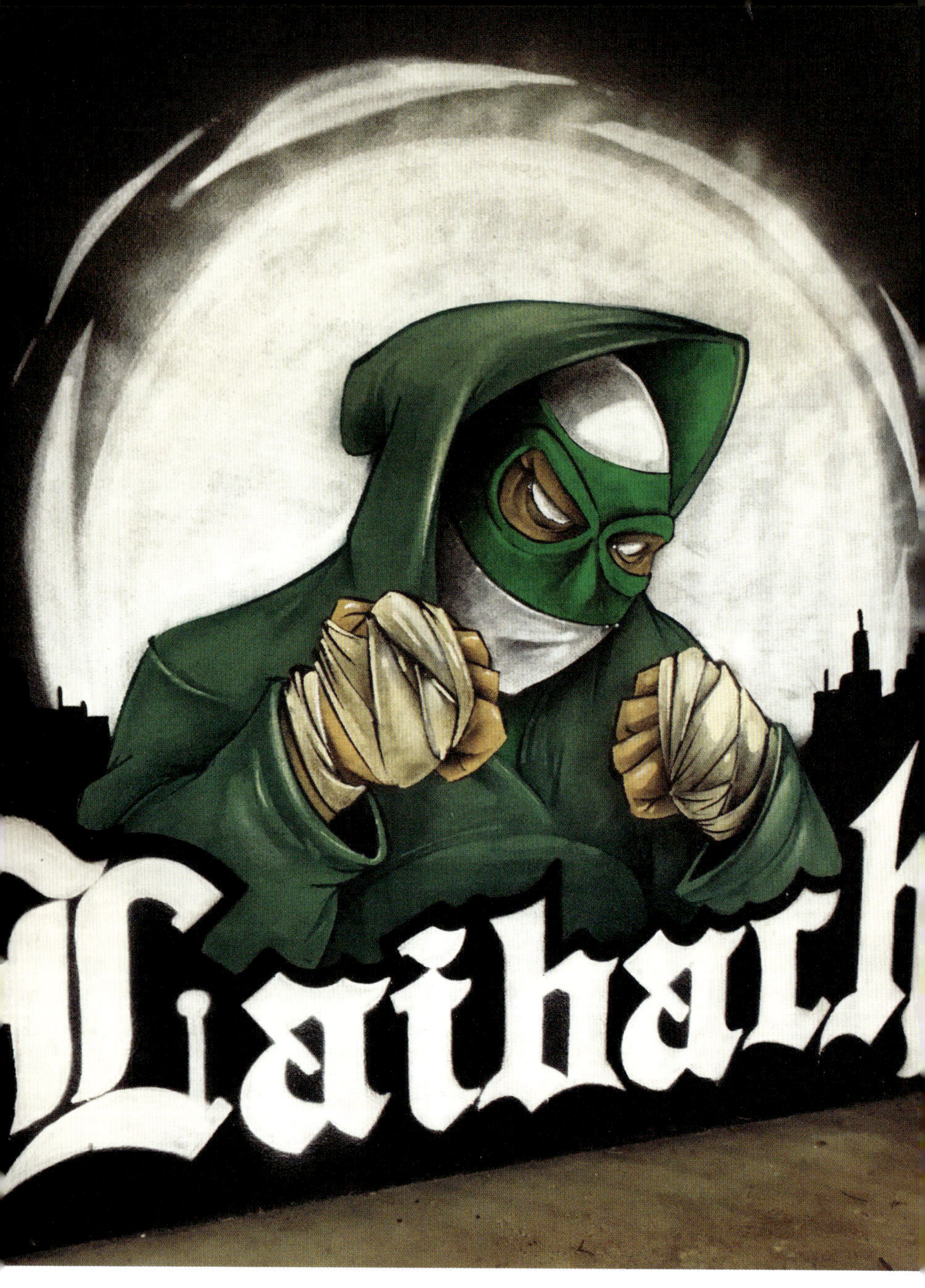

Above: *Laibach* (German for *Ljubljana*); by *Green Dragons*, fans of FC Olimpija Ljubljana; graffiti; Ljubljana, Slovenia; 2021.

it is often referred to as post-graffiti art. It augments the two spatial dimensions with a third one — on top of or incised into the surface — and compliments the graffiti spray cans with a whole range of other creative utensils.

Some of the most well-known types of these 3-D forms are stencils, stickers, and posters. See the following examples of fans of FC Hajduk from Vrsar, Croatia; the *Sparta Casuals* from FC Sparta Prague; and Partizan Belgrade's *Grobari*, which is actually an invitation to a party and features a hooligan with a tattooed cross on his forehead, a pit bull also with a cross on his forehead, and Death with a scythe, all with angry looks on their faces.

Other popular 3-D forms include murals like the large image of Dutch striker Robin van Persie in Rotterdam, where he started and finished his career in FC Feyenoord; public installations and visual interventions; scratchiti (for example: *Armada*, fans of FC Rijeka scratchiti) and scribbles in public spaces (like the one I found on the public telephone in Genova, calling out *Forza Juve /Forward Juventus/*); latrinalia and various other forms of visual interventions on any given surface (scratching, punching holes, chiselling, burning out, hollowing out, leaving prints or writing in freshly poured concrete, etc.).

Football-fan graffiti and street art — as opposed to recently co-opted graffiti practices — fall outside of the fine arts; they are neither an apology for the social inertia of their authors, nor depoliticized through a mediation of their illegality, publicness, aesthetic disruption, and ideological dissensus. They remain on external walls and not between four walls, and thus serve a critical public function: by destroying aesthetic harmony and the seamlessness of the political illusion around them in a Brecht-like manner, they provoke people into participation, into an aesthetic and ethical awakening.

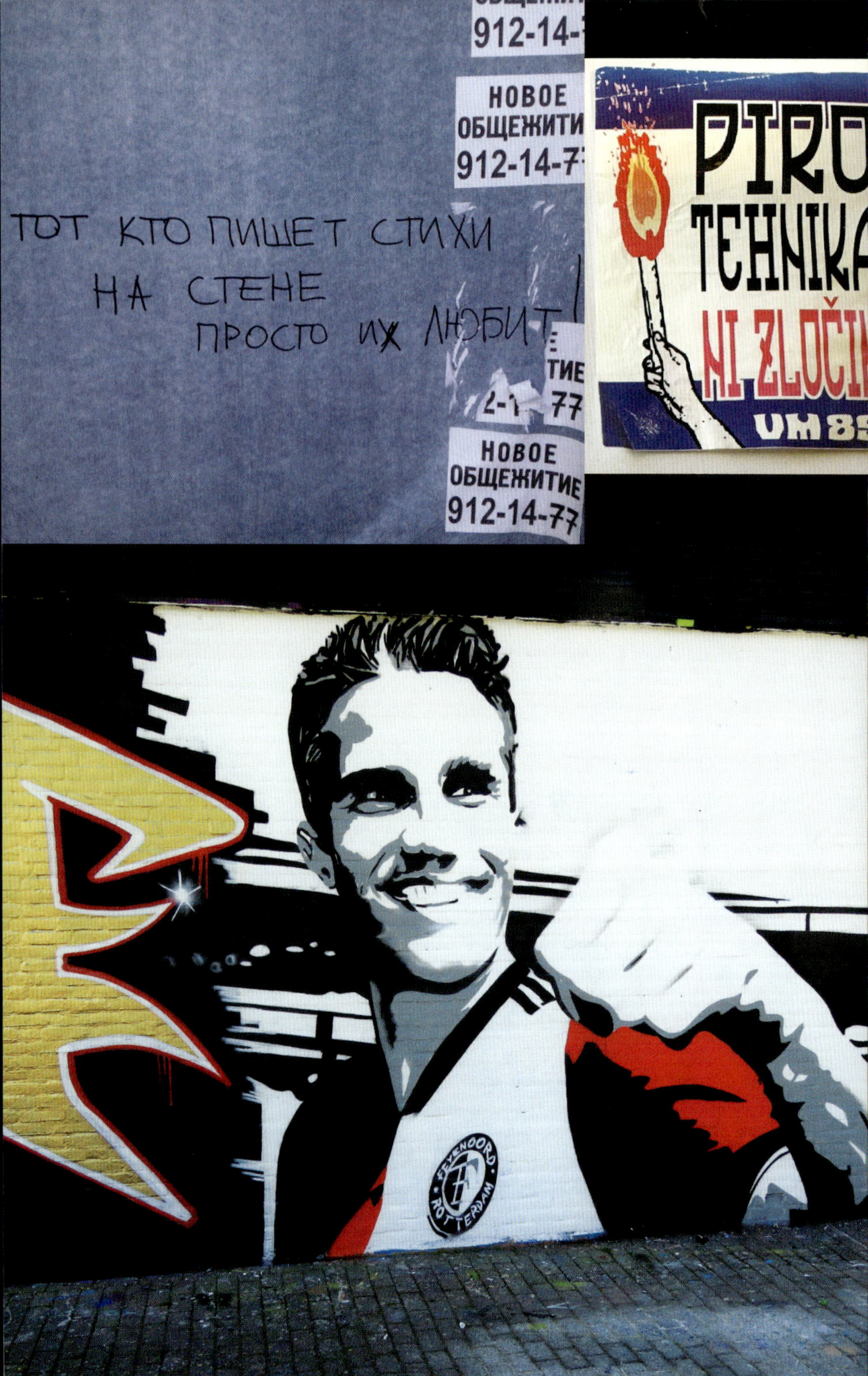

ОБЩЕЖИТ
912-14-7
НОВОЕ
ОБЩЕЖИТИ
912-14-7
ТОТ КТО ПИШЕТ СТИХИ
НА СТЕНЕ
ПРОСТО ИХ ЛЮБИТ
ТИЕ
2-1 77
НОВОЕ
ОБЩЕЖИТИЕ
912-14-77
PIRO
TEHNIKA
NI ZLOČI
UM 85
FEYENOORD
ROTTERDAM

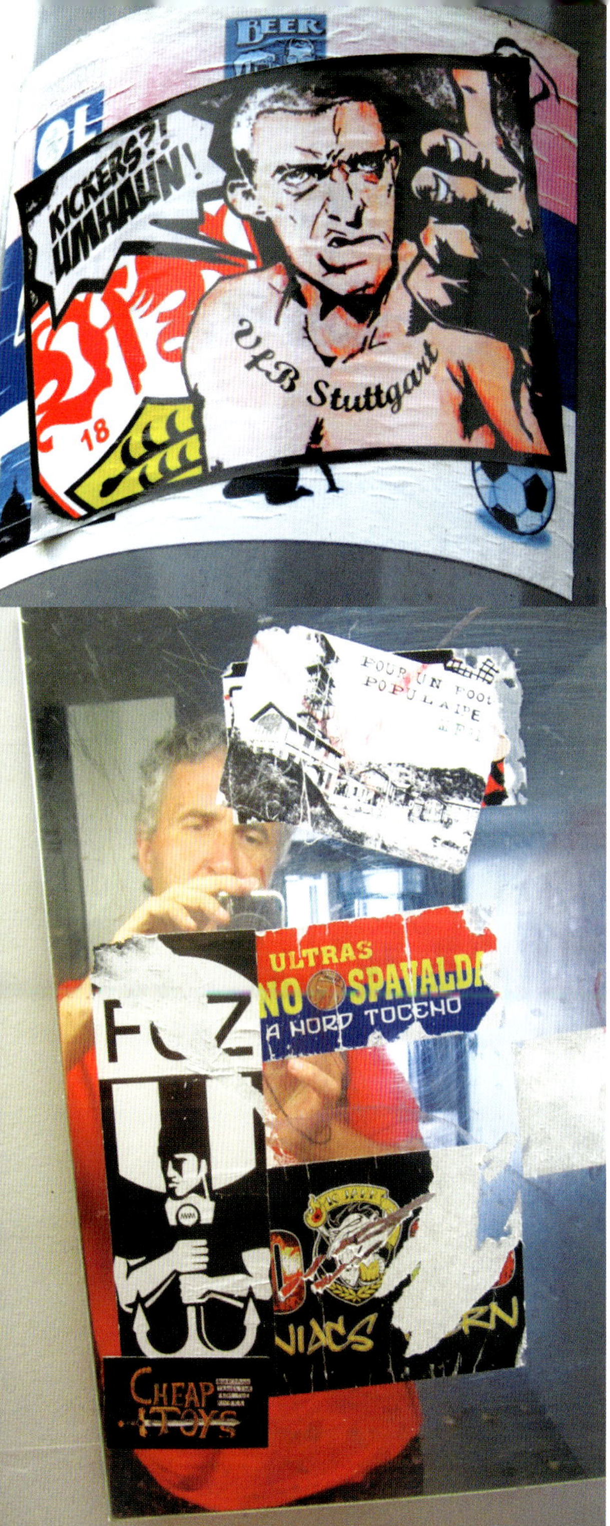

Clockwise from upper left:

Tot kto pishet stikhi na stene prosto ikh liubit! (*The one who writes verses on the walls simply loves them*); inscription; St. Petersburg, Russia; 2016.

Pirotehnika ni zločin — VM89 (*Pyrotechnics is not a crime — Viole Maribor, established in 1989*); by *Viole*, fans of FC Maribor; sticker; Maribor, Slovenia; 2014.

Kickers?! Hmhahn! — UFB Stuttgart; a sticker by fans of FC Stuttgart against their city rivals Stuttgarter Kickers; Vienna, Austria; 2020. Stylized image from *La Haine* (dir. Mathieu Kassovitz, 1995), starring Vincent Cassel.

Taking pictures of ultras' stickers in a public washroom; Laussane, Switzerland; 2016.

Robin van Persie; by fans of FC Feyenoord; mural; Rotterdam, Netherlands; 2019.

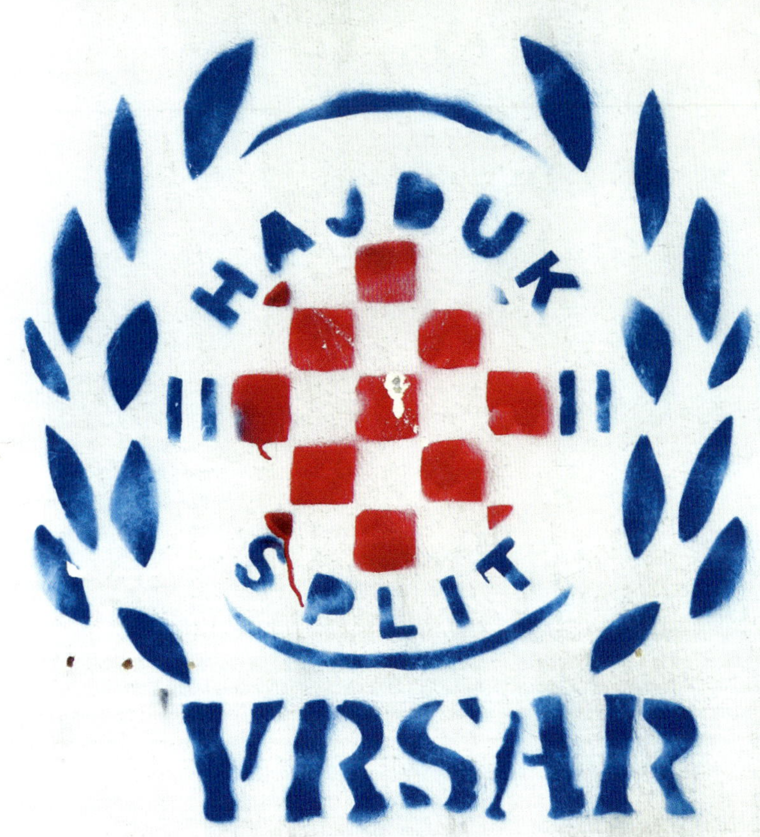
HAJDUK
SPLIT
VRSAR

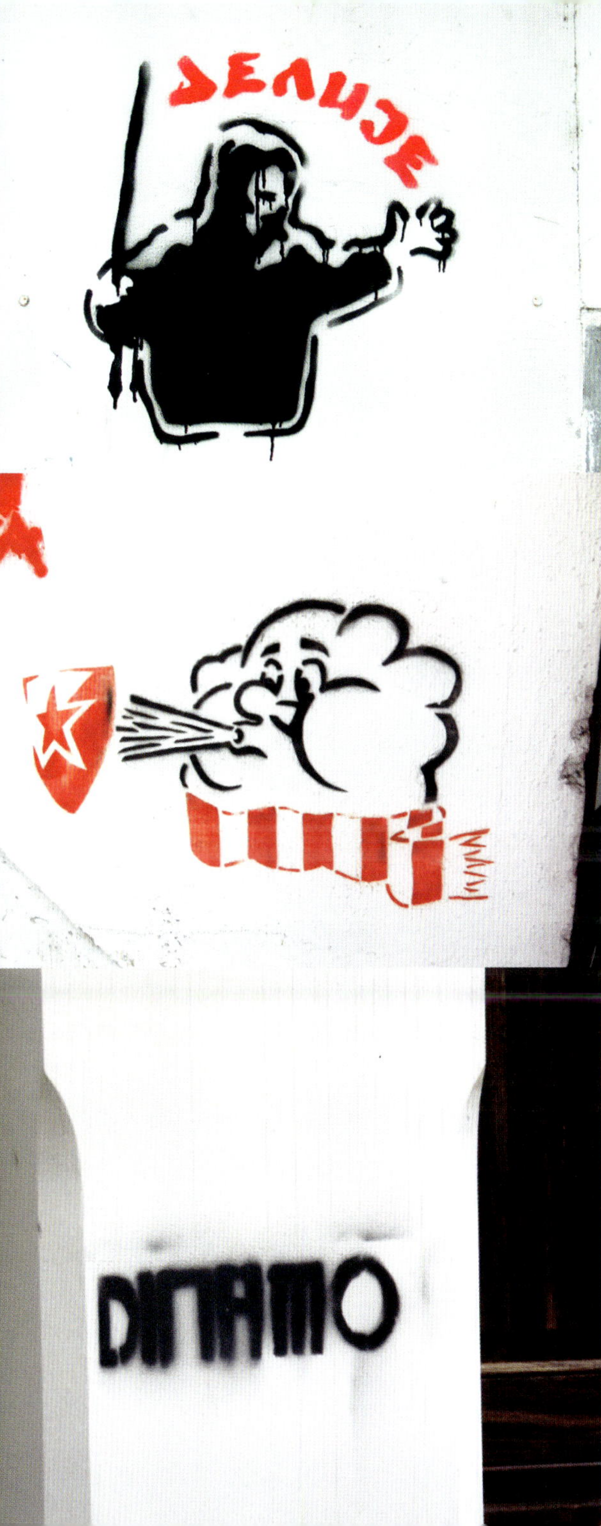

Opposite:
By *Torcida*, fans of
FC Hajduk Split,
from Vrsar;
stencil; Vrsar,
Croatia; 2014.

Above:
Delije (*Dukes*); by
fans of FC Crvena
Zvezda Belgrade;
stencil; Niš,
Serbia; 2016.

Center:
By *Delije* (*Dukes*),
fans of FC Crvena
Zvezda Belgrade;
stencil; Belgrade,
Serbia; 2018.

Below:
Dinamo; by *Bad
Blue Boys*, fans
of FC Dinamo
Zagreb; stencil;
Vukovar, Croatia;
2016.

Following page:
Invitation to
a party being
held by *Grobari*
(*Gravediggers*); fans
of FC Partizan;
poster; Belgrade,
Serbia; 2021.

Београд
БаШТА
рЕсТОРаН@
Партизана
ПФК
04.10.1945.
ЈУЖНА
ТРИБИНА
ГРУПА ЈНА
4.10

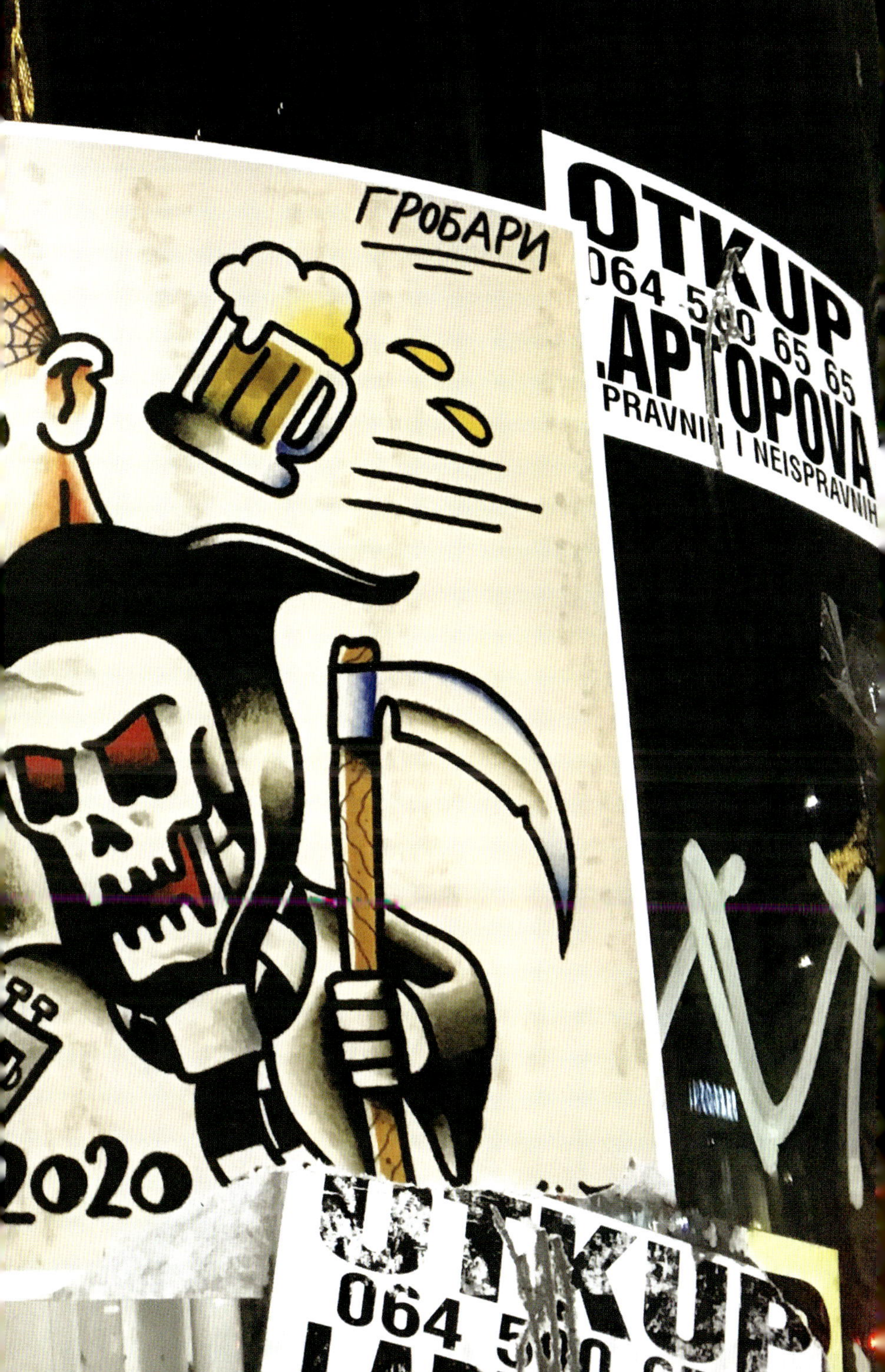

ГРОБАРИ
ОТКУП
064 5 0 65 65
.APTOPOVA
PRAVNIH I NEISPRAVNIH
2020
OTKUP
064 5 0 65

Unlike aesthetic, non-political graffiti, fan graffiti appear more uniform, are technically weaker, monotonous in their content, but much more numerous and incomparably more dramatic in their diction. Graffiti writers and football fans are similar in the search for street fame, respect, elevated status in a group's hierarchy and in strong self-concept (see Macdonald 2001: 66). Neither the former nor the latter wish to be heard in public except in their unconventional ways — they are seldom known by name.

Football-fan graffiti, specifically, can be seen among the graffiti that are "against apathy" (Lewisohn 2011: 10). This is what happens first with autonomous graffiti creativity or, as I call it, "the emancipation of aesthetics" ("aesthetical regime of the arts" in Rancière's terms) and second, with the emancipation of its usefulness, providing various ways to understand complications in "the aesthetics of emancipation" ("ethical regime"). In summary, they are visual political acts with a specific street connection between ethics and aesthetics, mediated by the culture of sports.

So, what happens when football-fanhood hits the wall, fandom that remains sprayed, glued, stuck, written, scratched, etc. on it? What do these *ultra vandal graffiti*, as described by an unknown *tifoso* writing near other football-related inscriptions I found in Graz, tell us about them, about their fan clubs, about their football clubs, about their cities, and about the social and political situation around them?

In this book, we hope to find out.

Opposite above: *Armada (Army)*; by fans of FC Rijeka; scratchiti; Buzet, Croatia; 2008.

Opposite below: *Forza Juve (Forward Juventus)*; inscription; Genova, Italy; 2020.

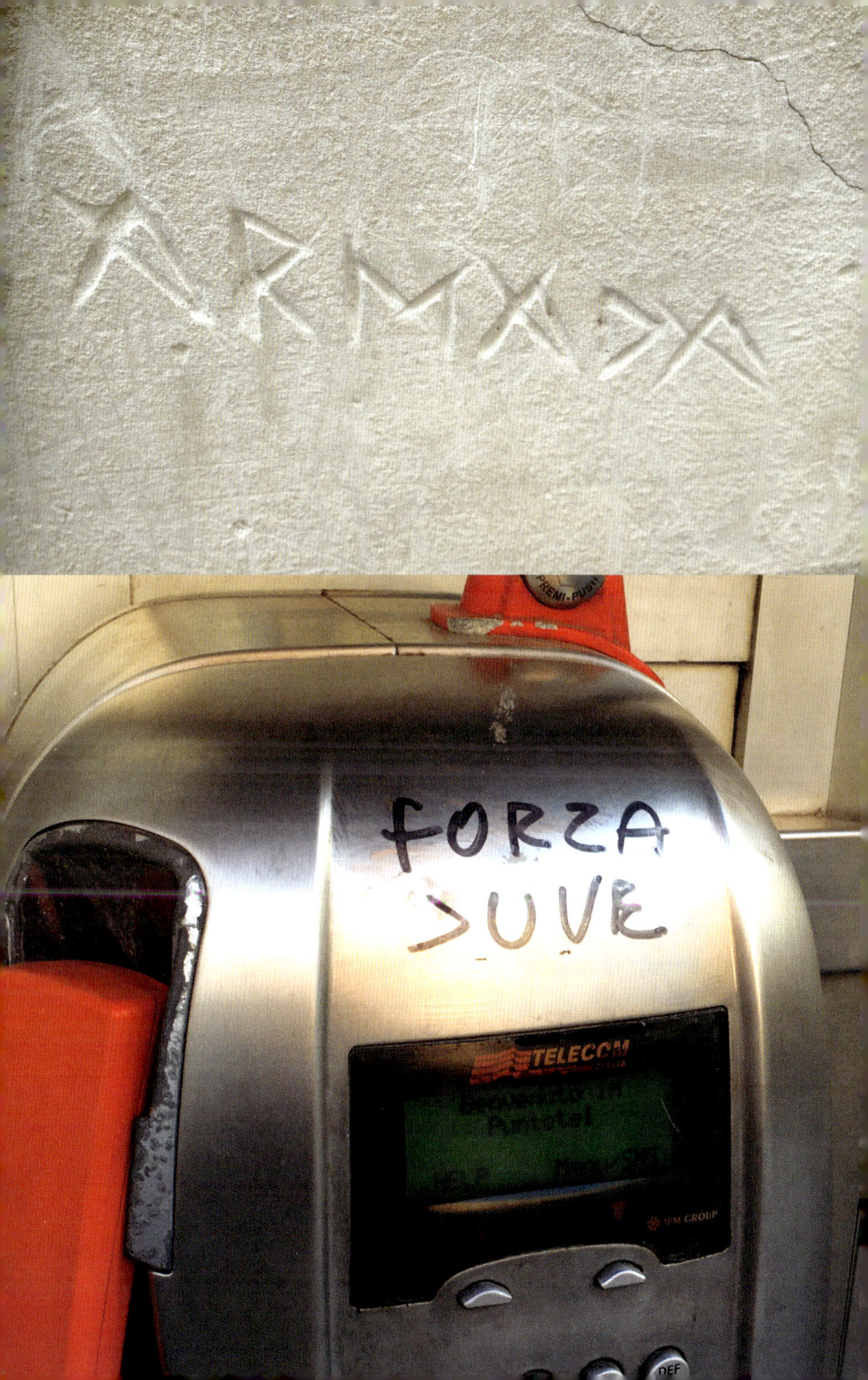
ARMADA
FORZA
JUVE
PREMI-PUSH
TELECOM
IFM GROUP

II. FOOTBALL––FAN GRAFFITI AND STREET ART IN THE CLASHING CONTEXT OF ART AND IDEOLOGY

During the FIFA World Cup in the summer of 2010, the Marxist culturologist Terry Eagleton wrote a well-circulated article in *The Guardian*, "Football: A Dear Friend to Capitalism," declaring, "If every right-wing thinktank came up with a scheme to distract the populace from political injustice and compensate them for lives of hard labor, the solution in each case would be the same: football." From a historical point of view, this was first a folk- and then a working-man's game, later capitalistically incorporated as the "opium of the masses" and an enormously profitable industry. In the words of another critical culturologist and activist, Gabriel Kuhn (2011: 18, 19), football can be seen as "a distraction from the political struggle, as a means by the powerful to keep the workers complacent, as a potential tool for nationalism, as a formula to pit workers against workers in competition, as a way to create stars, thereby undermining workers' solidarity" — therefore, instrumentalized in every possible way. It became a massive global corporate business, which is frankly admitted also by the owners of football clubs. Just recently, during the infamous attempt to create the European Super League in April 2021, one of its main supporters, businessman and chairman of FC Juventus Andrea Agnelli stated, "Football is not a game anymore. Today we are a 25-billion euro industry that needs stability."

But on the other hand, "football appeals to deeply rooted notions of collectivity and solidarity" (Kuhn, 51). This makes football — often referred to as "the most important of all unimportant things" — especially intriguing. The same goes for football-fan subculture, which is, looking at it as you may, not an ideologically neutral or apolitical action.

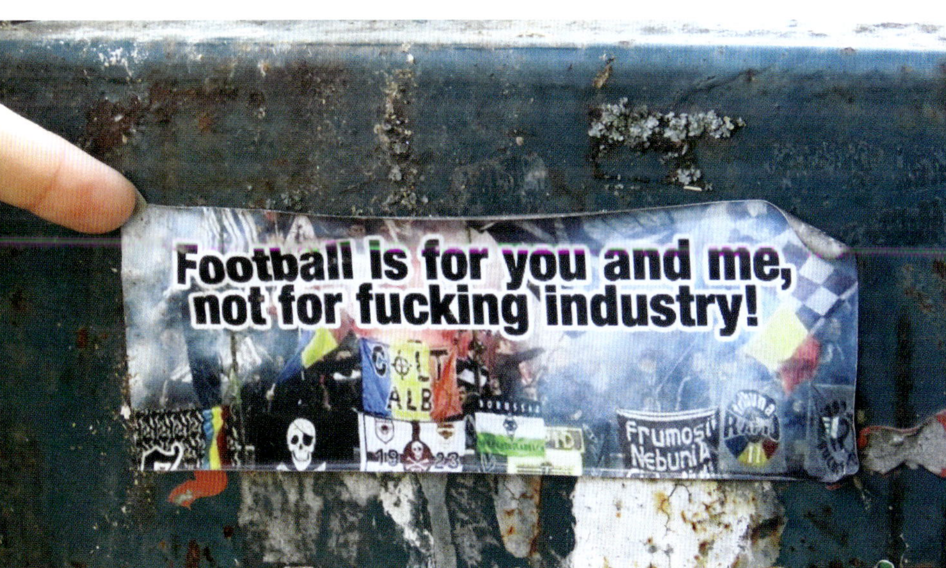

Football is for you and me, not for fucking industry!; a sticker by various Romanian club fans; Timișoara, Romania; 2017.

At first sight, football-fan graffiti and street art amaze with the variety in their form, color, technique and content, yet as a graffitologue, I am additionally interested whether this is also the case in the ideological sense. Neither can be easily understood. What, then, does this multicolored language say to the passers-by, to the "city users"; what does it call upon them to do, what does it communicate? Additionally, how are we to understand the ideological multitudes of the cultural variety that reside in fan graffiti and street art? Are these as heterogeneous as the ways in which they are expressed? Why do their visual ideologies feature not only so many differences but, foremost, so many ideological contradictions? A frequent criticism of football states that it "ignites, concentrates, and amplifies nationalist and sectarian feelings" (Kuhn 2011: 59). However, football also includes a variety of opposing, anti-nationalist and free-minded individuals, groups and tendencies (Ibid., 105–183, 198).

A few initial observations: First, it comes as no surprise that stickers have become the main medium — made in advance, they are cheap, mass-produced, less dangerous to post than a graffiti or stencil, require less skill, and can be spread over a vast area in a very short time. Murals remain a story in their own right; they are legal paintings of larger proportions, usually done by professional designers (mostly ones with a graffiti past) at the request of fan groups and in agreement with club management or even city authorities. Graffiti battles are also worth mentioning; sprayed or posted visiting-team- and fan-groups' symbols enrage home fans much like waving a red cloth would a bull — no sooner do they appear than they are already crossed out, doodled over, painted along, eradicated, laughed at, whitewashed or taken off.

Secondly, the temporal and spatial frequency of fan graffiti and street art rises with approaching important matches and with the proximity of a stadium — found on arteries and main roads leading to stadiums, at gas

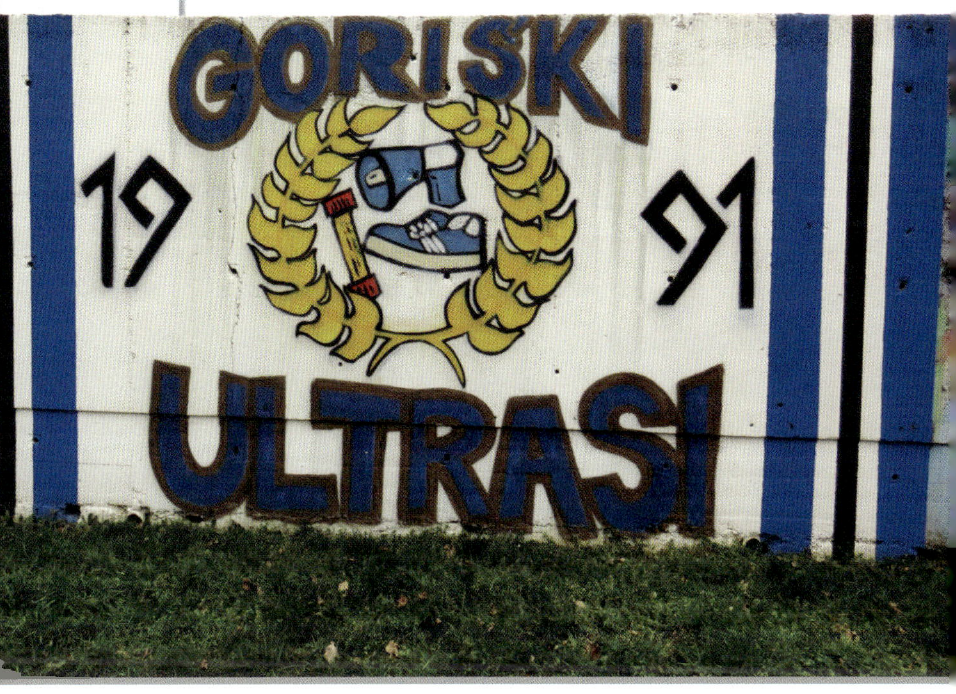

stations, and at bus- or train-stations that are popular arrival or departure points for the stadiums: a double *crescendo*, as important as the content itself if we wish to comprehend graffiti. There follow, of course, the "infamous" quarters, (self-proclaimed) ghettos and their sections of fan groups. Political graffiti writers in general and football-fan graffiti writers in particular appreciate *bombing* or stickering the city or even the stadium of the opposing team, with the intensity of painting/stickering increasing just before championships, their peaks, *fatal* away games, etc.

As I have written elsewhere, there is a constraint to this analysis which is worth repeating here. In my

Goriški ultrasi 1991 (*Ultras from Nova Gorica 1991*); by *Terror Boys*, fans of FC Gorica Nova Gorica; mural; Nova Gorica, Slovenia; 2020.

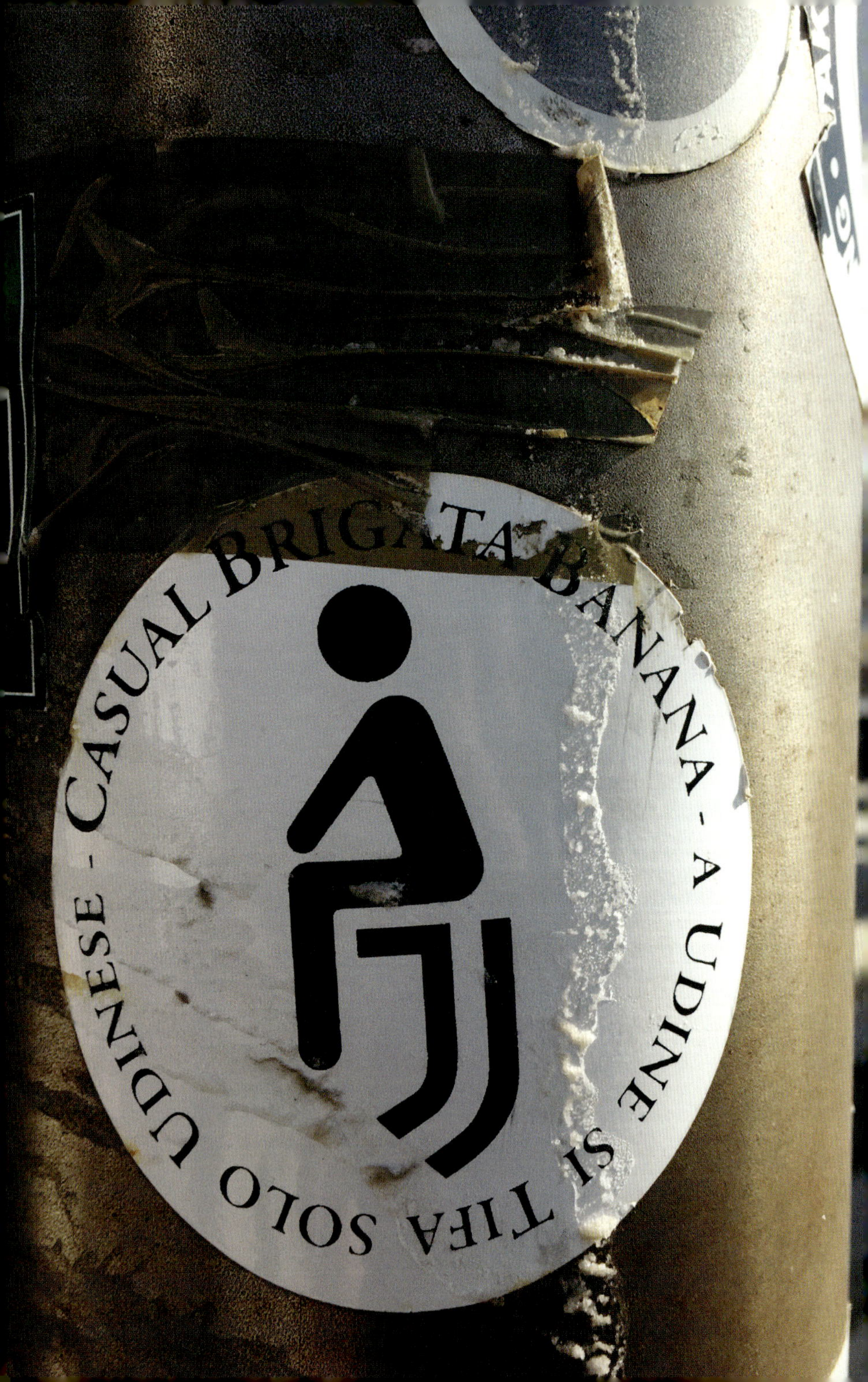

CASUAL BRIGATA BANANA - A UDINE - SI TIFA SOLO UDINESE -

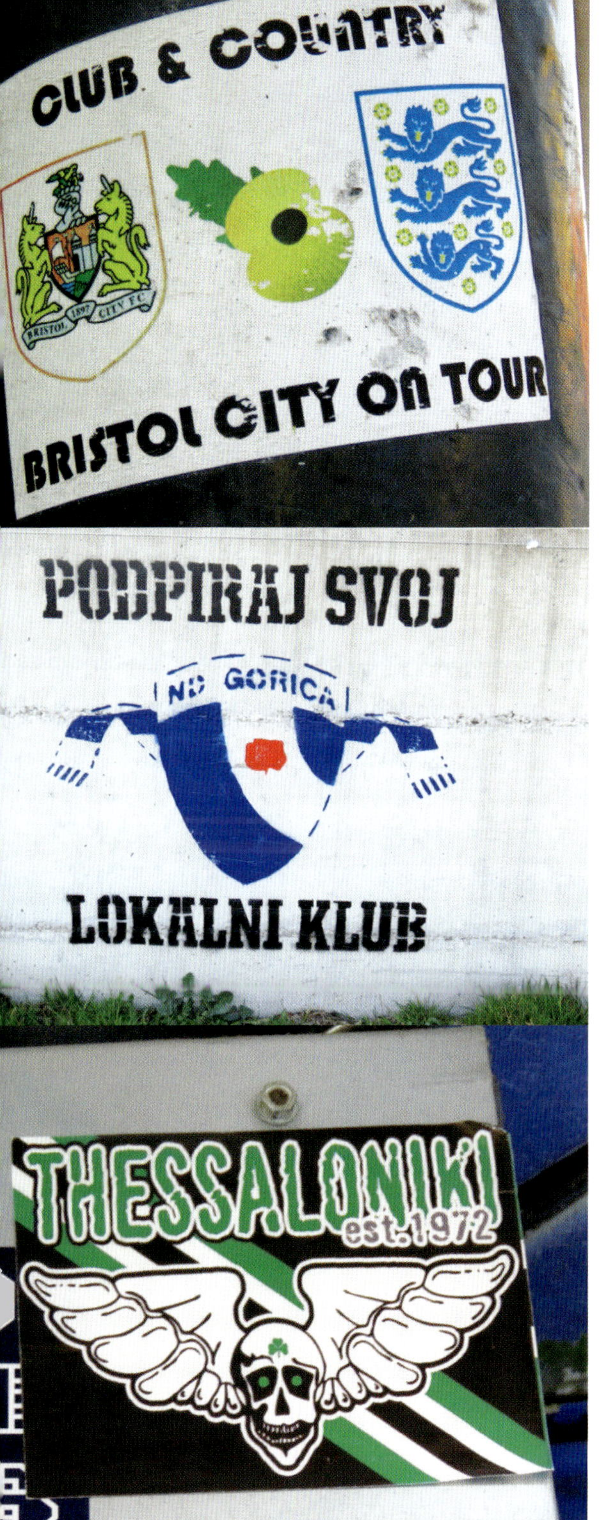

Opposite:
A Udine si tifa solo Udinese — Casual Brigata Banana (*In Udine we cheer only Udinese — Casual Brigade Banana*) — an image of a (Udinese) fan who is sitting on a toilet in the shape of "J" for Juventus; fans of FC Udinese Udine; sticker; Trieste, Italy; 2019.

Above:
Club & Country — Bristol City on tour; by fans of FC Bristol City; sticker; London, Great Britain; 2012.

Center:
Podpiraj svoj lokalni klub — ND Gorica (*Support your local club — FC Gorica*); by *Terror Boys*, fans of FC Gorica Nova Gorica; stencil; Nova Gorica, Slovenia; 2017.

Below:
Thessaloniki est. 1972; by *Gate 13*, fans of FC Panathinakos Athens, from Thessaloniki (this fan club was established in 1972); sticker; Skopje, North Macedonia; 2016.

definition, a work of graffiti is credible and authentic in its natural environment if it is an individual or collective illegal visual expression of an integral experience of an individual or a collective. As such, it is the raw urban *folk art* of anonymous people — their *pensée sauvage* — radical amateurism and not an elaborate urban fresco by sponsored graffiti craftsmen. A visual image of non-institutionalized power and simultaneously a tool for taking action.

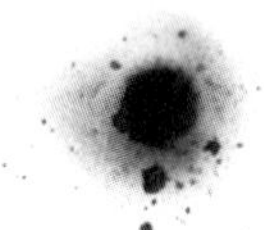

If Jackson Pollock stated that "a canvas is an arena in which to act," then graffiti writers could claim that "the street is an arena in which to act." Only by taking this position of understanding can one take brazen throw-ups, clumsy love statements on school benches, ever new visual inventions by ever new generations of street artists, witty interventions on posters — as well as the transitional graffiti by right- and left-wingers, nativists and cosmopolites, fans of different political options and football clubs, those who adore former and current heroes/countries, local vigilante groups and alter-globalists, and study them on the same level.

Graffiti are both the "power of the people" and the "power of the streets." The subversiveness of graffiti and street art lies in their participation and democracy: their public is more active than with the traditional artistic forms. Anyone can make graffiti; if they want to, if they are brave enough to, if they have something to say (or not, but spray-paints it anyway).

Affirming non-professionalism stands not only as praise to imperfection but also a confirmation of amateurism, non-alienation, unpretentiousness, unconventionality, and engagement. The art historian Véronique

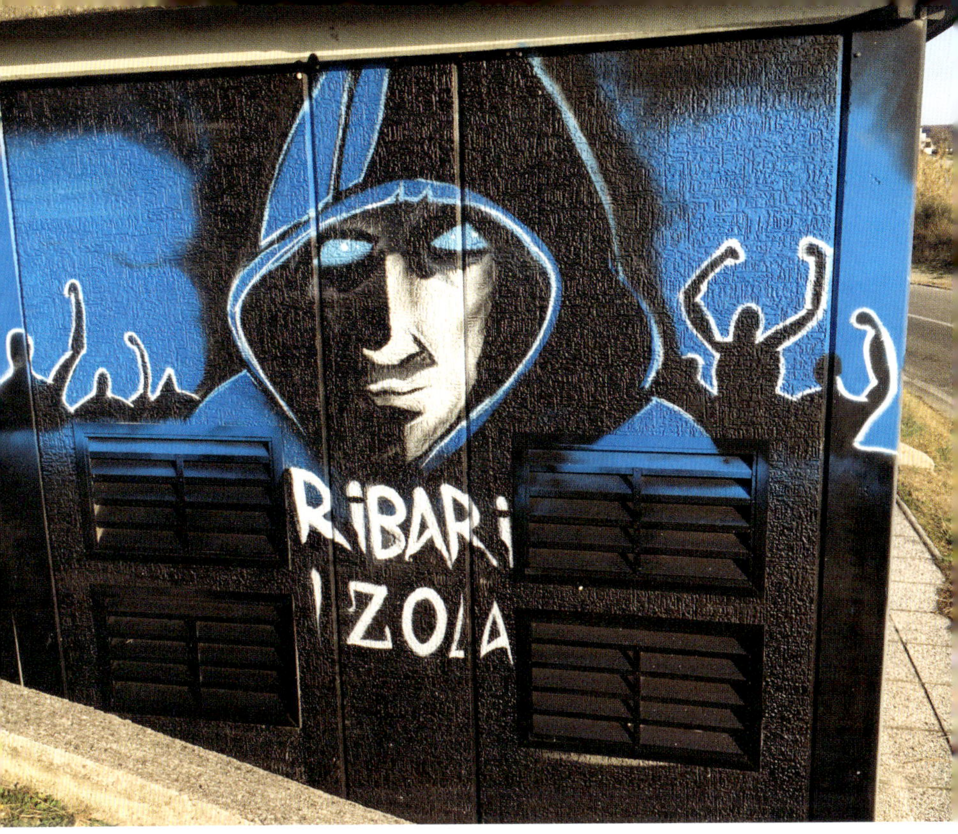

Plesch is convinced that "as long as quality — defined by criteria of aesthetic and technical excellence and by innovation — continues to determine what we study, … anonymous and 'damaged' works will be neglected" (2015: 55). Graffitiing and street art tear down the traditional divisions between creators and public, art and general creativity, the elite and the masses. Graffiti are made *by* the people, not only *for* the people. In the same way that Benjamin characterized film long ago, graffiti and street art carry progressive and transformative potentials within themselves; "every spectator is enabled to become a participant" (2007: 120).

In the following, I explore the cultural broadness and the ideological depth of football-fan graffiti and

Ribari Izola (*Fishermen Izola*); by *Ribari,* fans of FC Izola; mural; road to Izola, Slovenia; 2021.

street art with the help of two connected theoretical concepts: *rhizome* and *metamodern culture*. A rhizome, as defined by post-structuralists Gilles Deleuze and Felix Guattari, "ceaselessly establishes connections between semiotic chains, organizations of power, and circumstances relative to the arts, sciences, and social struggles" (Deleuze and Guattari 2005: 7). As such, "it has neither beginning nor end, but always a middle (*milieu*) from which it grows and which it overspills" (Ibid., 21, see also 25, 263) — in short, it "is reducible neither to the One nor the multiple" (Ibid., 21). Graphically, we can envision it as *polymorphous mycelium*; as open rings that develop multiple connections and lines all around, instead of establishing fixed spaces or positions; as a multiplicity, the multiple roots of these visuals need to be researched, as well as their intertwined organic structures and horizontal transfers, often internally contradicting.

Metamodernism has been typified by the Dutch cultural studies scholars Timotheus Vermeulen and Robin Van den Akker as the period that culturally replaces postmodernism. I prefer to perceive it as a not necessarily time-bound paradigm, yet "characterized by the oscillation between a typically modern commitment and a markedly postmodern detachment" (2010: 2; see also Nicolau 2016); "between hope and melancholy, between naïveté and knowingness, empathy and apathy, unity and plurality, totality and fragmentation, purity and ambiguity" (Ibid., 5–6). In metamodernism, meaning is a consequence of unsuccessful and ceaseless negotiations between two opposite poles, always somewhere and something "in between" and on the way. These negotiations are interconnected with other negotiations followed by yet other negotiations in endless rhizomatic multiplicities. If modernism can be summarized in a word *for* (which suggests determination, devotion, progressivism, even fanaticism), postmodernism with *neither, nor* (doubt, coming to terms with the free-floating), then the key word for metamodernism is *and*: constant negotiations between enthusiasm and irony, commitment and frivolity, permanency and transience, coherence and chaos, engagement and nihilism.

This book shows the presence of metamodern themes in this relatively narrow field of urban culture: football-fan graffiti, stickers, stencils, murals, and other forms of street art exhibit a variety of such ambiguities. They often, and at the same time, reveal sets of internal contradictions of their symbolic, political, social and cultural imaginarium and practice: rough & kind, dramatic & playful, expressing love & hate; referring to local & global inspiration; being socially rebellious & compliant, critical & affirmative, ideologically progressive & traditionalist; leaning left & right; emphasizing superiority & weakness; being pro- & against, inclusive & exclusive; looking aesthetically simple & complex, well-done & of poor quality; celebrating old & contemporary heroes, those from "their" history & those from global popular culture; seeming politically engaged & made for fun only, auratic & repetitive, DIY & ready-made, etc. & etc.

These operations between apparent binaries are elucidated by Marxist art historian Nicos Hadjinicolaou, who draws an analytically useful distinction between the "positive" or "affirmative visual ideology," i.e., the one that agrees with the ruling order of things, that perceives it in a positive way from every possible aesthetic angle and that adapts to it, and the "critical visual ideology" that questions this order and tries to demolish it. Both of these exist within football-fan graffiti and street art, as we will see, in a plethora of ways.

While positive visual or pictorial ideology, according to Hadjinicolaou, "ranges from the decoration of reality, or a simple affirmation of the existence of a reality, to its glorification" (1978: 147), critical visual ideology "exerts a critical function in regard to other non-visual kinds of ideologies, some elements of which are to be found in the work," including that it is "more or less openly opposed to particular class praxes or class

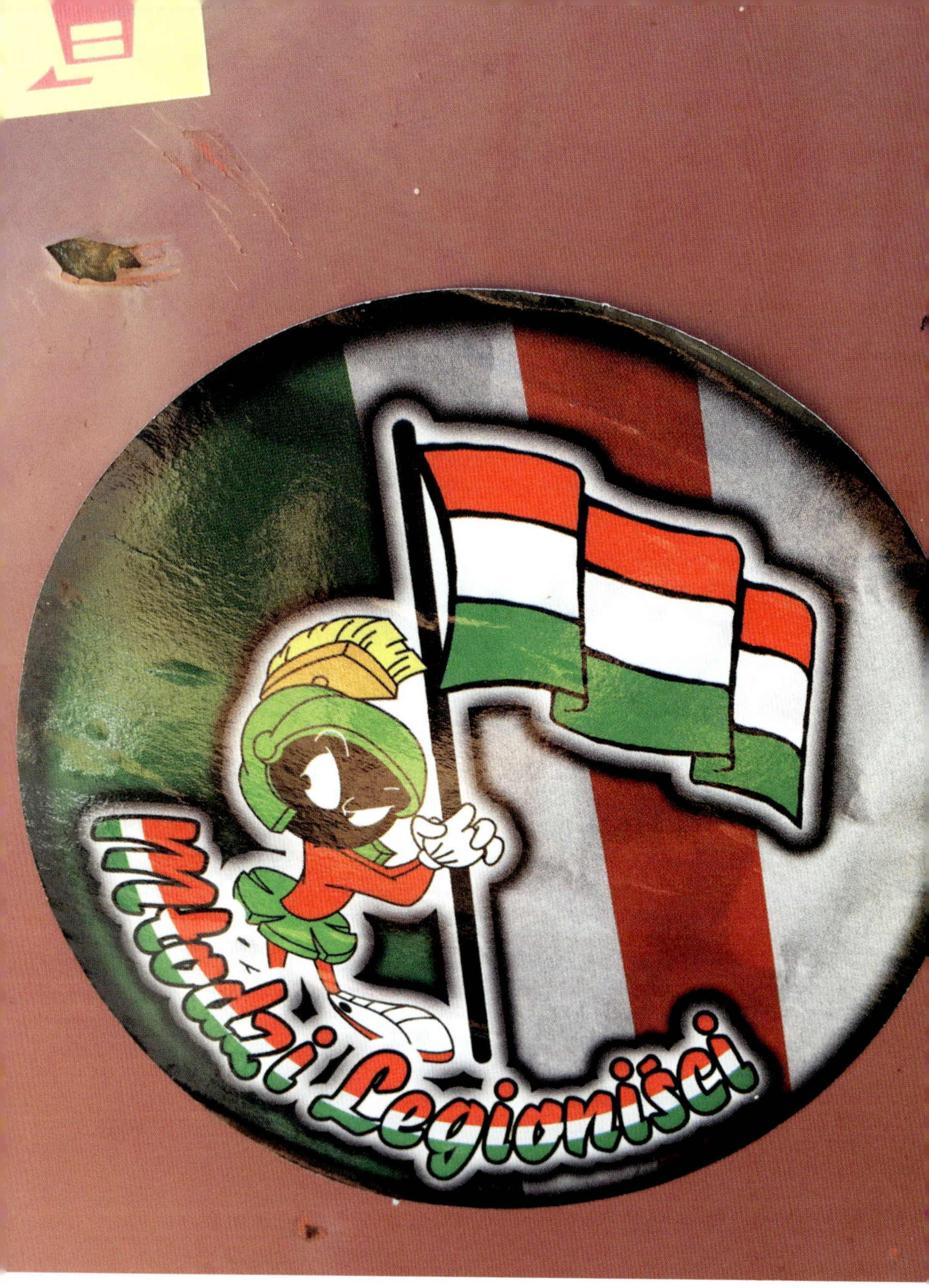

Młodzi legioniści (*Young legionnaires*); by fans of FC Legia Warsaw; sticker; Warsaw, Poland; 2009.

36

ideologies (usually ruling-class ideologies)" (Ibid., 148 and 12). Regardless of the adoring stance football-fan graffiti take about their home teams, overall they are non-conformist, *blasphemous, immoral* works that the dominant institutions (property owners, authorities) quickly recognize, condemn and treat accordingly. In this sense, graffitiing and street art simultaneously occupy both extremes of Hadjinicolaou's thesis in a metamodern way.

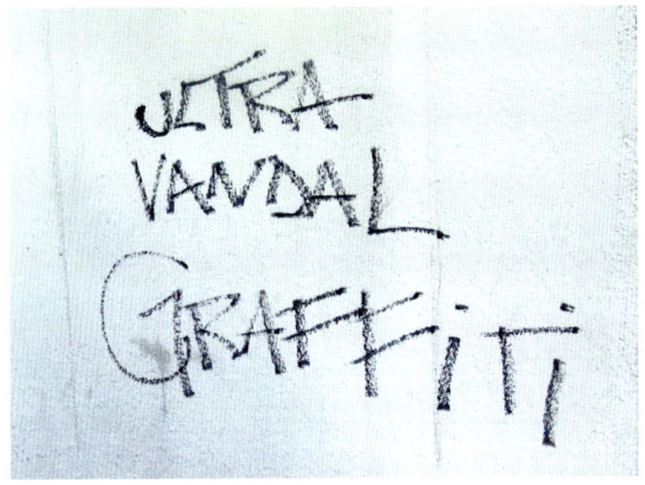

The four main content areas of football-fan graffiti and street art that we will look at now, in all their inclusive contradictions, are fans' visual self-image, recognizable aesthetics, presentation of fan values, and direct display of their political preferences. Included in these sections are many forms of expression: stickering, stenciling, graffitiing, wheatpasting, spraypainting, scraffito, and non-sanctioned murals. These eruptive forms play an important role in discovering the clashing context of art and ideology, and the role of sport in distilling and echoing the most potent, toxic, and motile societal themes.

Ultra Vandal Graffiti; by unknown authors; Graz, Austria; 2015.

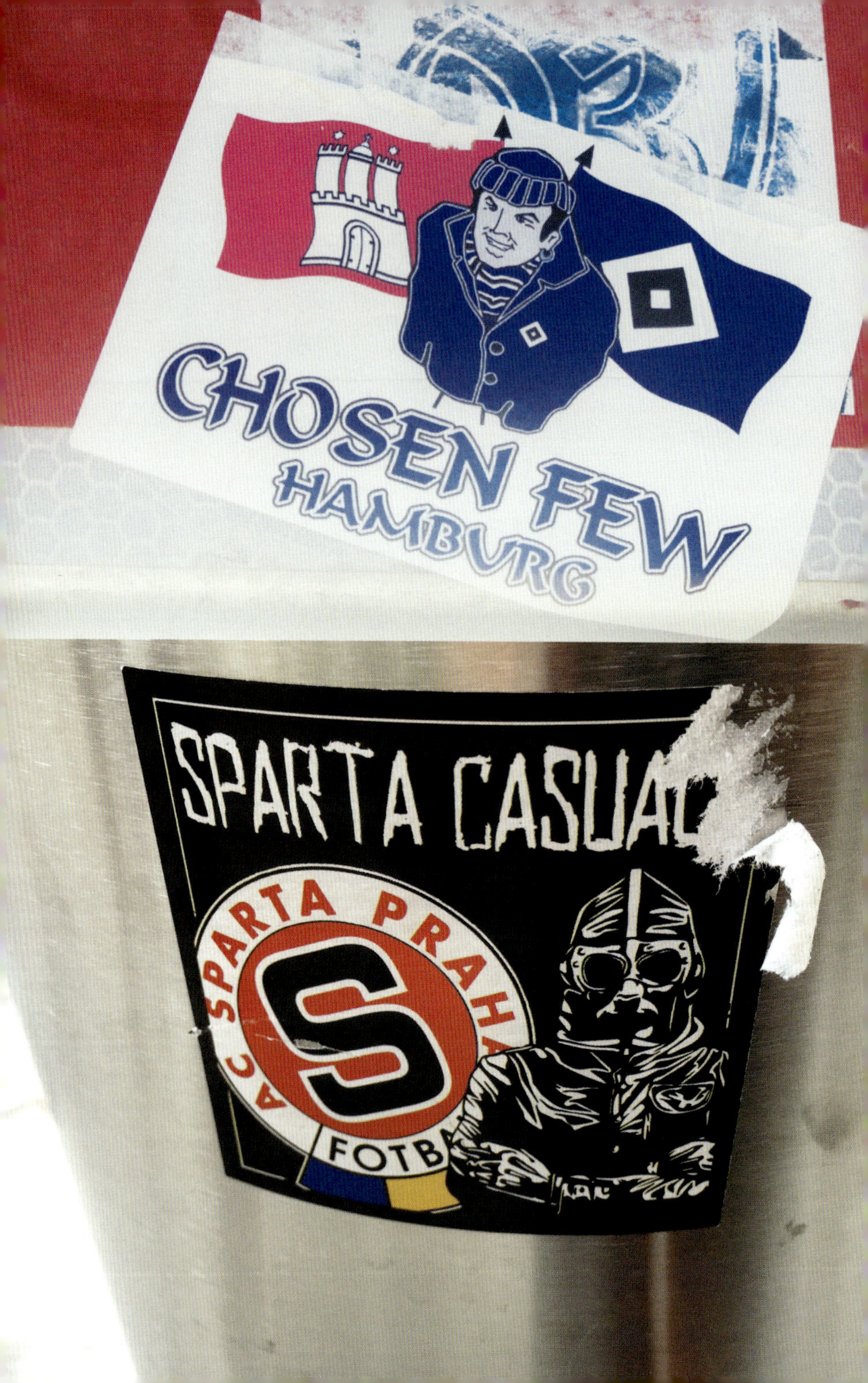

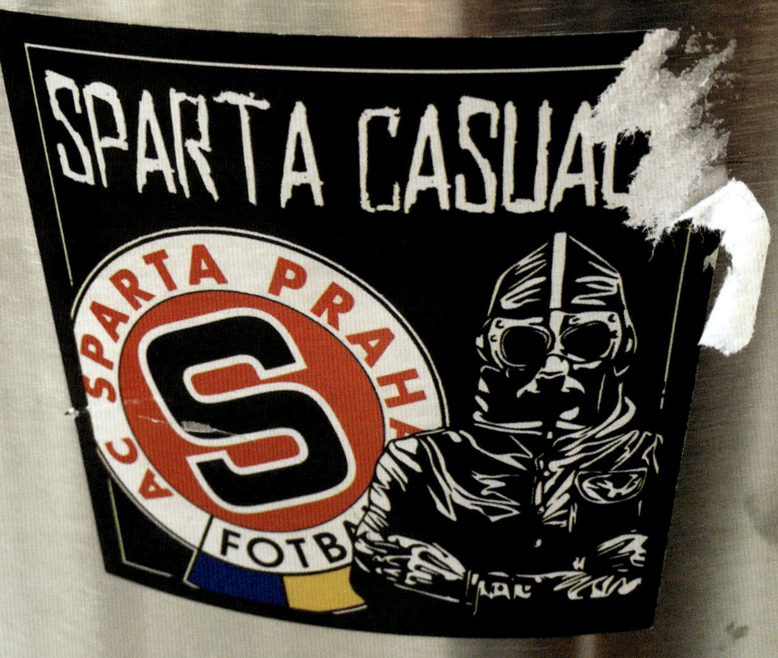
CHOSEN FEW
HAMBURG
SPARTA CASUAL
AC SPARTA PRAHA
S
FOTBA

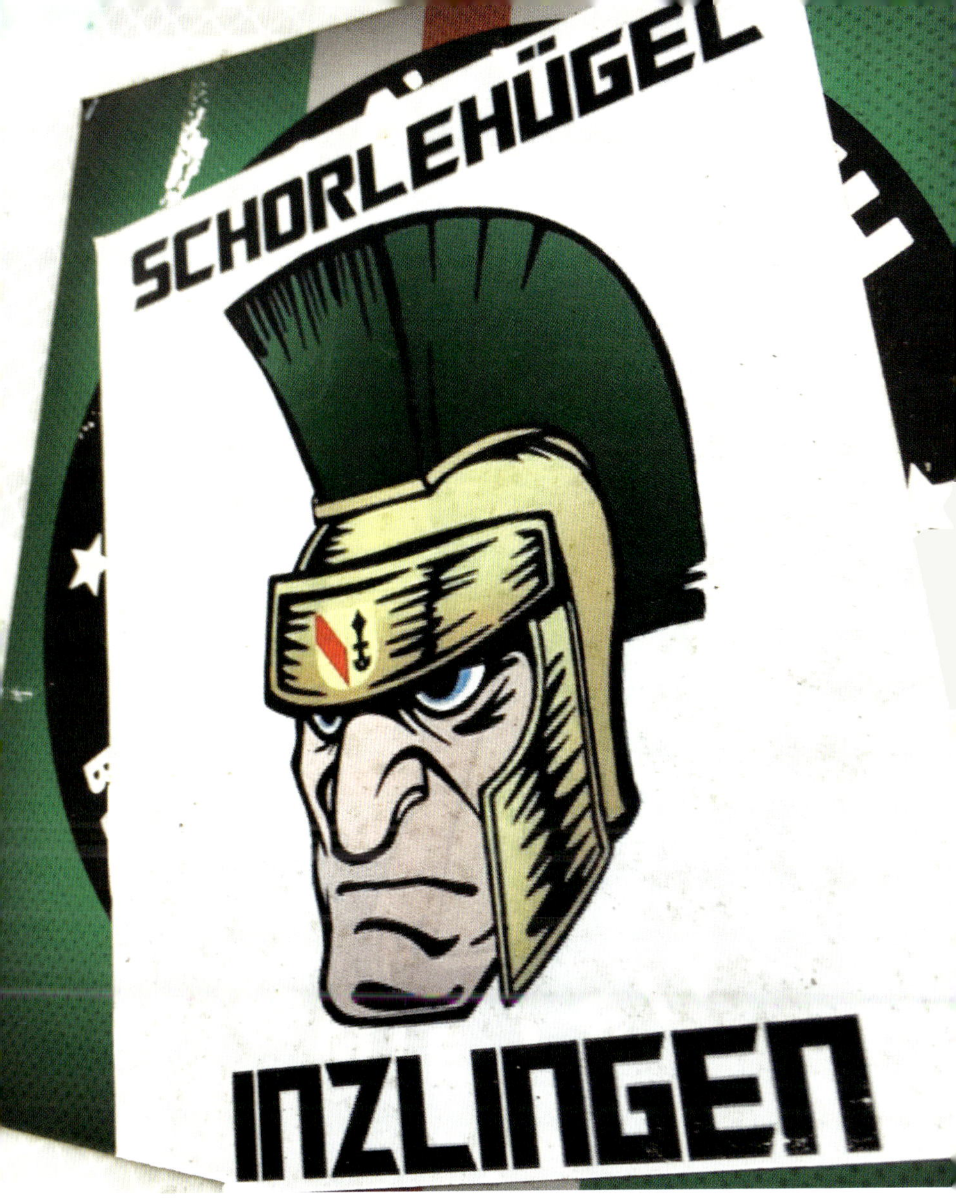

Opposite above: *Chosen Few — Hamburg*; by fans of (FC) Hamburger SV Hamburg; sticker; Berlin, Germany; 2011.

Opposite below: *Sparta casuals*; by fans of FC Sparta; sticker; Prague, Czech Republic; 2016.

Above: *Schorlehügel Inzlingen*; by fans of FC Inzlingen; sticker; Giessen, Germany; 2019.

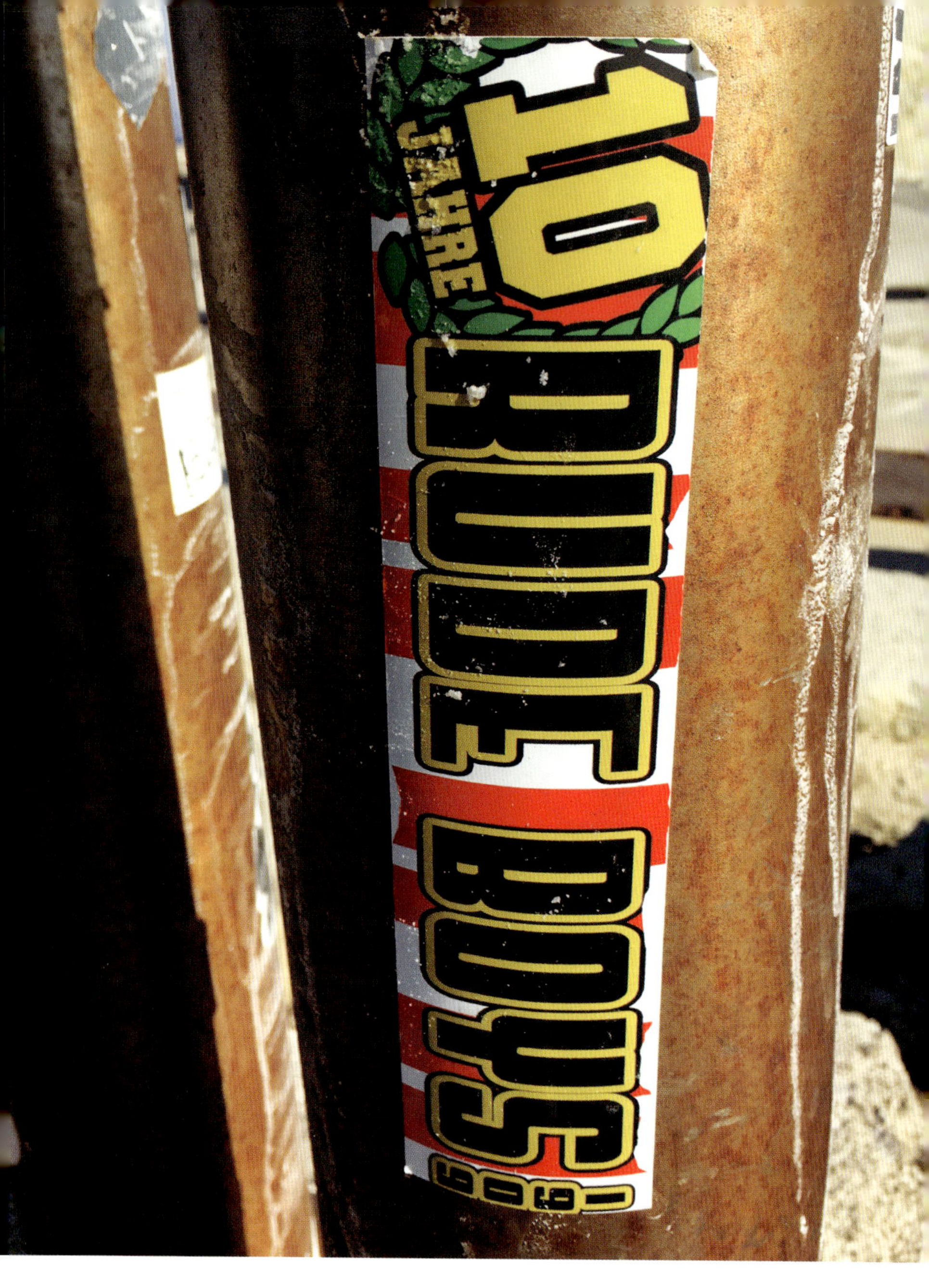

10 Jahre (10 Years) Rude Boys 1909; by an unidentified tifo club; sticker; Graz, Austria; 2015.

40

Self-image

Let us first address how fans present themselves through graffiti. In short: *Not arrogant simply the best*, as states an FC Anderlecht fans sticker.

Outlaws & defenders of tradition: at every step you can find the *Alone against everybody* cliché and other expressions of delight with an "us against the world" attitude (Thornton 2012: 120). On the other hand, there is the frequently seen *Ultras world* sticker that refers to a global alliance of all ultras featuring a daddy Ultra taking his son to a match with slogans such as *faithful to tradition* or *always faithful*.

Fans featured in the graffiti can be known & unknown: there are murals in homage to dead members, others pay tribute to arrested comrades. Greek scholar of youth and fan cultures Yiannis Zaimakis (2018: 260) noticed how graffiti images of Alexandros Grigoropoulos, a young fan of Panathinaikos killed by police in 2008, appeared in vicinity of football stadiums together with anti-systemic and anti-authoritarian messages. On the other hand, they hide in anonymous

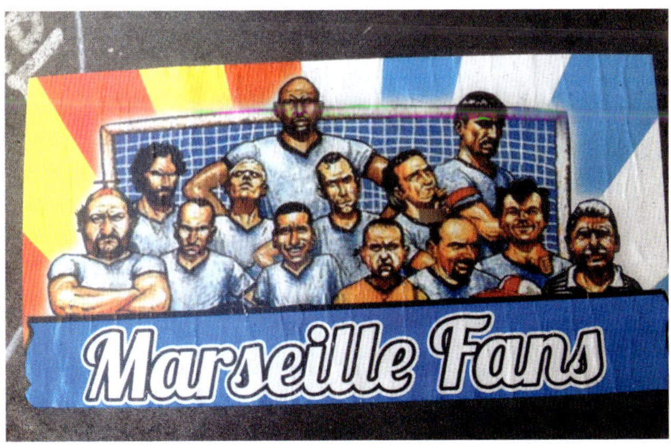

Marseille Fans; by fans of FC Olympique de Marseille; sticker; Modena, Italy; 2020.

collectivism: in graffiti and on stickers, they appear disguised, as mere silhouettes (e.g., the *Salt City Boys* or *Fukare /Lowlifes* of FC Sloboda from Tuzla, Bosnia-Herzegovina) or caricatures (e.g., one of the Marseille fans subgroups). Individually or together, known or unknown — always united, or in the words of a recurrent graffiti and sticker slogan: *You'll never walk alone.*

What is more, fans paint themselves at the same time as rough & kind, hyper-masculine and orderly: their artefacts sometimes present them as tough, full of *bad boyz* attitude, *Evil on the road*, as warns the sticker of *Horde zla* (*Hords of Evil*), supporters of FC Sarajevo. While at the same time I found a CSU Voința fan sticker from Sibiu, Romania that displays a loving motif symbolizing how belonging to the club is passed on *From father to son*. Another photo that I took in front of the stadium in St. Petersburg proudly presents *The hooligans family*. These stickers combine non-sequiturs: those by the Virtus Entella fans from Chiavari call themselves in Jamaican/ska style *Rude Boys*, and are visualized like dandies à la R. Valentino from the twenties or the heroes of Guido Crepax comics from the late sixties (see page 66). The FC Sturm fans from Graz and FC Krka from Novo Mesto self-ironically call themselves *Jewels* and *Manekeni* (*Models*), respectively.

They express their smallness & superiority, unimportance and holiness: stickers show them as nobodies, *riff-raff,* literally *small faces*, as one such group is called, while at the same time they use and paint metaphysical categories like *Holiness, Honor* and *Eternity* (e.g., the slogan *Honour — Glory* on FC Sporting Lisbon fan stickers, *Above all* on a Grobari graffiti, or *Sol Invictus, Unconquered Sun*, the official sun god of the later Roman Empire, in the name of a group of AIK Stockholm fans — see page 47).

They are sporty & not so sporty: images of the former appear among others on the stencils by above-mentioned *Delije*, the Belgrade Crvena zvezda fans; while

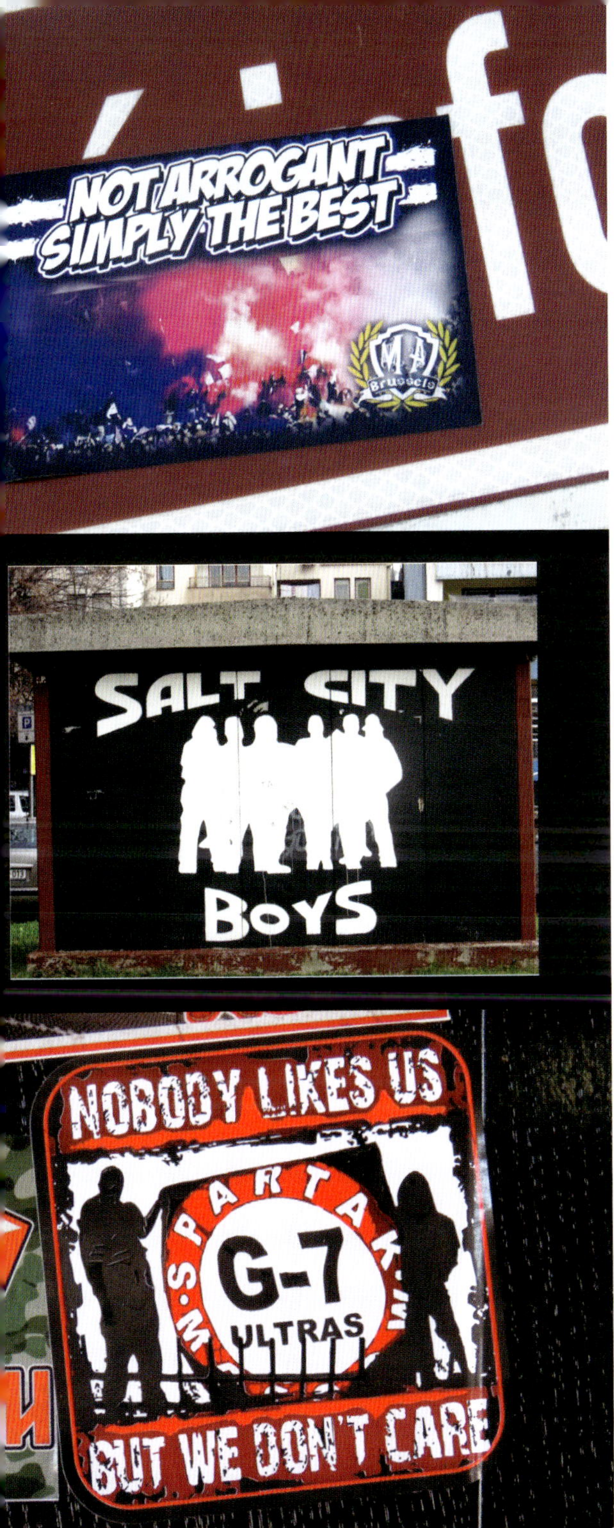

Above:
*Not arrogant
— Simply the
best*; by fans of
FC Anderlecht
Brussels; sticker;
Brussels, Belgium;
2017.

Center:
Salt City Boys; by
Fukare (*Low-lifes* or
Bums or *Wretched*),
fans of FC Sloboda
Tuzla; mural;
Tuzla, Bosnia-
Herzegovina; 2014.

Below:
*Nobody likes us, but
we don't care*; by
fans of FC Spartak
Moscow; sticker;
St. Petersburg,
Russia; 2015.

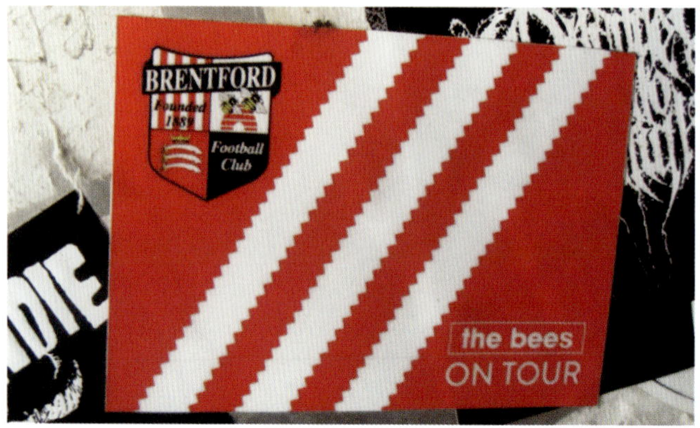

the FC Eintracht fans from Frankfurt proudly announce that they are *High Again* — their symbol, the eagle, spreading its wings among cannabis buds.

They are pro & contra: on the one hand they stand for the club and the mainstream values — on a FC Cibalia Vinkovci fan sticker, we can read *Let it be heard, let it be known/that there are only God and Croatia above Cibalija!* and notice a soldier wearing a nazi helmet (see page 88). On the other hand, they are against all of the usual Others in the ideological imaginarium of the postsocialist transition. For example, FC Lokomotiv fans from Moscow printed a sticker on which they proclaim in English (a language choice we will examine later) and in stylized (neo)nazi signs to be *Against tolerance* towards anarchists, communists, SHARP skinheads (that is, anti-racist: SkinHeads Against Racial Prejudices), Muslims, Jews and homosexuals.

In a very Deleuze-Guattari style, the graffiti and stickers are plain schizophrenia & paranoia: exaggerated images (or names) of themselves as madmen, lost or drunk people; opposed by outbursts of proud objections to unidentified persecutors, such as the *Bad Blue Boys* slogans *Nothing can stop us*; *You cannot extinguish our ideals*; *Always on the frontline, we'll fight for Dinamo till the end* or *Despised by everyone, controlled by none.*

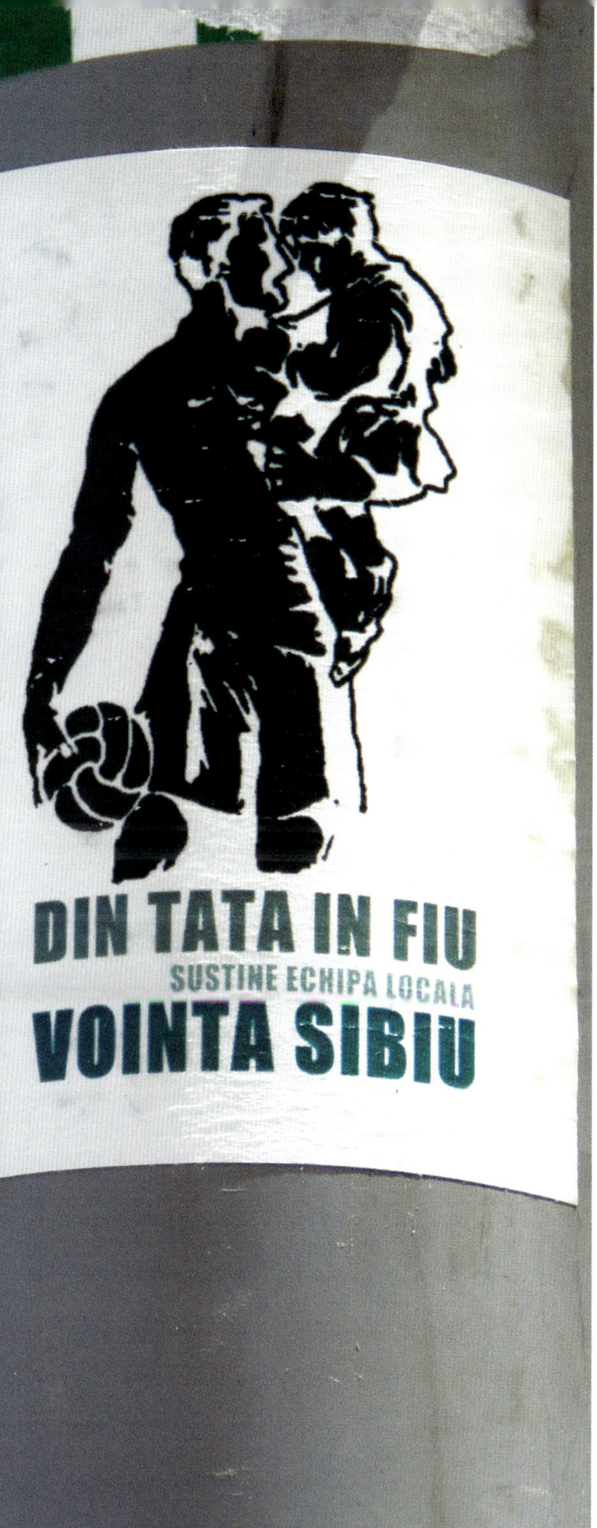

Opposite:
The Bees on Tour — Brentford Football Club; by fans of FC Brentford London; sticker; London, United Kingdom; 2012.

This page:
Din tata in fiu — Sustine Echipa locala — Vointa Sibiu (From father to son — Support the local team — Vointa Sibiu); by fans of (FC) CSU Voința Sibiu; sticker; Sibiu, Romania; 2017.

Following page left:
Diego Armando Maradona as a saint; sticker; Riomaggiore, Italy; 2020. Photo taken in July, before Maradona's death on November 25, 2020.

Following page right:
AIK — Sol Invictus (AIK - Unconquered Sun); by fans of FC AIK Stockholm; sticker; Malmö, Sweden; 2010.

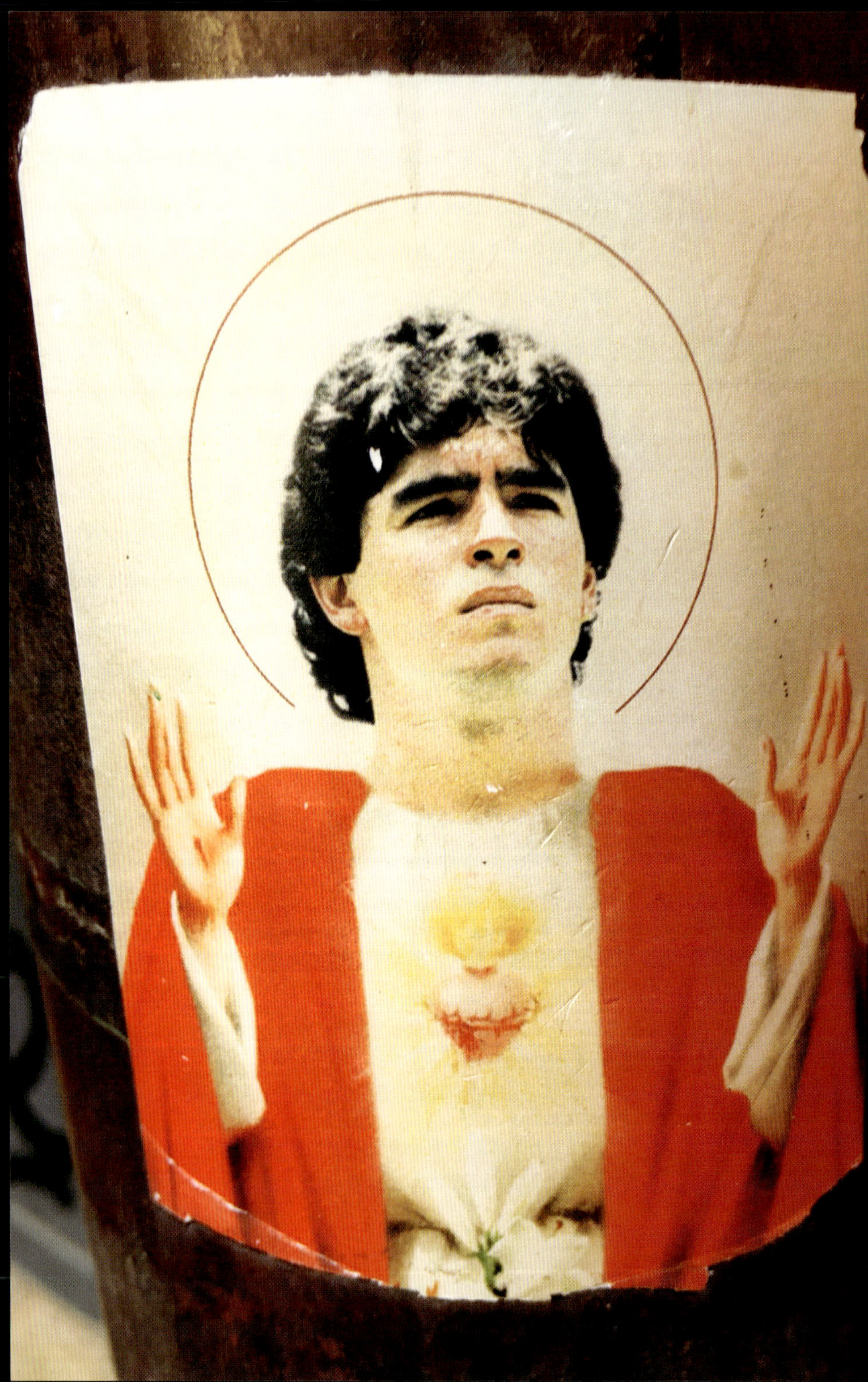

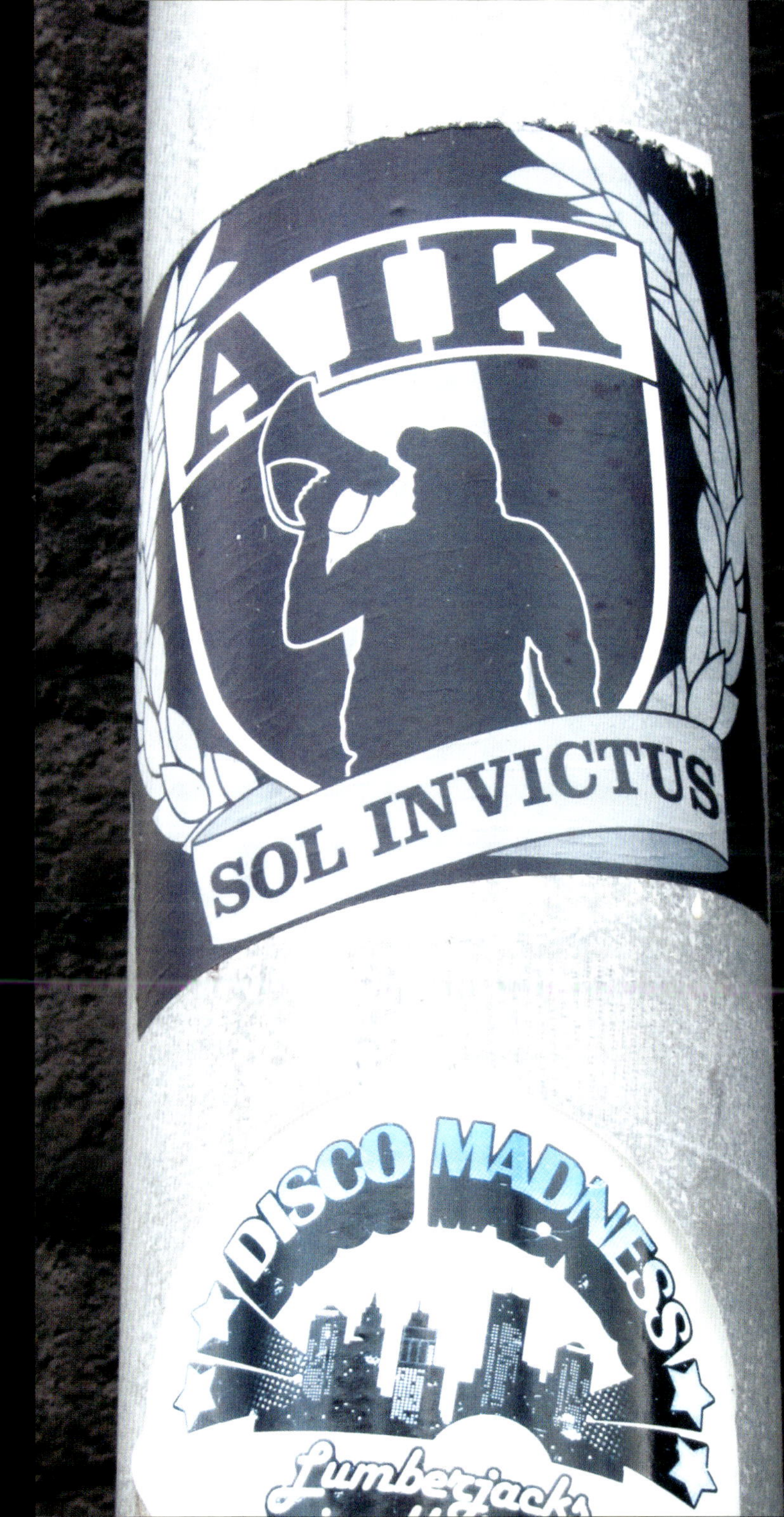

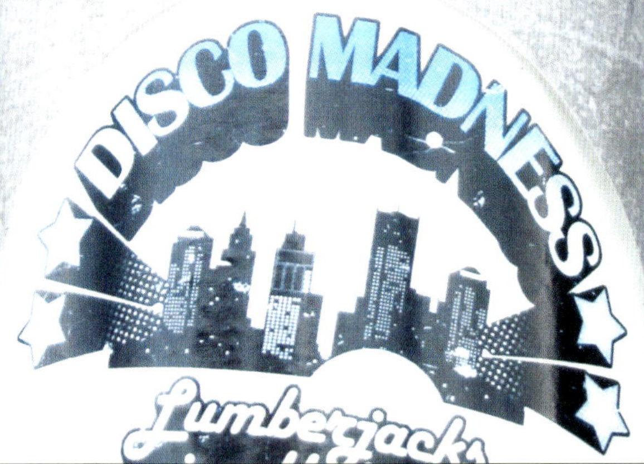
AIK
SOL INVICTUS
DISCO MADNESS
Lumberjacks

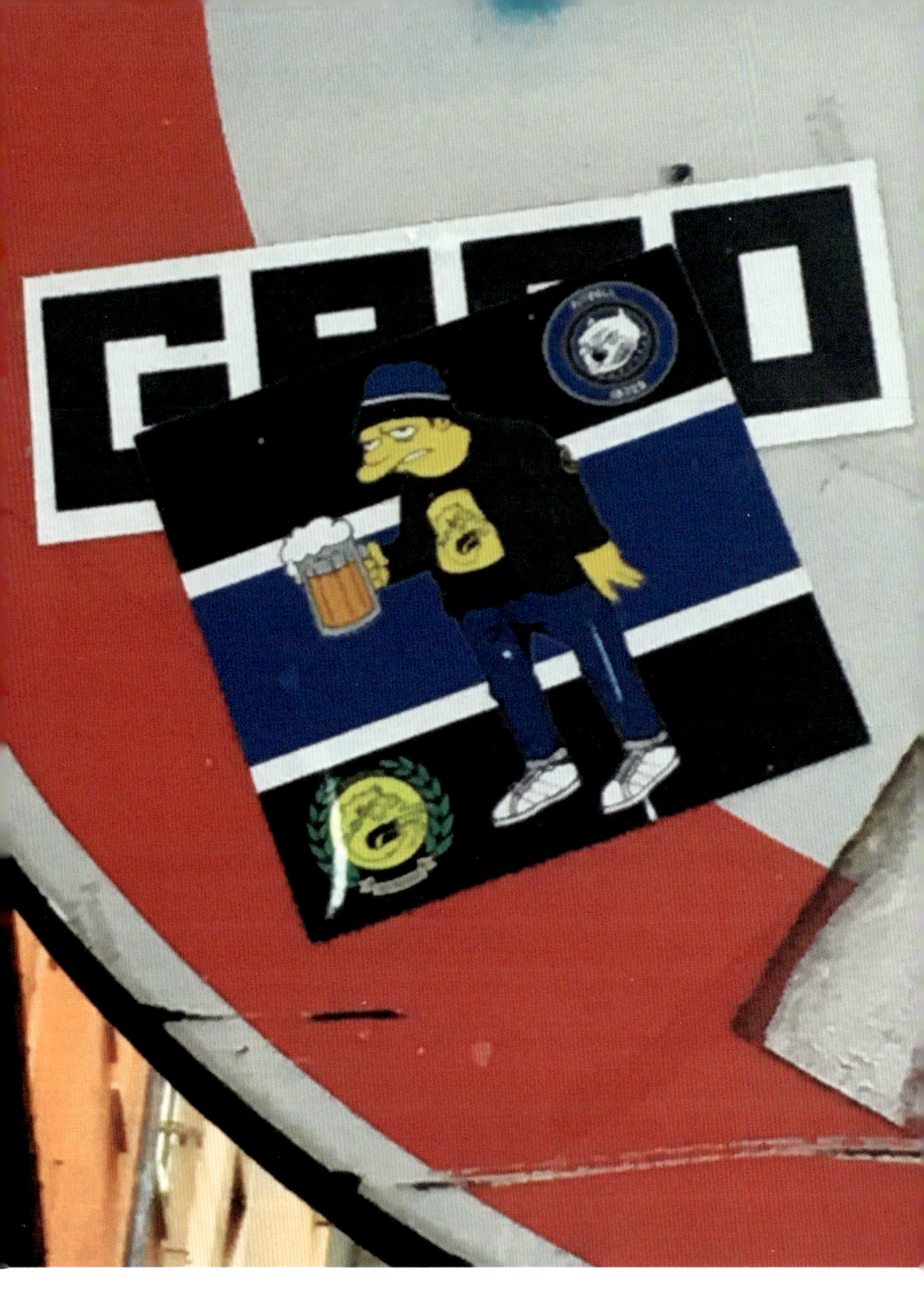

A sticker by the fans of FC Hellas Verona; Verona, Italy; 2020.

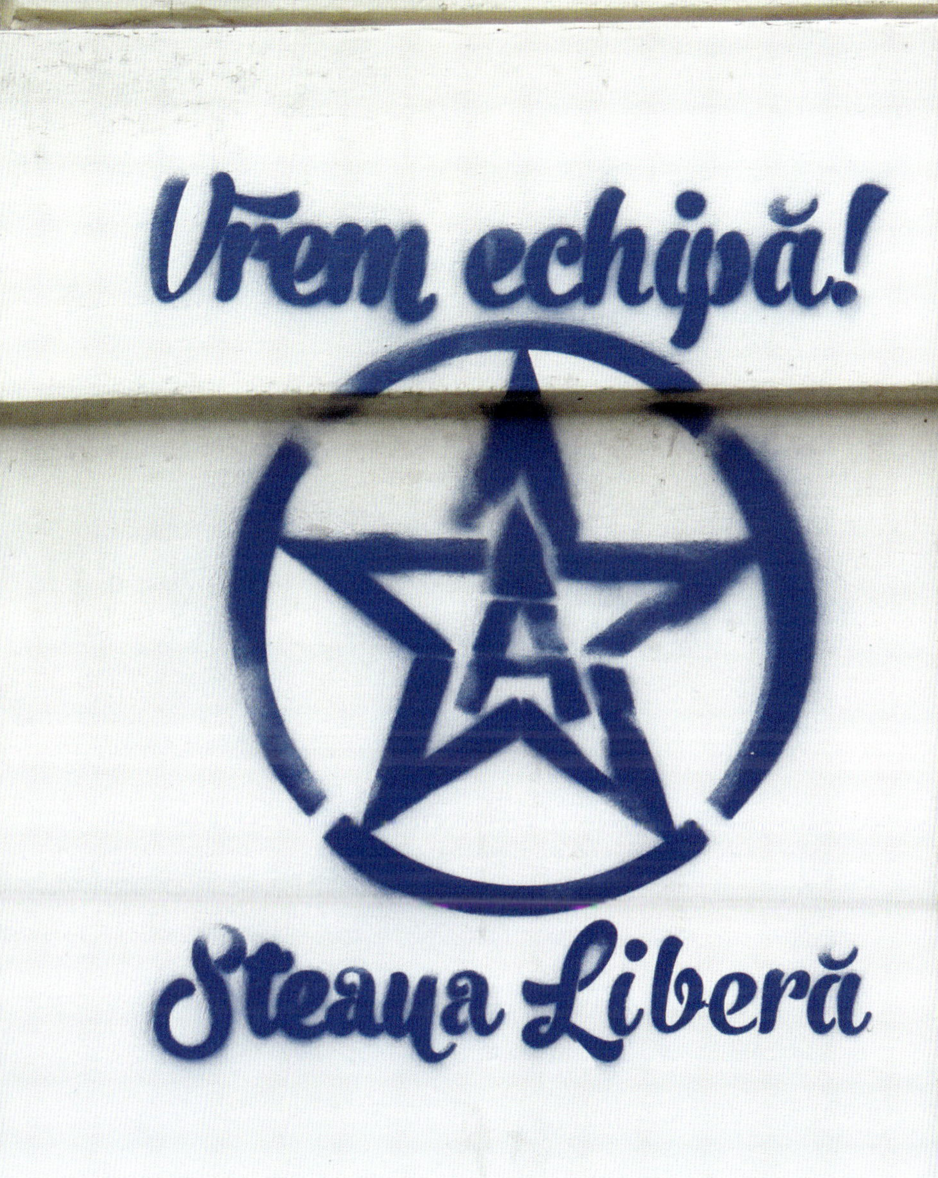

Vrem echipă! Steaua Liberă (*We want a team! Free Steaua*); by fans of FC Steaua Bucharest; stencil; Bucharest, Romania; 2017.

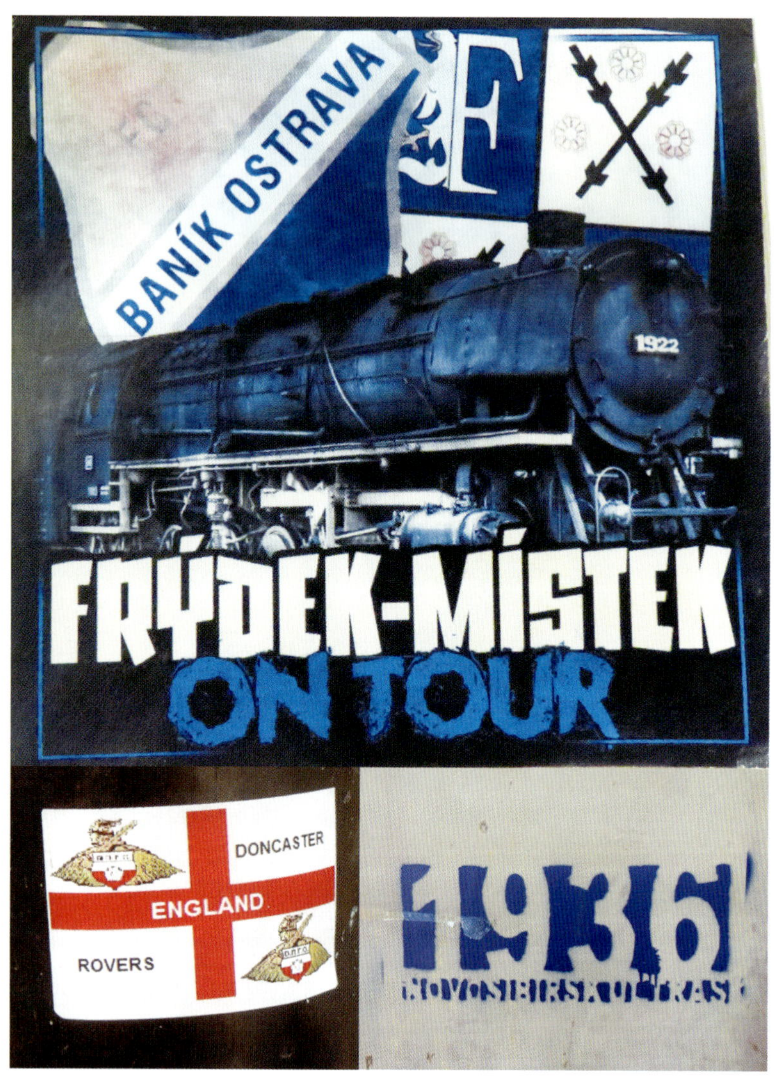

Above: *Frýdek-Místek on tour*; by fans of FC Baník Ostrava, from Frýdek-Místek; sticker; Prague, Czech Republic; 2016.

Below left: *Doncaster Rovers England*; by fans of FC Doncaster Rovers, South Yorkshire, United Kingdom; sticker; London, United Kingdom; 2011.

Below right: *Novosibirsk Ultras — 1936*; by fans of FC Novosibirsk; stencil; Moscow, Russia; 2016.

Aesthetics

There is both complexity & directness in football fan motifs. We can observe an intricate sticker with a lyre, old ornaments, local colors, and the FC Nantes *Brigade Loire* group acronym and year of establishment (page 77); or a similarly designed sticker by the FC Steaua from Bucharest featuring the Celtic cross, a skull, the Romanian national and club coat-of-arms, and *Combat Since 2009* in Gothic script, all in their club colors. Yet there are also: a simple stencil by those same Steaua fans with their star and script (page 49); FC Zürich or HJK Helsinki stickers with only script, year and club colors (page 55); and even straightforward spray-painted or stickered *punches in the face* by many fan groups.

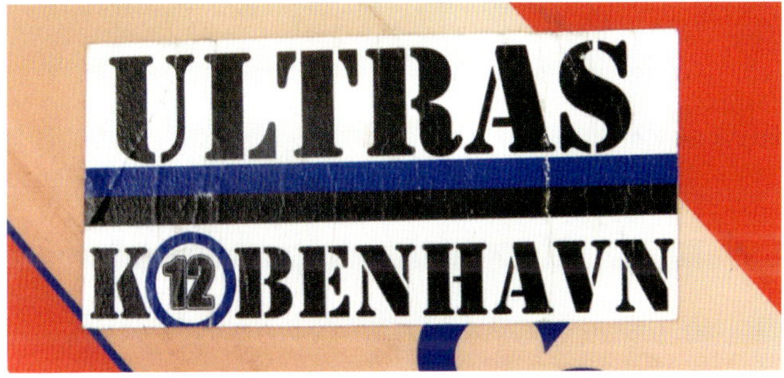

The dynamics of local & global inspirations that fuel their creativity is also interesting. At one end, we find local markers such as flags, coat-of-arms, insignia, geographic features, etc., creating the sense of *communitas*; for example, an old warrior and the English flag that represent the fans of Doncaster Rovers FC from South Yorkshire. Others symbolize industrial tradition, like the steam locomotive on the fan-sticker of FC Baník Ostrava from the Czech town Frýdek-Místek. Often, their discourse is marked by the use of local dialects.

Ultras København; by fans of FC København; sticker; Copenhagen, Denmark; 2012.

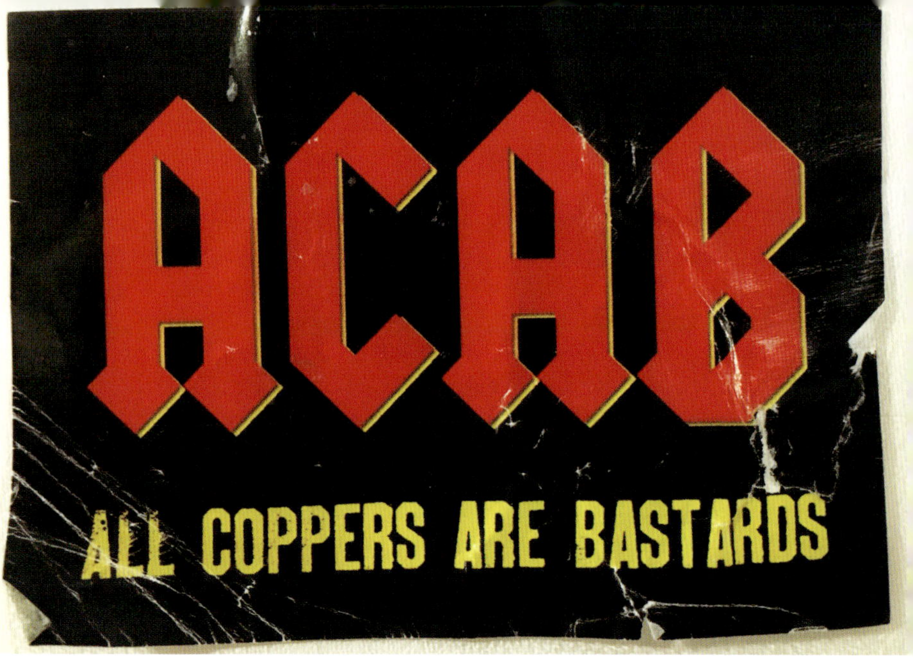

At the other end, however, there are those who belong to the symbolic inventory of the entirety of football-fan Europe: an RAF roundel or the Union Jack, originating from the early periods in the development of British subcultures (mods, skinheads, and later, punks), a laurel wreath, the acronym *ACAB* or the code 1312, which is a global abbreviation or cypher for *All Cops Are Bastards* (and the slogan *Fuck the Police!* in every European language...),[4] a skull, a fist, the Celtic cross, Gothic script or fasciofont, the middle finger, a megaphone, the police sketched as pigs, a pint of beer, and a bottle. I even found a Scottish-looking caricature on the sticker of *Eburg Hooligans* from Yekaterinburg, Russia (see page 72) and the

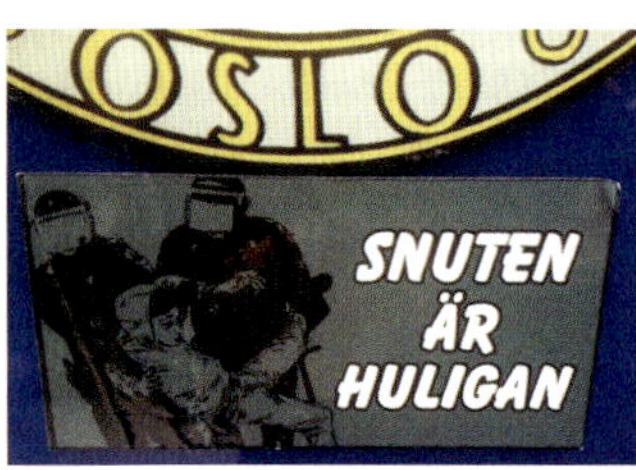

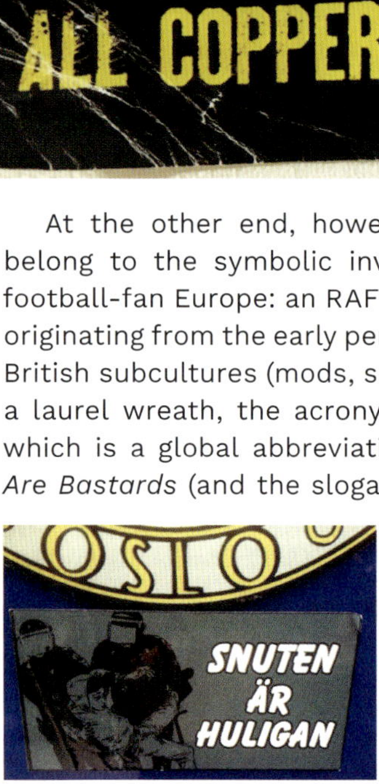

[4] Alternative readings of this acronym are *All Cats Are Beautiful, All Cops Are Brothers,* etc. In the end, they all mean the same, even if they don't use the exact words.

Above: *All Coppers Are Bastards*; sticker with heavy metal font; by unknown authors; Tallin, Estonia; 2015.

Below: *Snuten är huligan* (*The police are the hooligans*); by fans of FC Malmö; sticker; Malmö, Sweden; 2014.

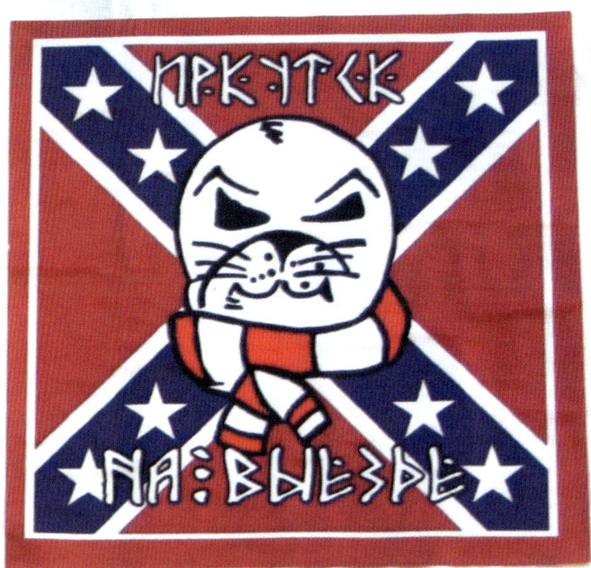

American Confederate *Rebel Flag* on FC Baikal stickers from Irkutsk, Siberia.

Consequently, fan graffiti also find inspiration in old & new symbols or icons, e.g., the Polish white eagle appears on a sticker by the Wisła Fan Club from Kraków with an explanation: *White star, white eagle, these are our ideals.* Alternatively, we find the three simple Adidas stripes on a sticker by The Bees fan-group of Brentford FC from Brentford (see page 44), or images of anime characters or the Joker from Batman on a couple of other stickers. You find pastism and presentism, pictures from another time and from the present, looking back and reflecting the current.

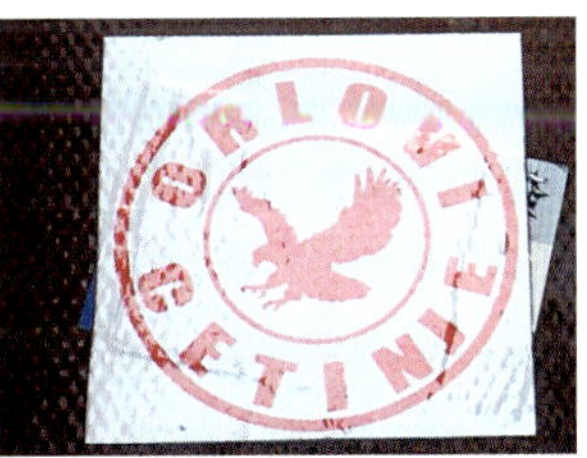

Above: *Irkutsk on Tour*; by *Baikal Ultras*, fans of FC Baikal Irkutsk; sticker; St. Petersburg, Russia; 2016.

Below: *Orlovi — Cetinje (Eagles — Cetinje)*; by *Orlovi (Eagles)*, fans of FC Lovćen Cetinje; sticker; Cetinje, Montenegro; 2017.

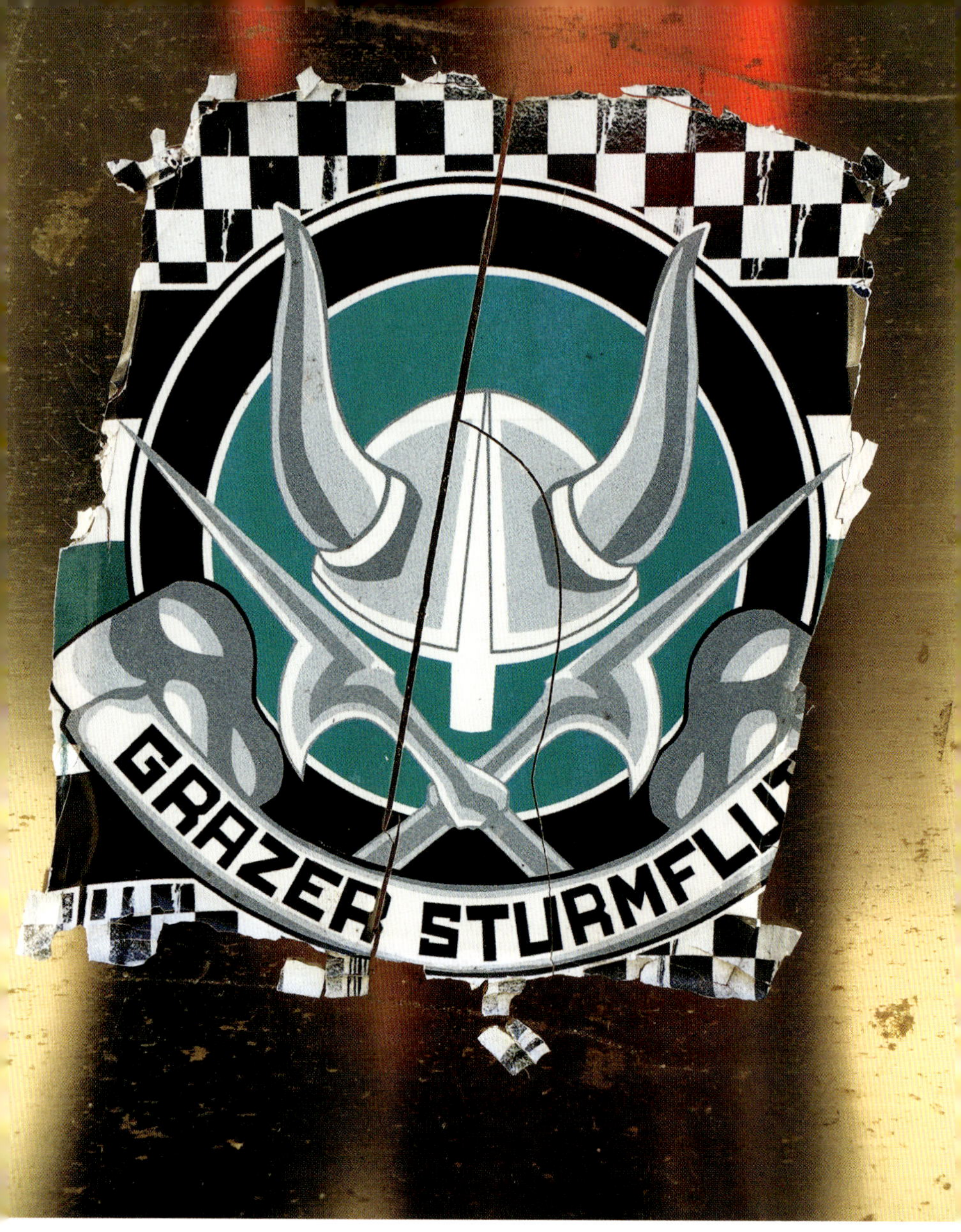

Grazer Sturmflut; by fans of FC Sturm Graz; sticker; Graz, Austria; 2013.

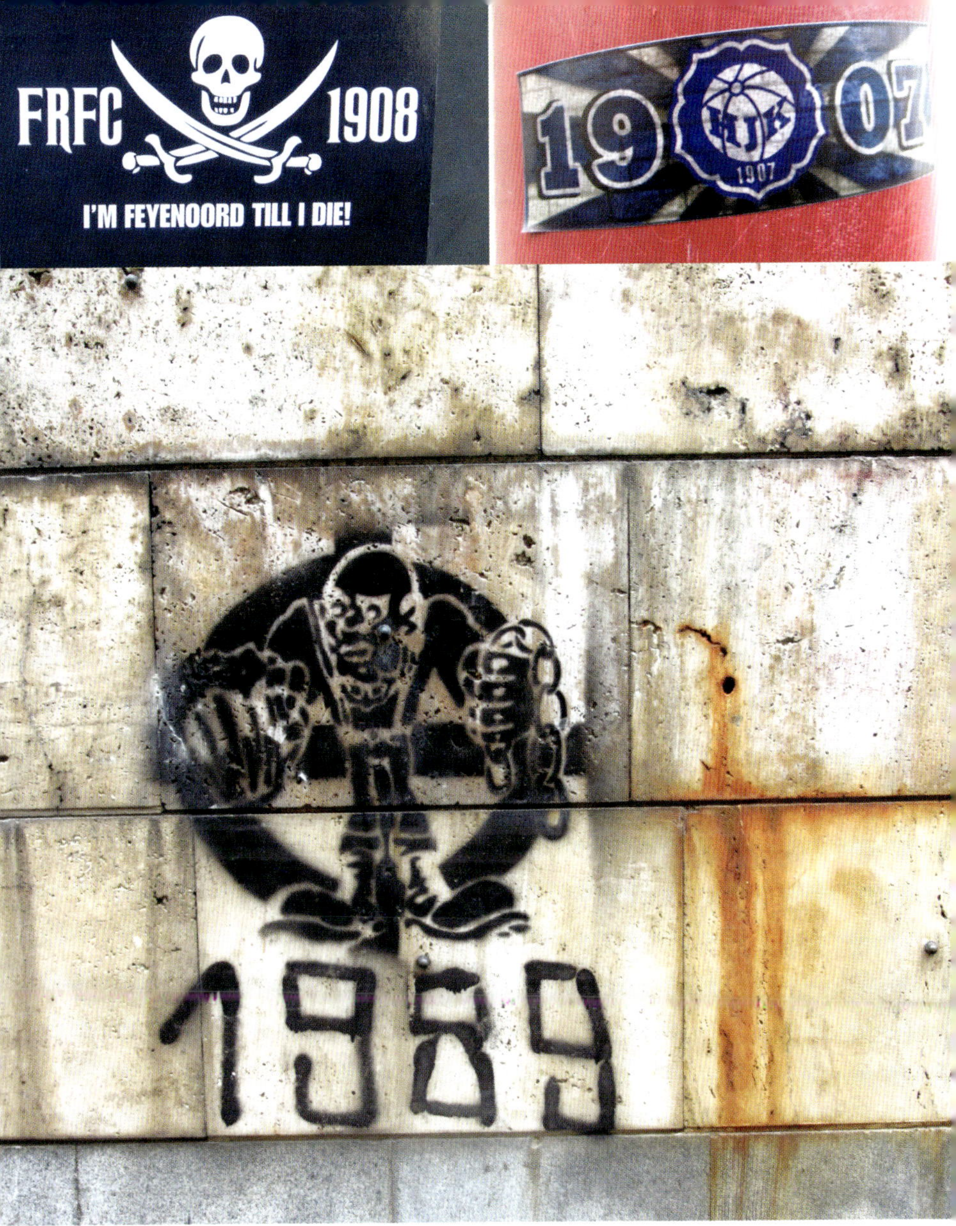

Above left: *FRFC 1908 — I'm Feyenoord till I die!*; by fans of FC Feyenoord; Rotterdam, The Netherlands; 2015.

Above right: *HJK 1907*; by fans of FC Helsinki; sticker; Tallinn, Estonia; 2015.

Below: *1989*; one of the symbols used by *Viole*, fans of FC Maribor, established in 1989; stencil; Maribor; 2012.

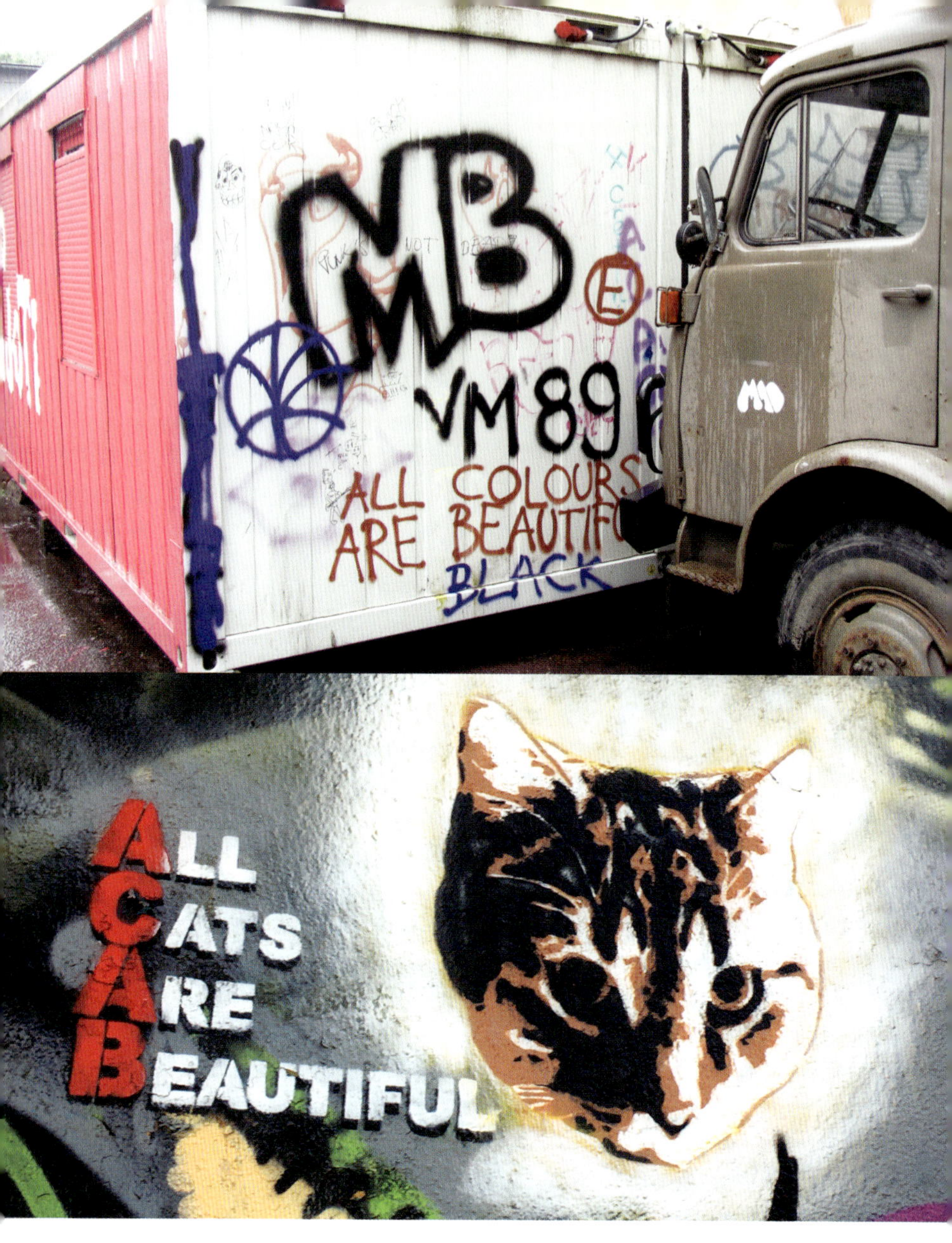

Above: *All Colours Are Beautiful — MB VM 89* (abbreviations for *Maribor, Viole Maribor, 1989*); by *Viole*, fans of FC Maribor; graffiti; Maribor, Slovenia; 2012.

Below: *All Cats Are Beautiful*; by unknown authors; stencil; Ljubljana, Slovenia; 2021.

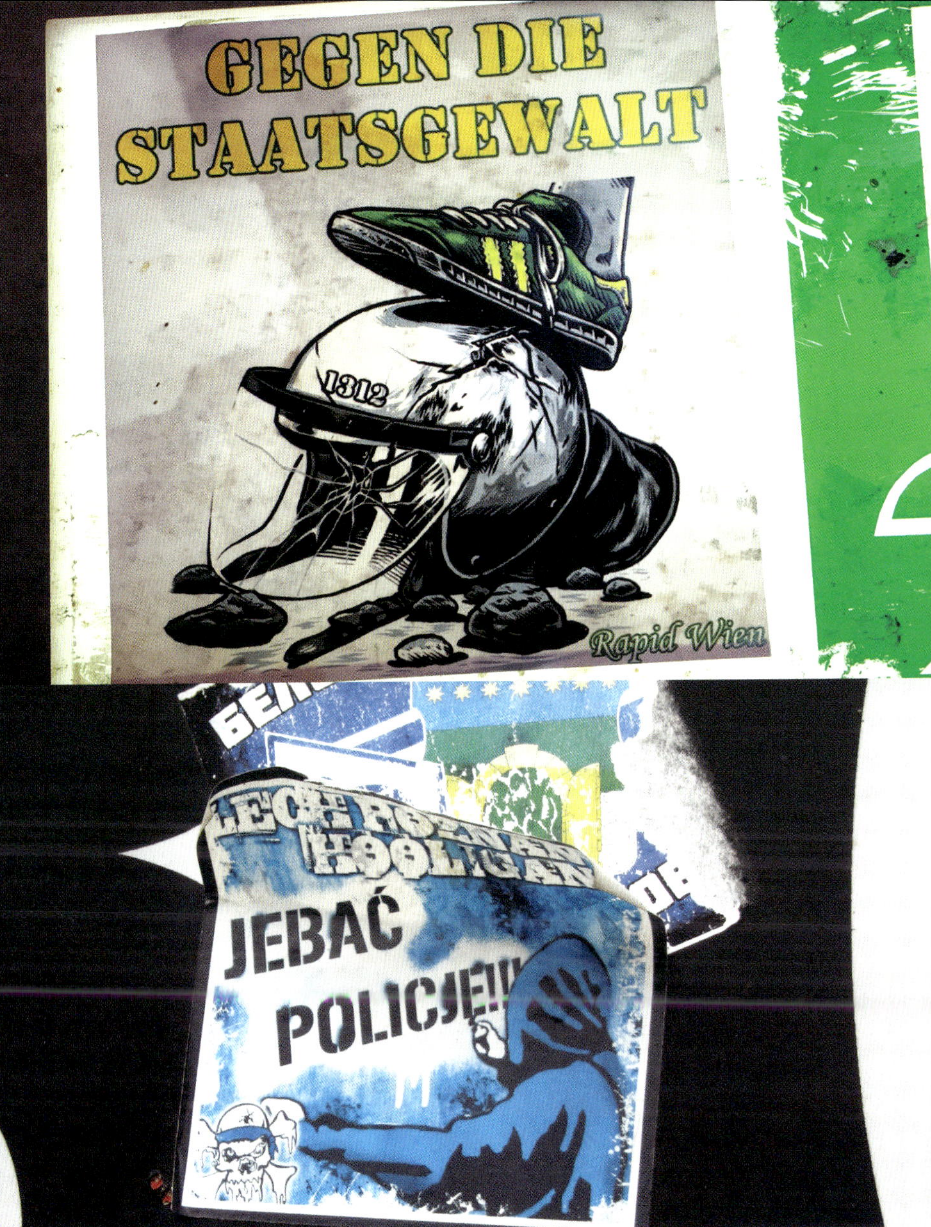

Above: *Gegen die Staatsgewalt* (*Against the violence of the state*) *1312 — Rapid Wien*; by fans of FC Rapid Vienna; sticker; Vienna, Austria; 2020.

Below: *Lech Poznan Hooligans — Jebać policje!!!* (*Fuck police!!!*); by fans of FC Lech Poznań, Poland; sticker; Krakow, Poland; 2009.

Typography

Football fans write their messages in random & very specific typography. Not being skilled graffiti writers, they improvise and use most different types of fonts; however, two of them are very typical. The first one is Gothic script (or Blackletter), often used also in heavy-metal, goth and biker subcultures, symbolizing toughness. The other is fasciofont (or Ultras Liberi) deriving from the typography of Italian avant-gardes (which were to a certain degree connected with the fascist regime): we can find it in graffiti and other football-fan visuals, but also in Italian right- and left-leaning political sub-groups.

For this book, our designer Tauras Stalnionis created an updated version of Ultras Liberi to connect it to the digital age. (For more on the history of this typeface and his analysis of Ultras Liberi's readability issues, see his contribution in the Appendix, pages 160–163.)

Writers of football-fan graffiti and authors of their stickers use, beside these two highly recognizable typographies, also a variety of other less specific ones, in many cases their "handwriting" is very bad, ugly. Yet, football-fan writers never use wildstyle letters or other typographies of the graffiti subculture because they are too cryptic. Their message to the public must be immediately and clearly understood.

And, finally, a note about their pure technical quality: most fan graffiti, stickers, murals, stencils, etc., are made crafty and on a do-it-yourself basis. Among the many cases of really extremely elaborate murals from my region, I must definitely mention those by the *Armada* (*Army*) of FC Rijeka, *Demoni* (*Demons*) of FC Istra 1961 from Pula and *Horde zla* (*Hords of Evil*) of FC Sarajevo; as well as aesthetically unpolished — or, to say frankly — really poor looking graffiti included in this book.

Ragazzi di Lubiana (*Ljubljana lads*); by *Green Dragons*, fans of FC
Olimpija Ljubljana; sticker (fasciofont); Ljubljana, Slovenia; 2018.

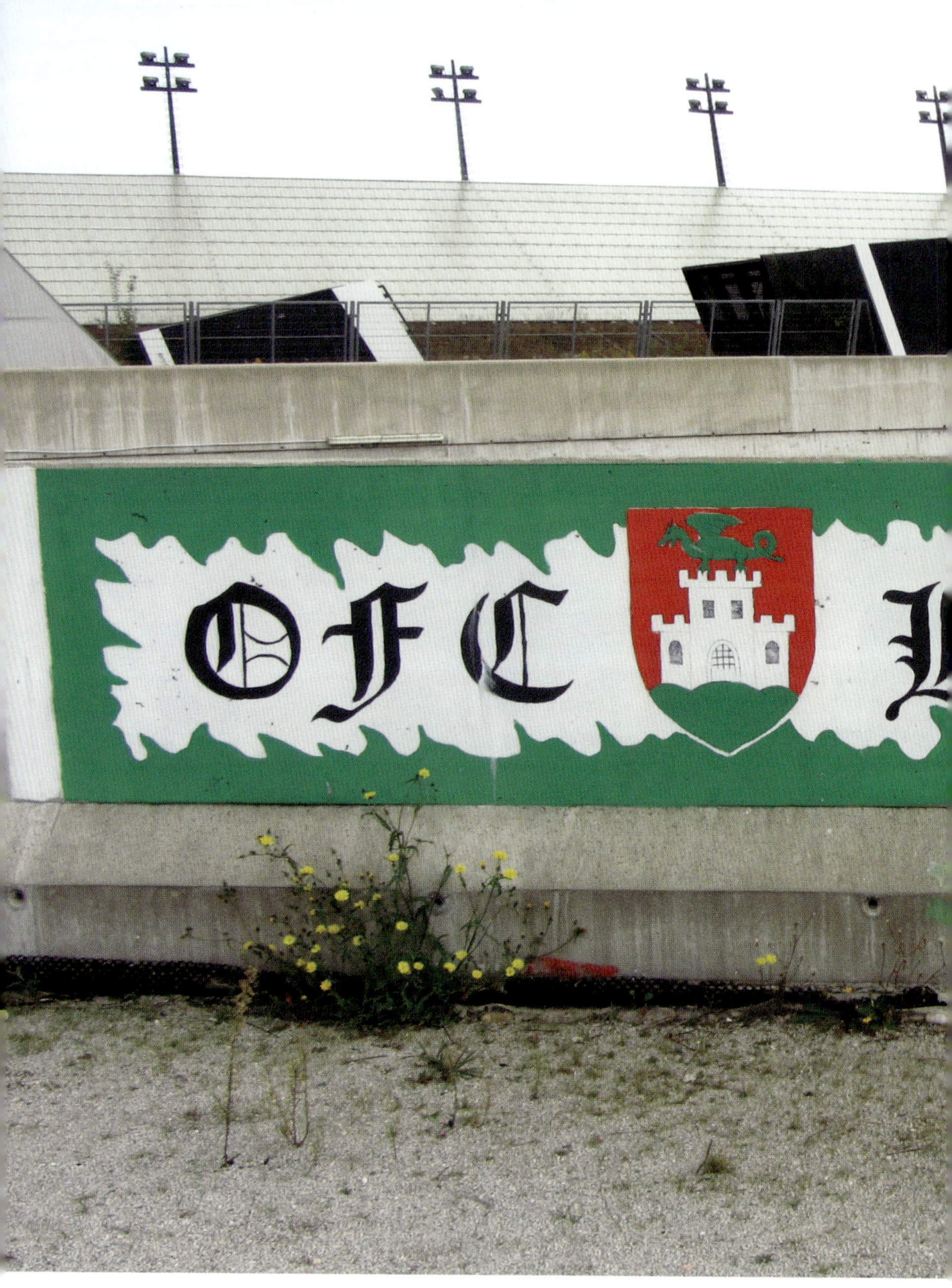

OFC Hooligans (*FC Olimpija Hooligans*); by *Green Dragons,* fans of FC Olimpija Ljubljana; mural (Gothic script); Ljubljana, Slovenia; 2014.

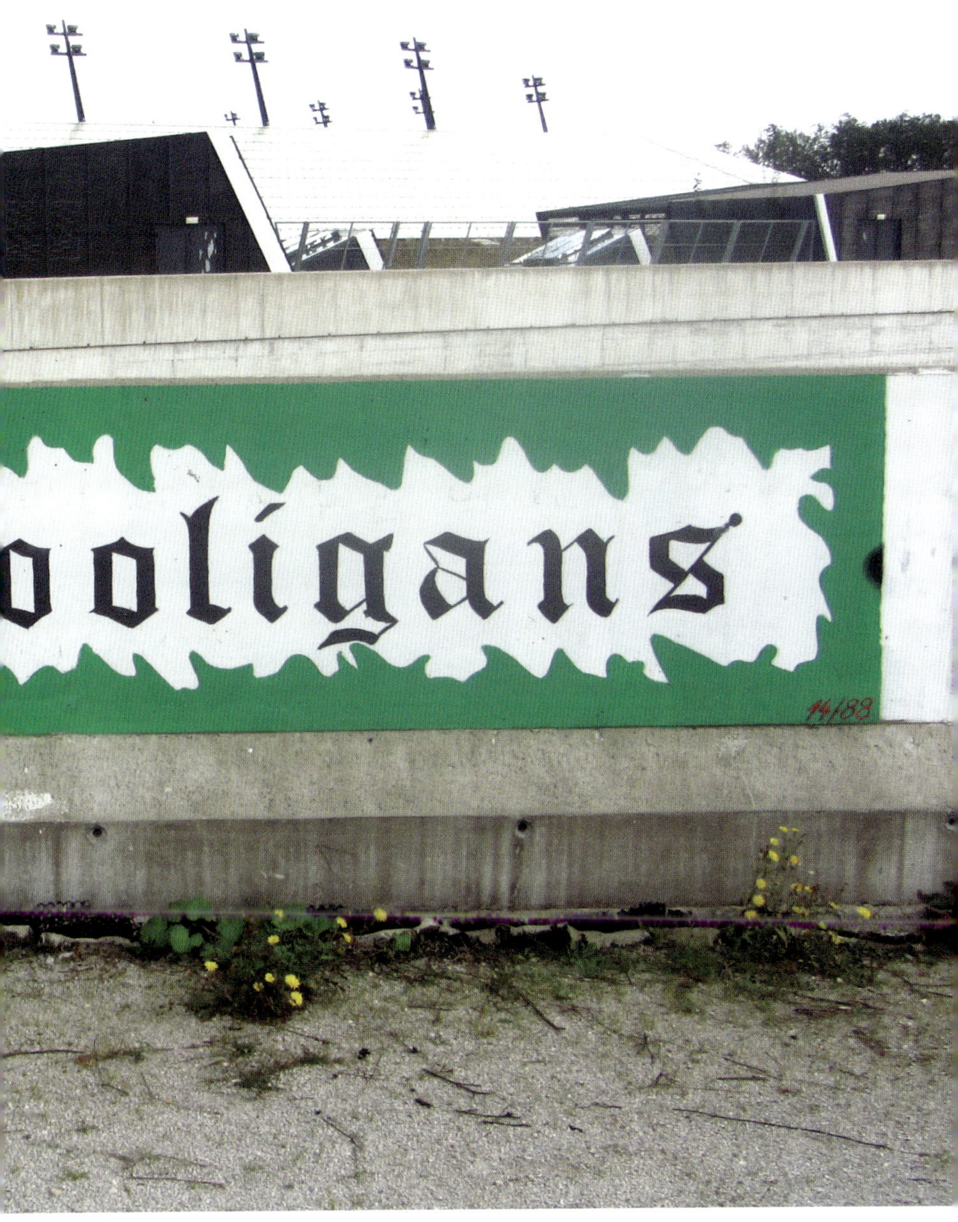
ooligans
14/88

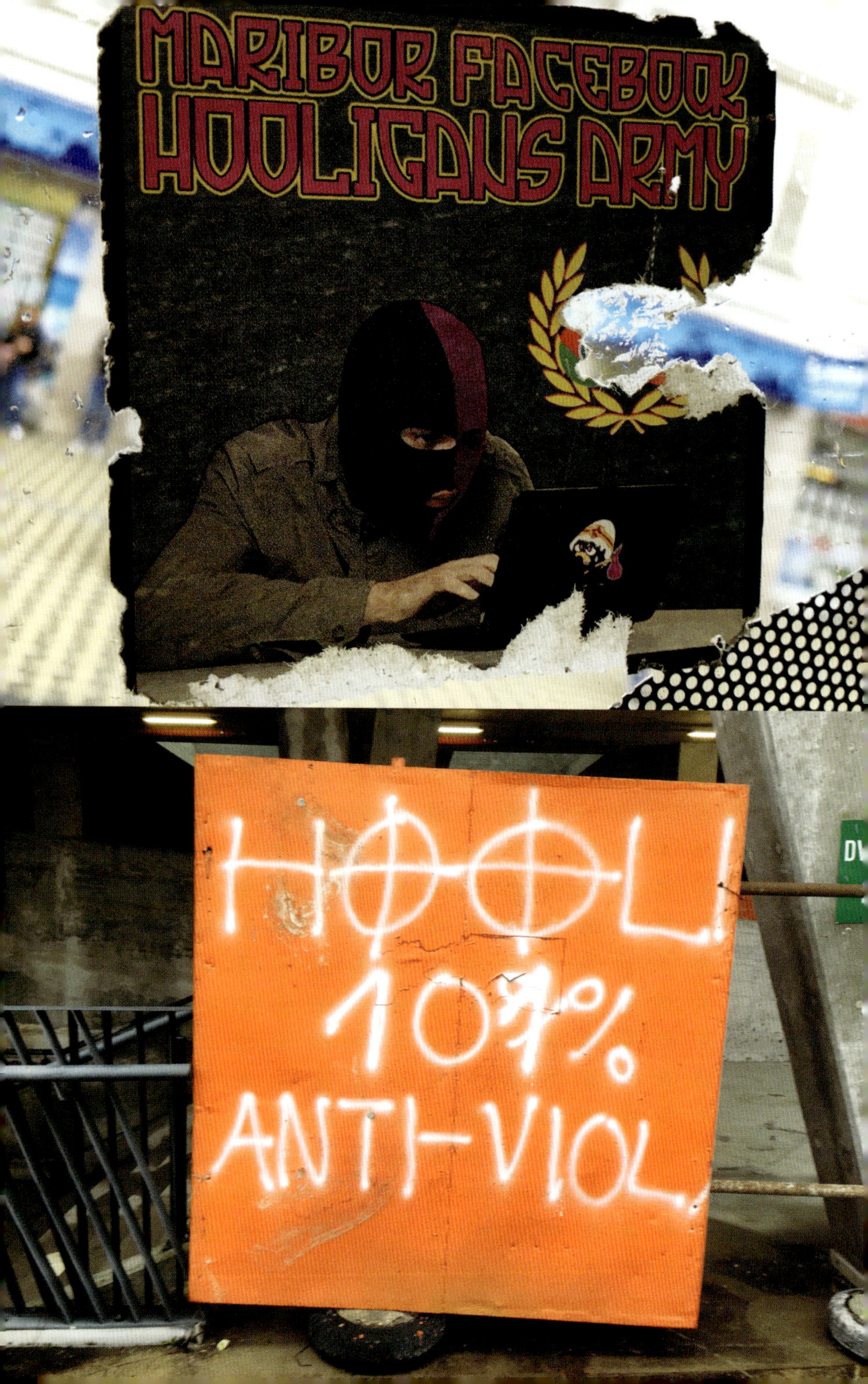
MARIBOR FACEBOOK
HOOLIGANS ARMY
HOOLI
107%
ANTI-VIOL

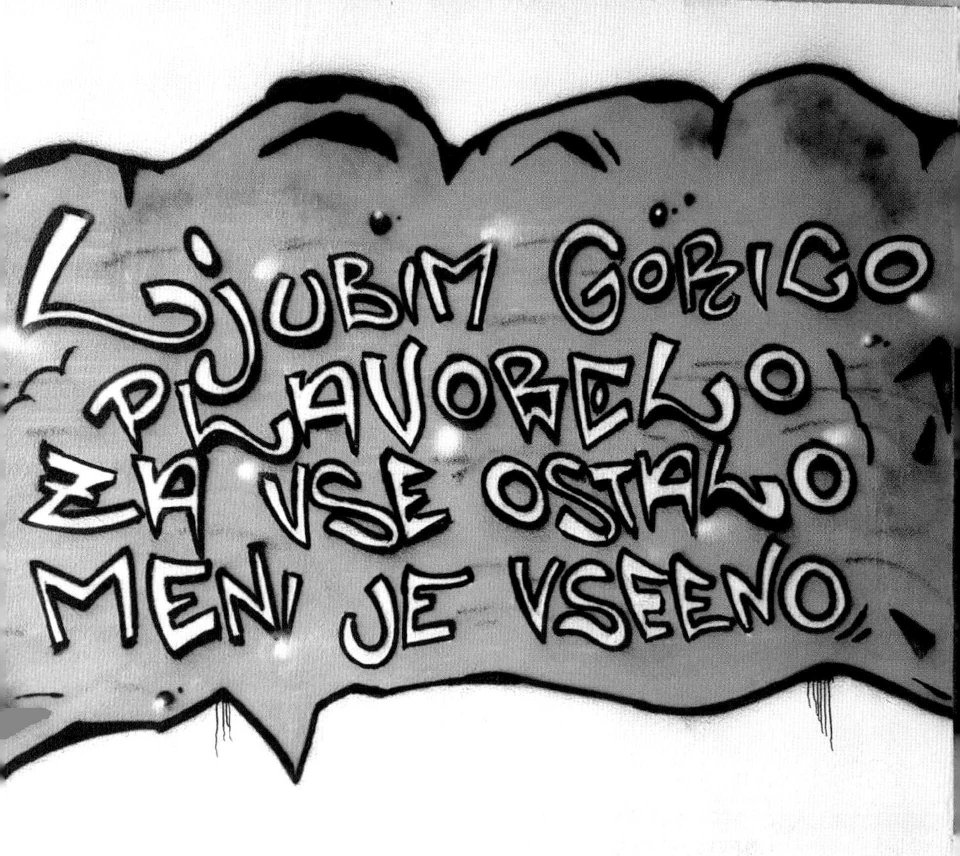

Opposite above: *Maribor facebook hooligans army*; by *Viole*, fans of FC Maribor; sticker (fasciofont); Maribor, Slovenia; 2017.

Opposite below: *Hool 101% Anti-Viola*; graffiti (poor style) made by *Green Dragons*, fans of FC Olimpija, against their rivals *Viole*, fans of FC Maribor; Ljubljana, Slovenia; 2021.

Above:
Ljubim Gorico plavobelo, za vse ostalo meni je vseeno (*I love blue-white Gorica, and I don't care for anything else*); by *Terror Boys*, fans of FC Gorica Nova Gorica; mural; Nova Gorica, Slovenia; 2019.

Following page:
Moje mesto, moj klub, FC OL (*My city, my club, FC Olimpija Ljubljana*); by *Green Dragons*, fans of FC Olimpija Ljubljana; mural; Ljubljana, Slovenia; 2018.

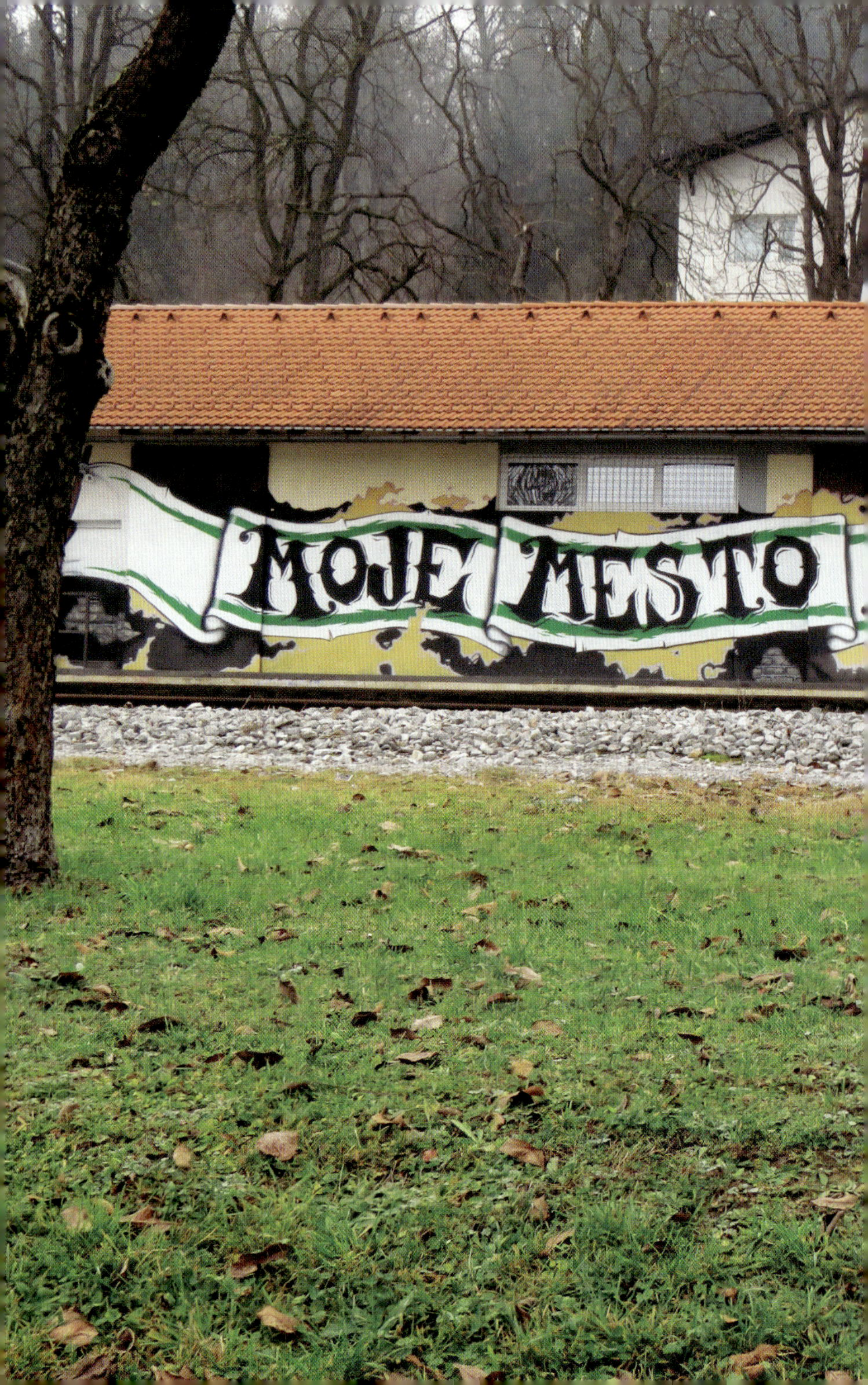
MOJE MESTO

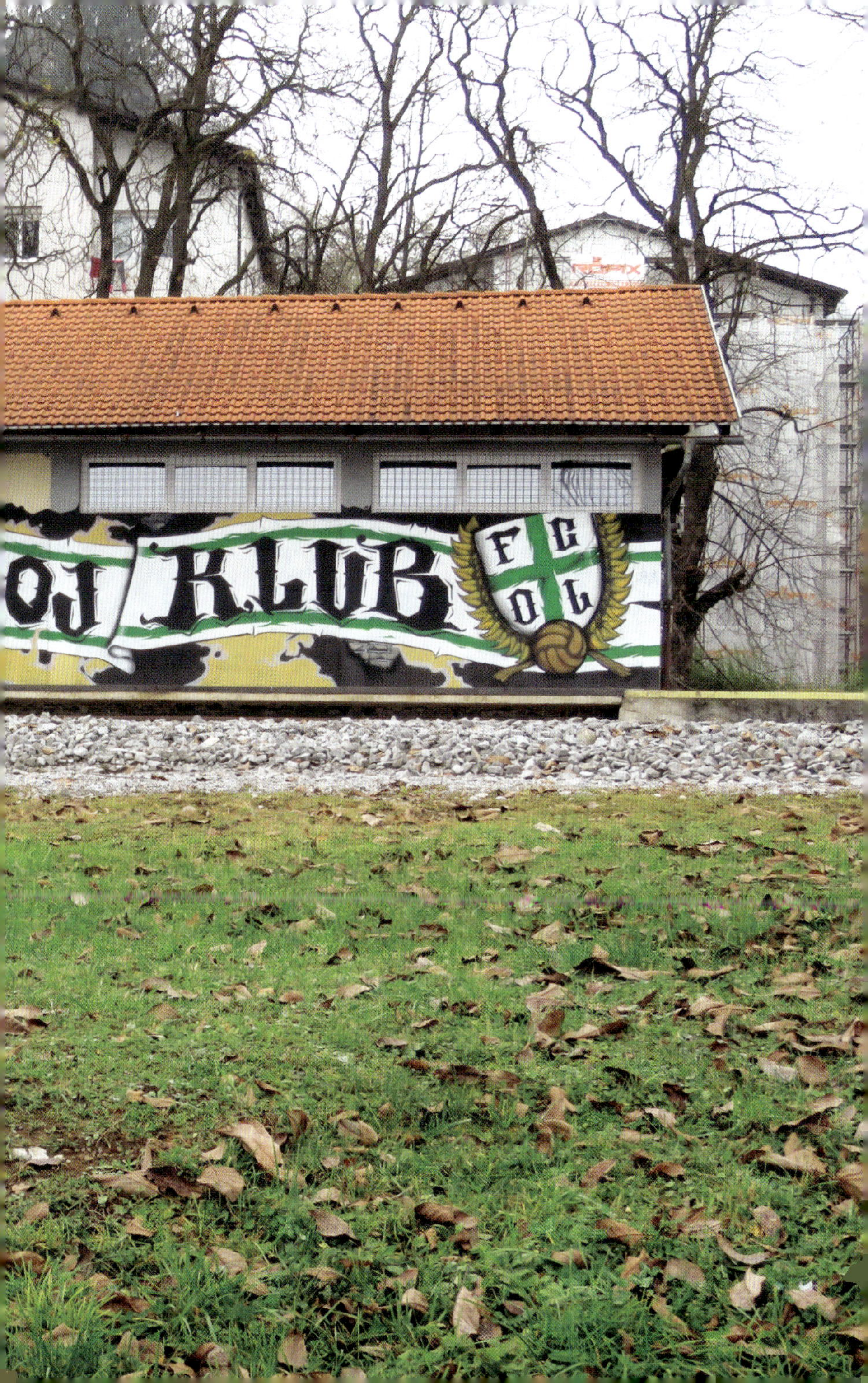
OJ KLUB
FC OL

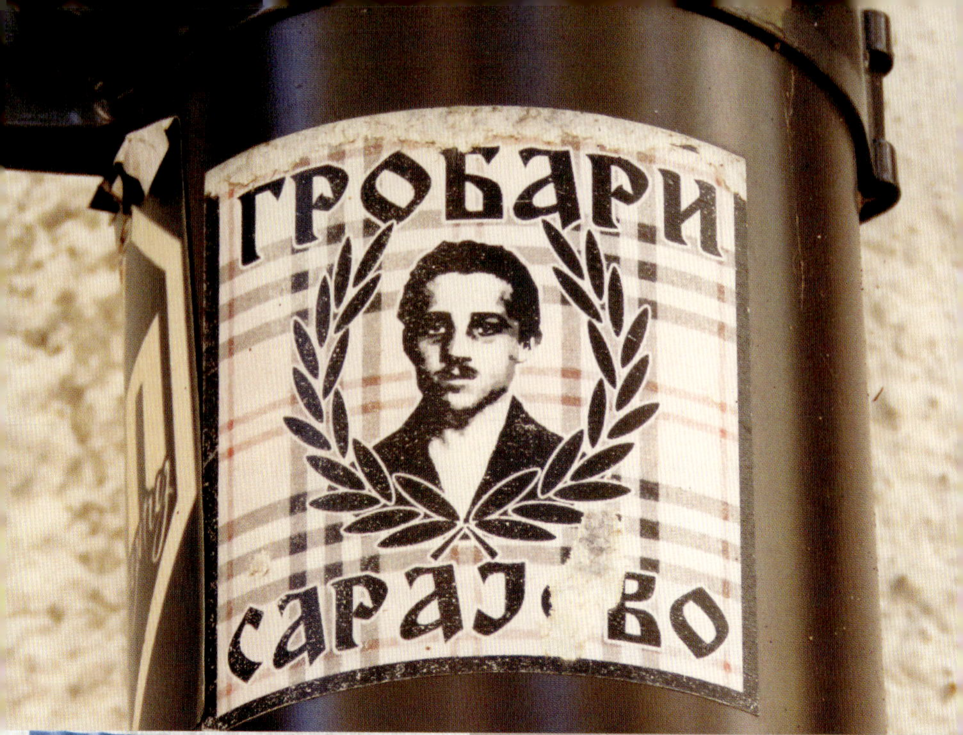

ГРОБАРИ
САРАЈ ВО

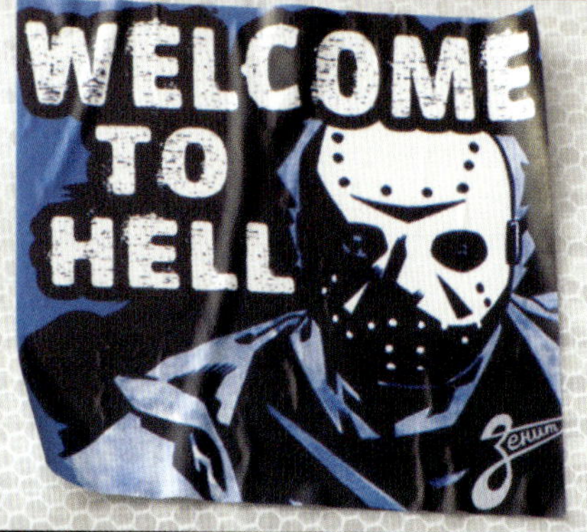

WELCOME
TO
HELL

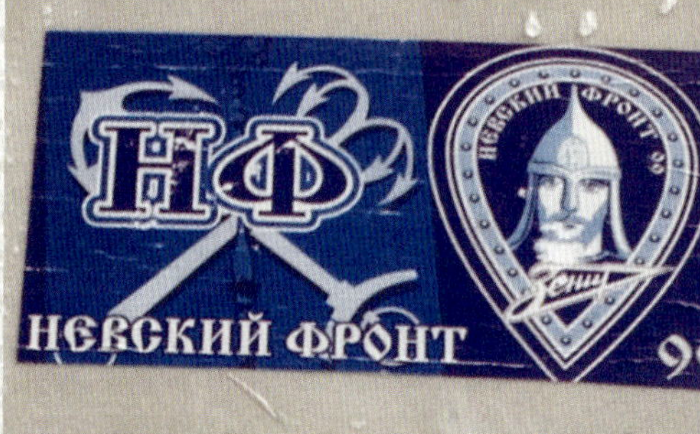

НФ
НЕВСКИЙ ФРОНТ

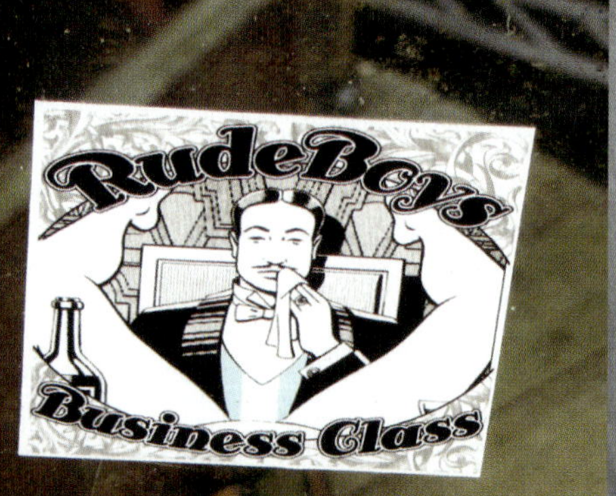

RudeBoys
Business Class

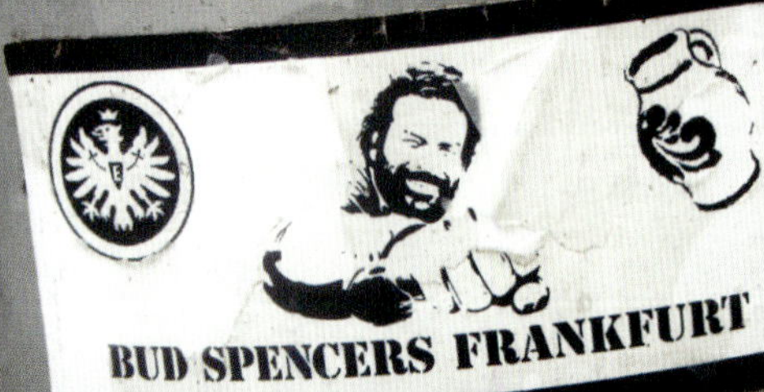

BUD SPENCERS FRANKFURT

Values

Love & hate: a First Vienna FC fan-sticker's centerpiece is a heart resembling an old leather football ball (page 77), while *Sezione Ostile* (*Hostile Sector*) of the FC Olimpia from Satu Mare, Romania, produced a sticker featuring a fan throwing a Molotov cocktail. Along these lines, violence & peacefulness are common motifs: there is a Banja Luka fan graffiti saying *We are Serbian fans, Europe be afraid of us* with the added Serbian Orthodox Church coat of arms, while the opposite pole is represented by a fairly flower-power-inspired sticker of *Rubin Ultras* of FC Rubin Kazan.

Old & new heroes: St. Petersburg's FC Zenit fan stickers show Jason Voorhees, the *Friday the 13th* series killer wearing a hockey goalie mask, while the one from FC Nevsky Front includes an image of Saint Alexander Nevsky. Pro-Yugoslav hero, an assassin of the Archduke and heir presumptive to the Habsburg throne Franz Ferdinand in Sarajevo in 1914 Gavrilo Princip can be found on the Sarajevo *Grobari* (*Gravediggers*) stickers, iconic Italian comedy actor Bud Spencer on those by FC Eintracht, Frankfurt, and controversial Croatian general Ante Gotovina on *Torcida*'s (see page 91).

Fan graffiti and street art can be both dramatic & playful, dead serious and ironic: a Novi Sad (Serbia) graffiti announces that *Death is being prepared for the*

Opposite above: *Grobari Sarajevo* (*Gravediggers Sarajevo*); by *Gravediggers,* fans of FC Partizan Belgrade; sticker; Doboj, Bosnia-Herzegovina; 2014.

Center left: *Welcome to Hell*; by fans of FC Zenit Saint Petersburg; sticker; Saint Petersburg, Russia; 2015.

Center right: *Nevsky Front*; by fans of FC Nevsky Front Saint Petersburg; sticker; Saint Petersburg, Russia; 2016.

Below left: *Rude Boys — Business Class*; by *Rude Boys*, fans of FC Virtus Entella Chiavari; sticker; Trieste, Italy; 2017.

Below right: *Bud Spencers Frankfurt*; by fans of FC Eintracht Frankfurt am Main; sticker; Frankfurt am Main, Germany; 2015.

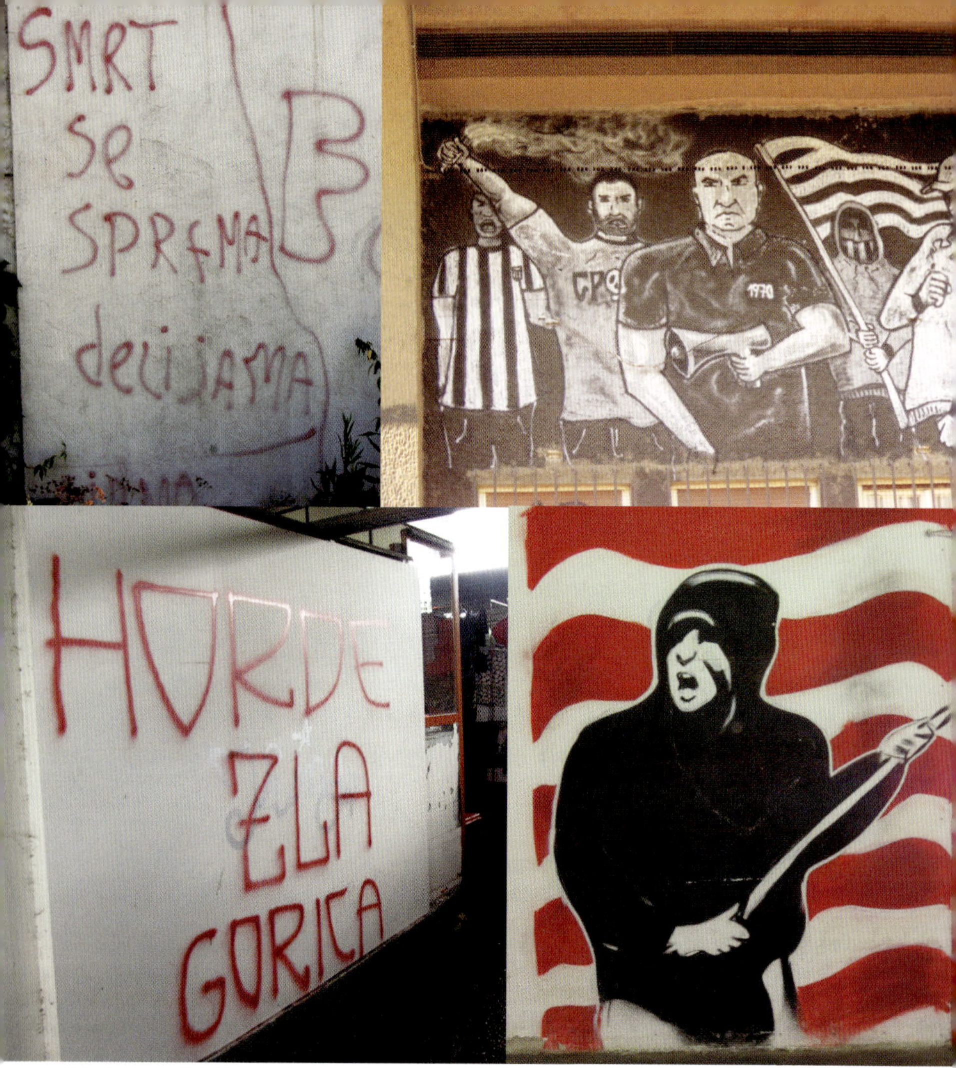

Above left: *Smrt se sprema Delijama* (*Death is being prepared for Delijas*); graffiti against *Delije* (*Dukes*), by fans of FC Crvena Zvezda Belgrade; Novi Sad, Serbia; 2013.

Above right: *Grobari* (*Gravediggers*), fans of FC Partizan Belgrade; mural; Belgrade, Serbia; 2017.

Below left: *Horde zla Gorica* (*Hords of Evil Gorica*); by *Horde zla*, fans of FC Sarajevo from the neighborhood of Gorica; graffiti; Sarajevo, Bosnia-Herzegovina; 2015.

Below right: *Delije* (*Dukes*), fans of FC Crvena Zvezda Belgrade; mural; Belgrade, Serbia; 2016.

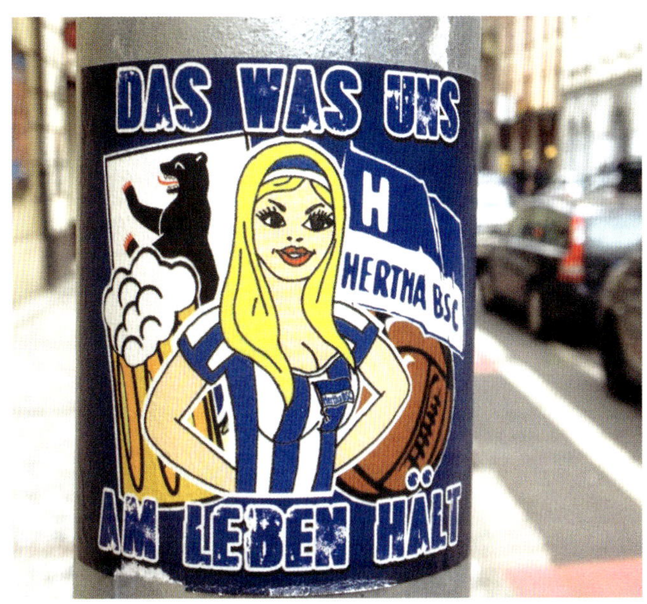

Delijas (fans of FC Crvena zvezda from Belgrade), and a Banja Luka graffiti (from the capital of the Serbian part of Bosnia-Herzegovina) promises *Death to Cops*. On the other hand, the *Society Graz* group of Grazer AK wishes to be seen as the sharp-dressed criminals from *Reservoir Dogs*, and a mischievous busty cheerleader smiles from a FC Hertha Berlin sticker.

Pro-Europe & anti-Europe, global and local: while some football fans clearly oppose the Union of European Football Associations (UEFA) and International Federation of Association Football (FIFA), which they perceive as multinational corporations destroying the local football scene and repressing football fans, some fan stickers celebrate the success of their respective teams in *Europe*. There is one by the *Viole* fans of FC Maribor, Slovenia, saying *Viole Maribor on Tour — Europe, here we are/We will conquer you!* At the other end of the spectrum, walls bearing graffiti of Serbian

Das was uns am leben hält — BSC Hertha (What keeps us alive — BSC Hertha); by fans of FC Hertha Berlin; sticker; Berlin, Germany; 2008.

tifosi speak that *UEFA* (or alternatively *FIFA*) *Supports Terrorism* because both organizations accepted Kosovo as a full member.[5]

In April 2021, the strong reactions by football fans to the proposed — and quickly extinguished — idea of The Super League of twenty of the most powerful football clubs in Europe (around the core dozen of them from Italy, England and Spain) show they want different football than that planned by a handful of football moguls and monopolists. Beside spontaneous protests of fan groups, also their official body, Football Supporters Europe (FSE) clearly opposed the Super League initiative. The fans' desires for more pluralistic, less commercialized, community-oriented, fan-based and not profit-based development of football competition finally came to the fore, although for years this was already distinctively and consistently displayed in their graffiti and street-art production. They were joined by not only UEFA and FIFA, leading British, Italian, and French politicians, but also by sport commentators and some current and former players.

Fans clearly prefer *old football* to the corporative one, and they hate its gentrification. Illustrative of this are the AFC Ajax fan sticker with its clichés *Fuck*

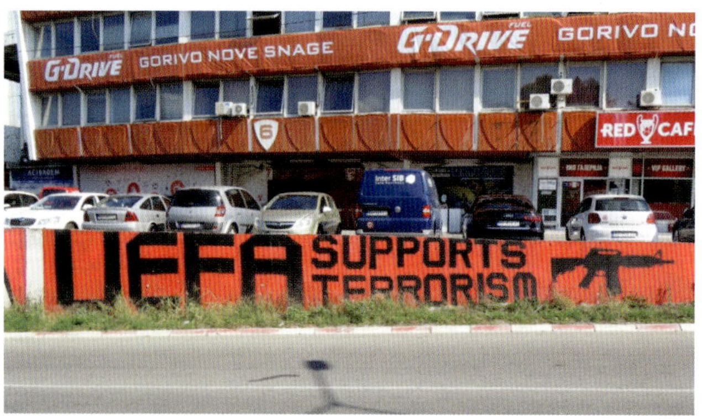

UEFA supports terrorism; unknown fans; mural; Belgrade, Serbia; 2014.

[5] To understand football and football fanhood as political resistance, see the case of Kosovo in O'Connor (2021: 34–35).

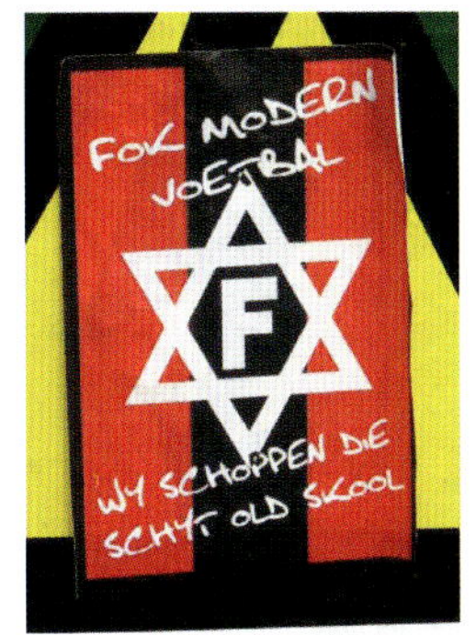

Modern Football and *We kick that shit, old school*; or the FC Paris Saint-Germain fan sticker with the same nostalgic message (in English) and a '40s or '50s black-and-white photo of boys chasing a ball on the street (see page 74). It is interesting to note that many football clubs, playing in the second or third tiers of national championships or even in regional leagues, have fervent fan bases, which shows also in their graffiti, stickers and stencils. But on the other hand, football fans in general have absolutely no problems wearing global sport brands or prestigious casual labels like Fred Perry, Stone Island or Everlast which have become (as such or as an aesthetic inspiration) a kind of informal symbol for them.

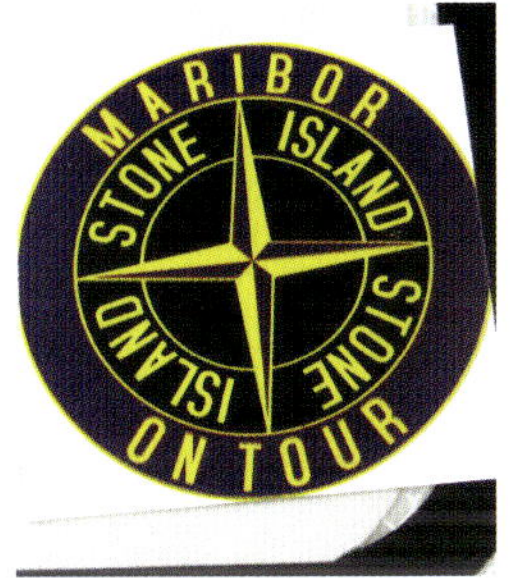

Plus, without a broader regional, European or global framework, football would remain on the level of an informal game of local lads. Global organization goes hand in hand with professionalization, which brings football as a game to entirely new levels. Football develops and is by definition changing, "modern."

On a related note, fans are locally patriotic & internationalistic: the *Vojvode* (*Dukes*) of FC Teteks, Tetovo (North Macedonia), choose to be represented by the Orthodox cross, and the FC Dinamo Zagreb fans *Bad Blue Boys* maintain to be *Defending the city, then*

Above: *Fok modern voetbal — Wyschoppen died schyt old skool* (*Fuck modern football — we kick that shit, old school*); by fans of FC Ajax Amsterdam; sticker; Leiden, The Netherlands; 2012.

Below: *Stone Island - Maribor — Gentlemen's Choice*; by *Viole*, fans of FC Maribor; sticker; Radlje, Slovenia; 2020.

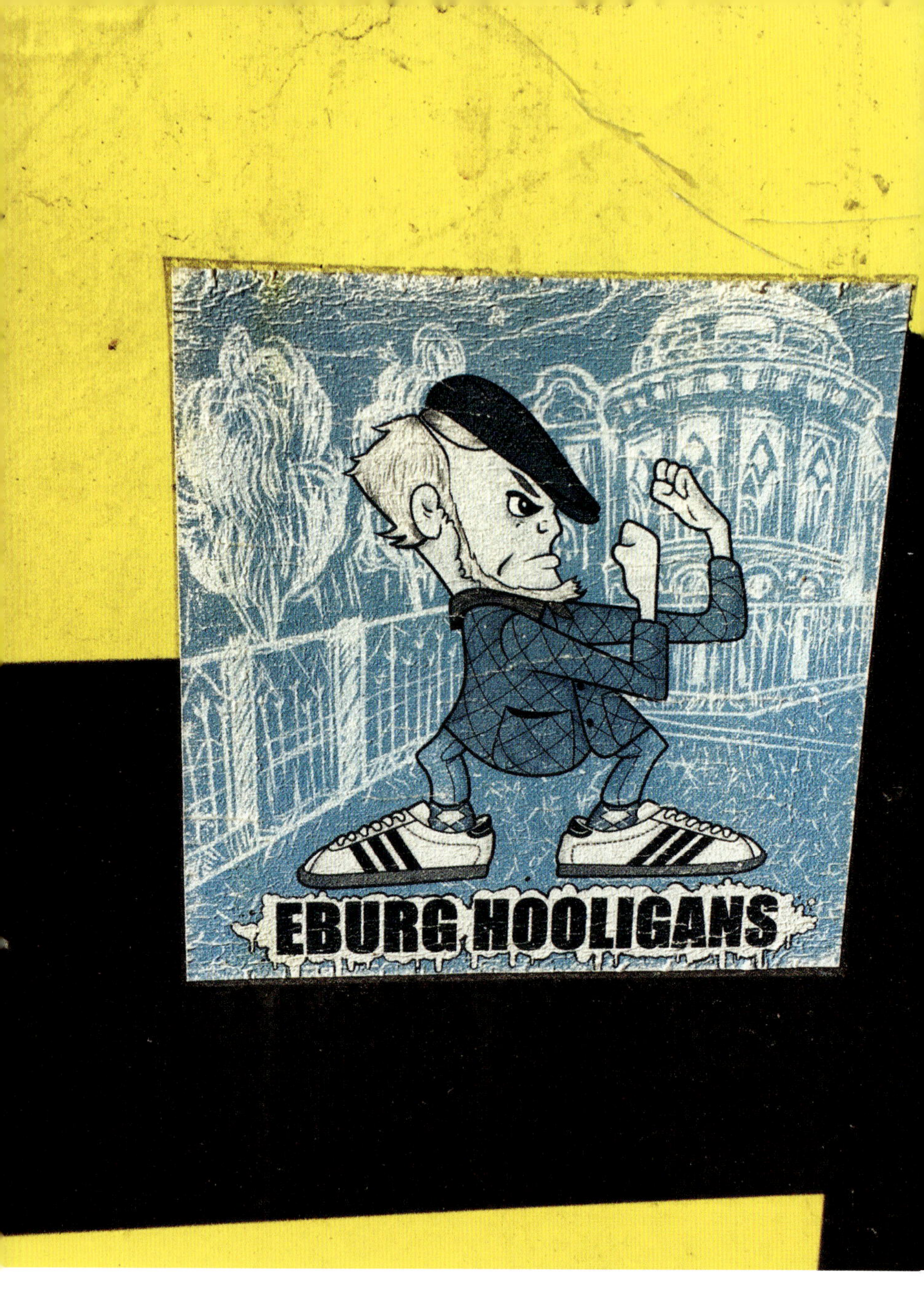

Eburg Hooligans; by fans of FC Ural Yekaterinburg, Russia;
sticker; Belgrade, Serbia; 2017.

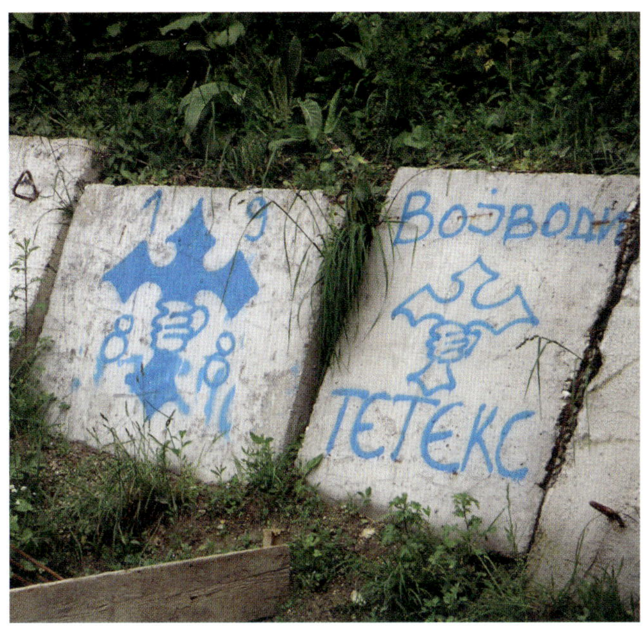

and now. Their localism goes as far as claiming the symbolism or the language of the conquered native inhabitants, one example being a sticker by the fans of FC Baltika Kaliningrad, which depicts one of the fans with a baseball bat and a killer's smile, accompanied by the words *Königsberg Ultras* (see page 167).[6] On the other hand, fans of FC CSKA Moscow, and FC Partizan Belgrade, issued a sticker proclaiming *Russians and Serbs, brothers forever* (see page 75).

Fans mark their terrain at home & abroad: we are well aware of the former — home-based fans make sure to mark their turf by occupying every visible space in the town and its vicinity. However, they also zealously spray-paint their love for their club/hate towards others as far away as they can. One of the most bizarre examples I found was scribbled *Forza Lecce* (*Forward Lecce*), a football club from Italian town of the same

Vojvodi, Teteks (Dukes, Teteks); by fans of FC Teteks Tetovo; graffiti; Tetovo, North Macedonia; 2011.

Kaliningrad is the capital of the most westernmost region, in fact an enclave of Russia, situated between Poland and Lithuania. Until 1945 it belonged to Germany, and its old name Königsberg was changed in 1946. However, local football fans, Russians by ethnicity, perform their subcultural eccentrism by using the old name.

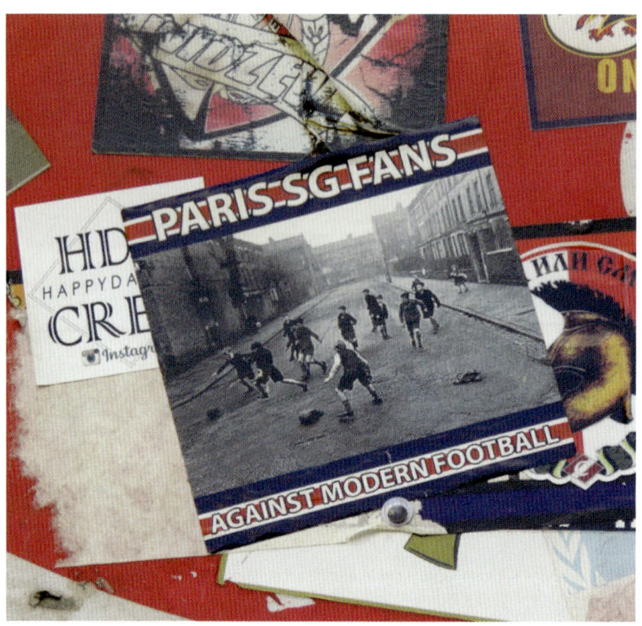

name), deep underground, in a Wieliczka Salt Mine elevator near Kraków.

It is also true that they often love their club & oppose its management: this can be seen on stickers by the *Bad Blue Boys* for whom *Love is measured in kilometers*, i.e., visiting matches, yet who hate the club president Zlatko Mamić (crossed out on stickers and called *Serb, Gypsy,* etc., in graffiti).

In another (apparent) paradox, fans of bigger clubs simultaneously love their city & have to fight for it, as they are on bad terms with other fans from the city and stand against them as much as they would stand against fans of other clubs. This is apparent from mutually hateful graffiti by the fans of two Kraków-based teams, Wisła and Cracovia, two Rijeka-based teams, Rijeka and Orijent, two Belgrade-based teams,

Paris SG fans against modern football; by fans of FC Paris Saint-Germain; sticker; Leiden, Netherlands; 2012.

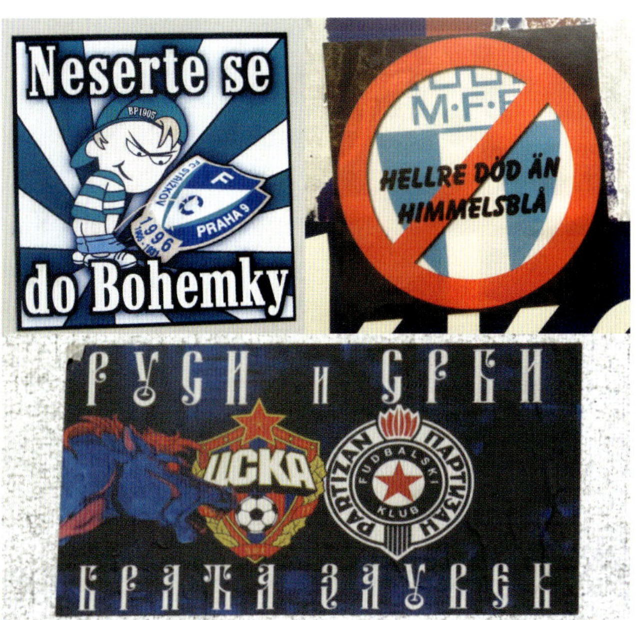

Crvena zvezda and Partizan, and two Graz-based teams, Sturm and Grazer AK (GAK). There is also the dispute between the Prague-based clubs with practically identical names FC Bohemians and Bohemians 1905 about the right to use the name "Bohemians": the "Bohemka" (Bohemians 1905) sticker warns "Střížkov" (Bohemians), *Don't fuck with Bohemka!* Yet there are also shows of camaraderie, as displayed in the joint loyalty sticker of tifo club *Grobari* and FC CSKA Moscow.

Above left: *Neserte se do Bohemky (Don't fuck with Bohemka)*; by fans of Bohemians 1905 against FC Bohemians Prague (Střížkov); sticker; Prague, Czech Republic; 2016.

Above right: *Hellre Död Än Himmelsblå (Rather Dead Than Sky Blue) Copenhagen*; anti-FC Malmö fans; sticker; Copenhagen, Denmark; 2013.

Below: *Rusi i Srbi — Braća zauvek (Russians and Serbs — Brothers forever)*: joint sticker by *Grobari*, fans of FC Partizan Belgrade and fans of FC CSKA Moscow; Moscow, Russia; 2008.

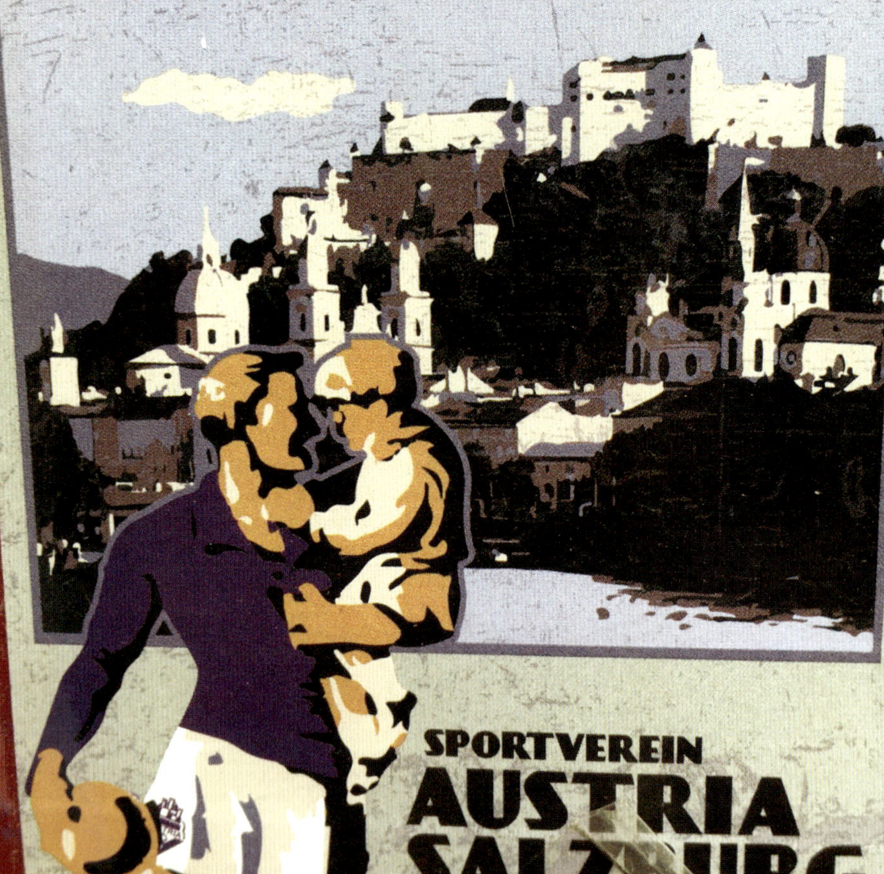

FUSSBALL
ROMANTIKER
SPORTVEREIN
AUSTRIA
SALZBURG
VON 1933

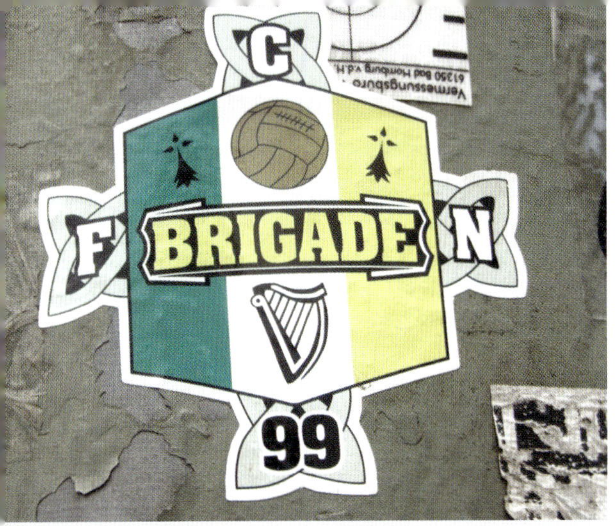

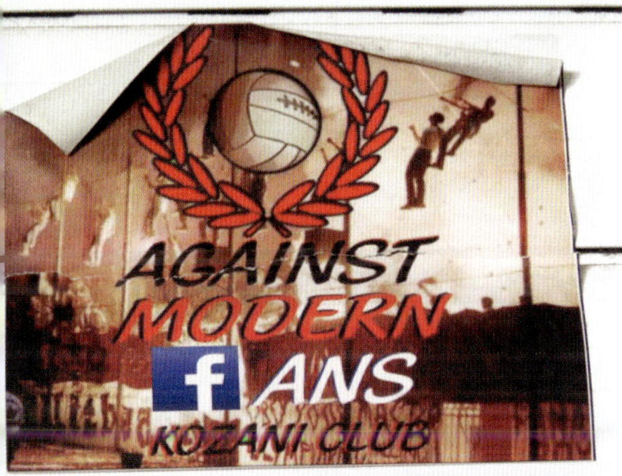

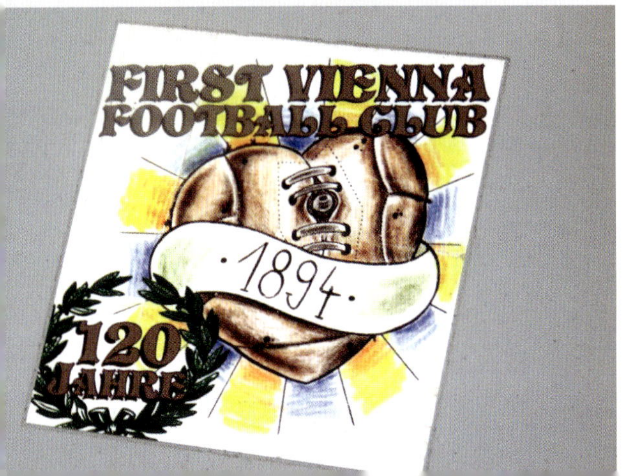

Opposite:
Fussball Romantiker — Sportverein Austria Salzburg von 1933 (Football Romantic — Sports club Austria Salzburg since 1933); by fans of FC Austria Salzburg; sticker; Gorizia, Italy; 2021.

Above:
By fans of FC Nantes; sticker; London, United Kingdom; 2011.

Center:
Against modern fans (Facebook fans) — Kozani club; by fans of FC Kozani, Greece; sticker; Skopje, North Macedonia; 2016.

Below:
First Vienna football club — 1894 — 120 Jahre (120 years); by fans of First Vienna FC; sticker; Vienna, Austria; 2020.

Political messages

A frequent criticism of football states that it "ignites, concentrates, and amplifies nationalist and sectarian feelings" (Kuhn 2011: 59). But at the same time, football includes a variety of opposing, anti-nationalist and free-minded individuals, groups and tendencies (Ibid., 105–183, 198). We will look at some of the polarizing examples of all these, and in a later section will closely examine the echoes and dissonance between fan art and ideology.

Football-fan graffiti can be seen as both apolitical & political. Supposedly, they are only interested in playing ball, which is expressed by images of old balls, pints of beer and megaphones: there are examples from *Terror Boys* of FC Gorica — murals showing their usual "props" of beer (this page) and a loudspeaker (see page 29) and from FC Maribor's *Viole* (sticker featuring Andy Capp with a pint of beer, signed by *Alco corps Maribor*). Yet I regularly also notice (current) political

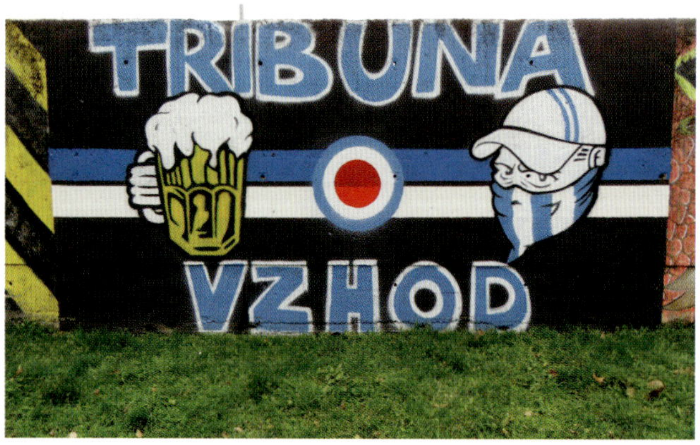

Above: *Tribuna vzhod* (*Terrace — east*); by *Terror Boys*, fans of FC Gorica Nova Gorica; mural; Nova Gorica, Slovenia; 2019.

Opposite: *BBB Zaprešić*, image of count Josip Jelačič (1801–1859) (*Bad Blue Boys*); by *Bad Blue Boys*, fans of FC Dinamo Zagreb; sticker; Zagreb, Croatia; 2019.

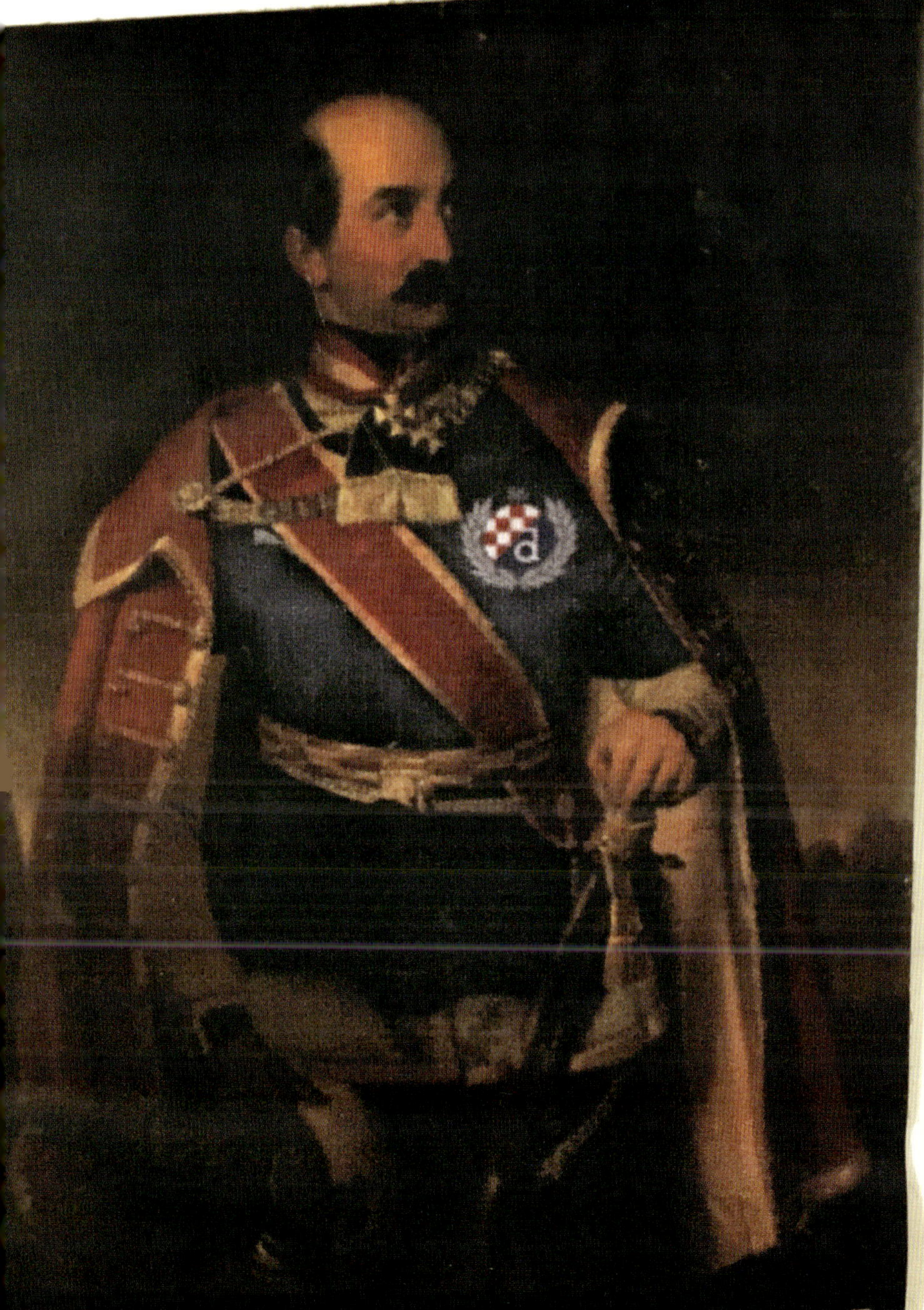

BBB ZAPREŠIĆ

and nationalistic topics in them. The Hajduk's *Torcida* often does visual marketing with ustasha (the name of Croatian nazis during the World War II or present-day advocates of extreme Croatian Right) or nazi symbols (like the nazi-eagle), or renames itself in graffiti as *Hajduk Jugend* (derivative of *Hitlerjugend*).[7] Fans of Serbian football clubs obsessively spray messages like *Kosovo is Serbia* or *1389* (which is the year of the traumatic Kosovo battle that marked the beginning of the Ottoman domination over the medieval Serbian state) or post stickers with a crossed out Albanian national symbol over Kosovo.

[7] For a profound study of the history and present of the Torcida ultras, see Lalić 2011.

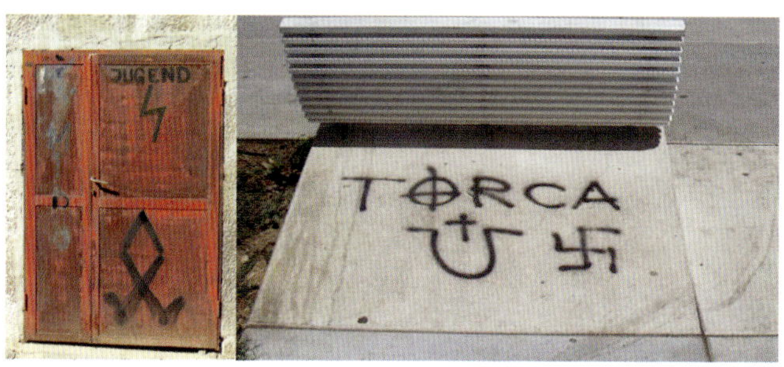

Stickers, graffiti and stencils mix sports & politics: a ball combined with a Celtic cross by the Sofia CSKA fans promises *Loyalty to the nation and the club!*, while the Moscow CSKA fans prefer a combination of the city-quarter name, club coat of arms (with a red star!) and the nazi version of the *Totenkopf*. The majority of various Croatian fan groups feature an ustasha version of the Croatian coat-of-arms. Furthermore, lots of football-fan street-art pieces are inspired by signifiers of political totalitarianisms of the 20th century,

Above left: *Jugend* and neo-nazi Odal rune (used by several SS units in WWII); graffiti; Partizan Stadium, Belgrade, Serbia; 2016.

Above right: *Torca* (*Torcida*) swastika, Celtic cross / neonazi symbol / ustasha clerico-fascist symbol; by fans of FC Hajduk Split; graffiti; Split, Croatia; 2011.

Opposite: Map of Kosovo with crossed-out Albanian black eagle; by *Delije* (*Dukes*), fans of FC Crvena Zvezda Belgrade; Belgrade, Serbia; 2021.

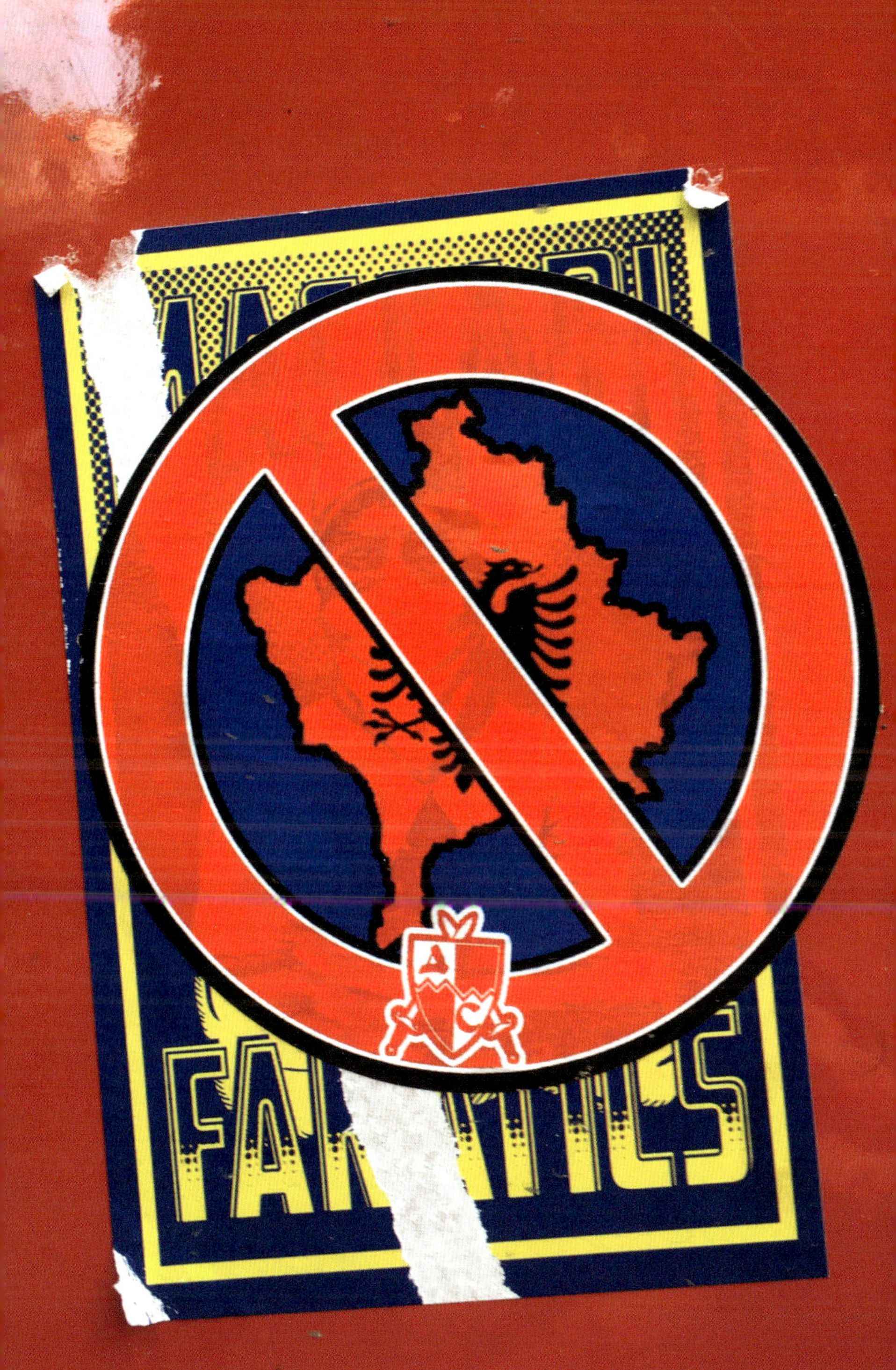

MA...
FANATICS

symbolizing toughness and fanaticism, like nazi aesthetics & socialist avant-gardism. The former is popular with the fans of FC Senezh, Solnechnogorsk, and the latter with the fans of CSKA or FC Lokomotiv, Moscow.

Graffiti, stencil and sticker themes can be left-wing & right-wing, yet it is obvious from fans' traditional

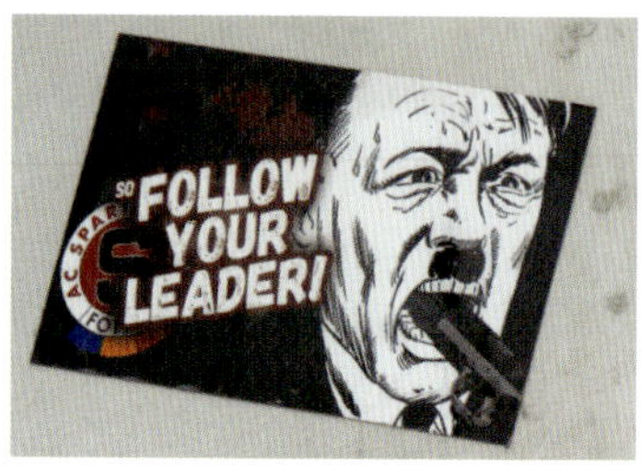

values, (local-)patriotism and conservative political agenda that the latter prevail. Leftist stickers are produced by the fans of Ajax, Amsterdam (*Always Anti Racist*), FC Rapid Vienna (a fist shattering a swastika, and the inscription *Never go right*) and FC Sparta Prague (an image of A. Hitler with a gun in his mouth, and a classic antifa slogan *Follow Your Leader!*).

Examples of right-leaning messages include a *Diósgyőr Hooligans* sticker by the FC Diósgyőr, Hungary, that shows the nazi *Totenkopf* and, in Gothic script, the name of the German Romantic movement *Sturm und Drang*, a common reference in extreme nationalism; or a sticker by the Moscow-based Spartak fans with a German military helmet, the *Stahlhelm*.[8] (See page 87.)

They often contradict themselves: the largest Belgrade and Zagreb clubs have typical

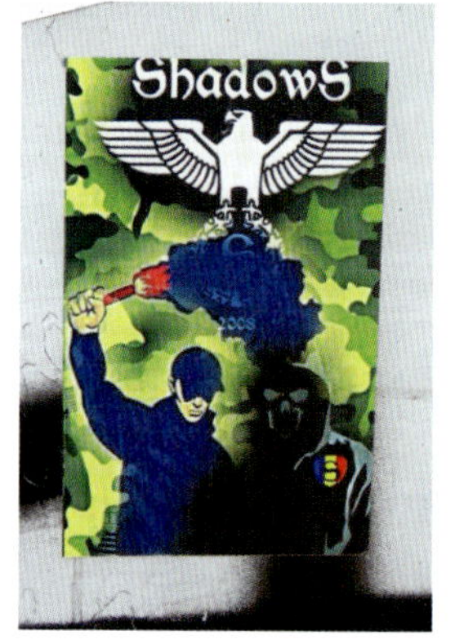

[8] For a concise overview of history and present of very similar political aspects and dimensions of th[e] Greek football-fan culture, see Zaimak[is] (2018).

Above: *Follow Your Leader! — AC Sparta*; by fans of FC Sparta Prague; sticker; Prague, Czech Republic; 2016.

Below: *Shadows 2008*; by *Shadows 08,* one of the fan groups of FC Steaua Bucharest; sticker; Constanța, Romania; 2017.

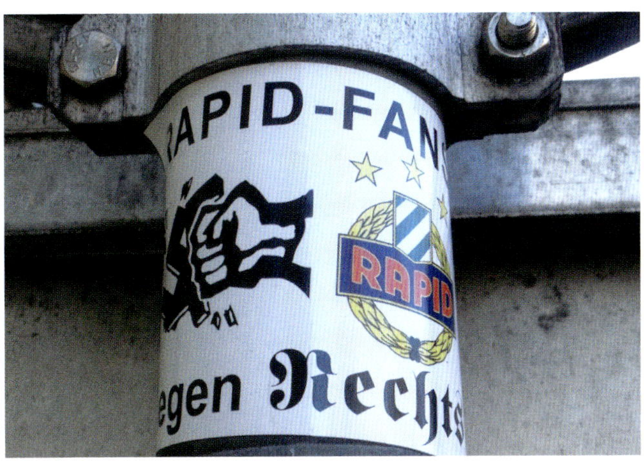

socialist names carrying over from Yugoslav times and some even have the red star in their coat of arms (Crvena zvezda, Partizan and Dinamo). In contrast, the iconography of their fans, *Delije, Grobari,* and *Bad Blue Boys*, is distinctively right-wing, nationalist, often even fascist, as they celebrate the Quisling commanders of World War II or war criminals from the recent Bosnian War, going as far as donning the name of their formations.

Football-fan graffiti can also be non-chauvinistic & chauvinistic: transparents and graffiti by Hamburg-based St. Pauli state *Refugees Welcome*, and the FC Levadia Tallinn (Estonia) fans' sticker appeals to the passers-by in both Russian and Cyrillic script (see page 87). Unidentified football fans post stickers *Love Football — Hate racism* and they reverse the usual meaning of the 1312 in *All colors are beautiful* (see pages 56 and 171).

Football clubs with strong left-wing *tifosi* are, beside St Pauli, also Livorno, AEK Athens, Olympique de Marseille, Adana Demirspor from Turkey, Werder

Rapid Fans / Gegen Rechts (Fans of FC Rapid Against the Right-wing); by fans of FC Rapid Vienna; sticker; Vienna, Austria; 2011.

Bremen, Scottish Celtic, the Israeli Hapoel, the English Liverpool and the Spanish Rayo Vallecano. Their icons (Che Guevara), symbols (red stars, red banners, hammer and sickle), songs (*Bandiera Rossa*) and slogans (*For a Coloured Terrace!*) are diametrically opposed to the right-wing ones. There's only a small number of left-leaning clubs in the Balkans: the FC Zagreb *White Angels*, the Velež *Red Army* from Mostar, and the Čelik *Robijaši* (*Convicts*) Zenica, both from Bosnia-Herzegovina.

Meanwhile, the *Patriot Boys* or the *Lešinari* (*Vultures*), both fans of FC Borac Banja Luka, Bosnia-Herzegovina 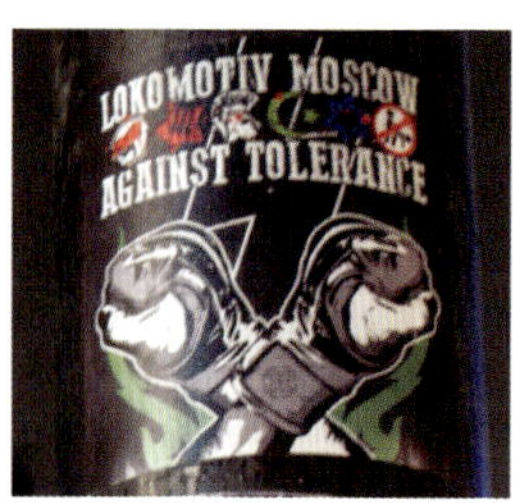 produce stencils with the Serbian nationalist sign (the first three-finger salute) and the words *Because I hate Bosnia*. Players and fans of Ajax, a club with Jewish roots, regularly receive antisemitic insults,[9] while the fans of Korona Kielce

[9] Similarly received by fans of FC Cracovia Krakow, known as *The Jude Gang*.

Above: *Patriot Boys — Jer mrzim Bosnu* (*Because I hate Bosnia*, with the symbol of the *Lešinari* ultras and the Serbian nationalistic three-finger salute); by *Lešinari* (*Vultures*), fans of FC Borac Banja Luka, capital of the Serbian republic in Bosnia-Herzegovina; combination of stencils and graffiti; Banja Luka, Bosnia-Herzegovina; 2015.

Below: *Lokomotiv Moscow against tolerance*, symbols of anarchism, antifascism, sharp skinheads, Islam, Judaism, and homosexual acts; by fans of FC Lokomotiv Moscow; sticker; Moscow, Russia; 2015.

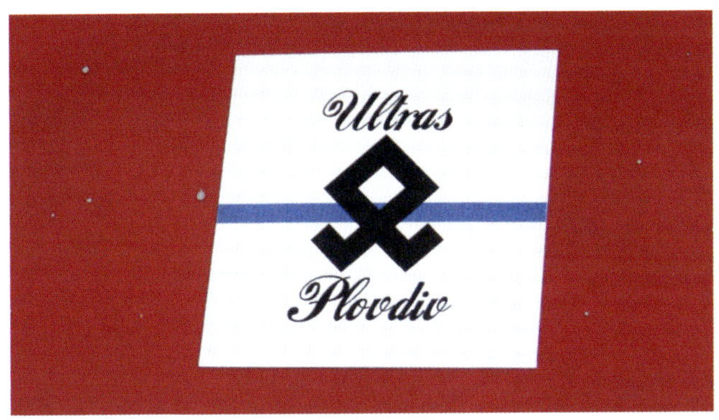

(from Poland) display images of KKK members and burning crosses, together with English inscriptions *We stand for god, race & country*. Unidentified Russian fans post stickers against their regional southern neighbors *Against Caucasian football* with upside-down coats of arms of Caucasian football clubs playing in Russian leagues. All the while, these extremists manage to overlook the fact that clubs from Europe they consider *white continent* attract more and more players of different races, from other continents, and from what they consider as not totally integral parts of Europe, such as the Balkans and the Caucasus.

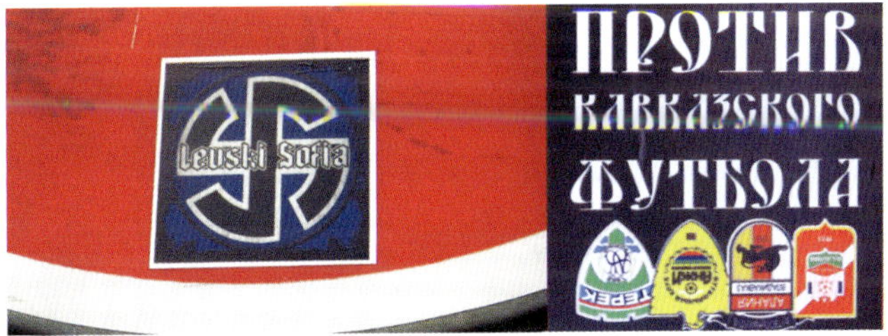

Above: *Ultras Plovdiv* and Odal rune; by *Napoletani Ultras Plovdiv*, fans of FC Lokomotiv Plovdiv; sticker; Plovdiv, Bulgaria; 2019.

Below left: *Levski Sofia*; by fans of FC Levski Sofia (also known as the *Animals*); sticker; Sofia, Bulgaria; 2018.

Below right: *Protiv kavkazskogo futboli* (*Against football from the Caucasus*); by unknown fans; sticker; Saint Petersburg, Russia; 2016.

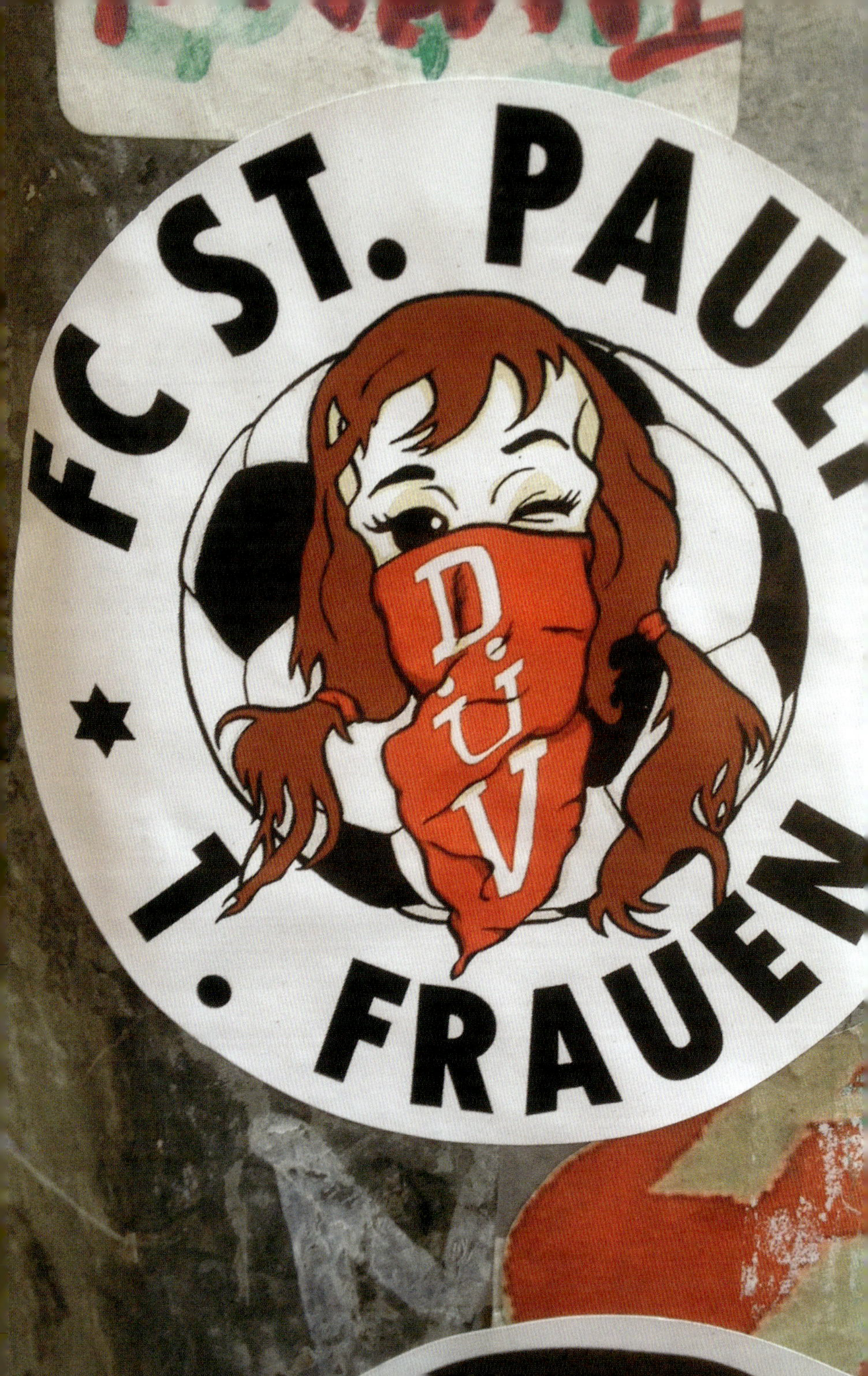

FC ST. PAULI
T. FRAUEN
DUV

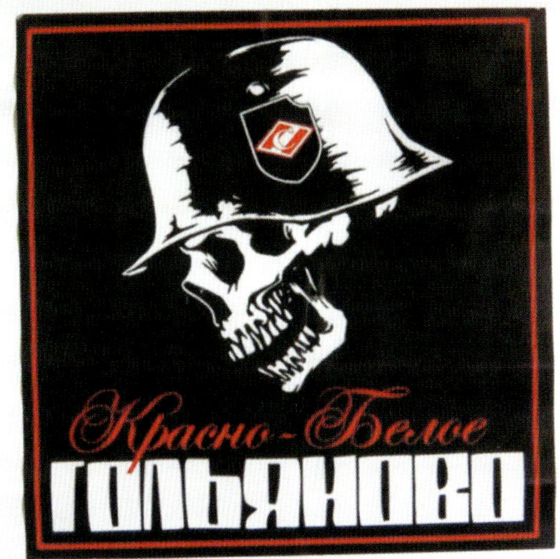

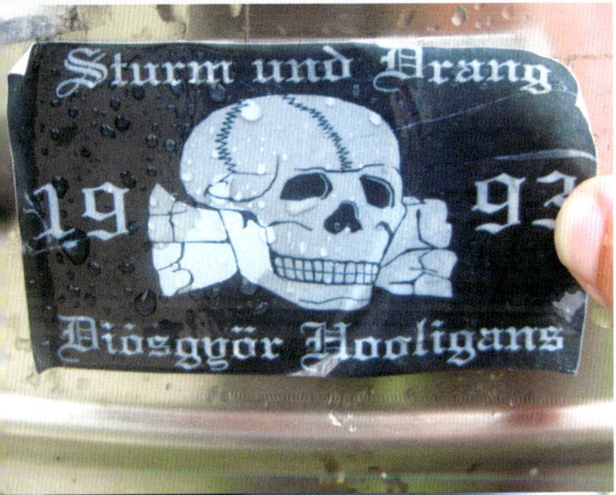

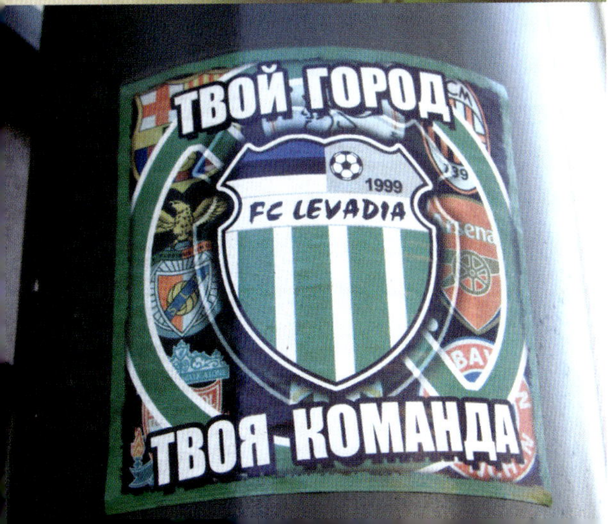

Opposite:
FC St. Pauli — 1. Frauen (FC St. Pauli — Women); by fans of FC St. Pauli Hamburg; sticker; Giessen, Germany; 2019.

Above:
Red-white Golyanovo; by fans of FC Spartak Moscow from the district of Golyanovo; sticker; Moscow, Russia; 2008.

Center:
Sturm und Drang — Diósgyőr Hooligans 1993 with *Totenkopf* (*Storm and stress*); by fans of FC Diósgyőr Miskolc; sticker; Szenendre, Hungary; 2017.

Below:
Tvoi gorod — tvoia komanda (*Your city, your team*) *FC Levadia*; by fans of FC Levadia Tallinn; sticker; Tallinn, Estonia; 2015.

War, peace, and football in (post-)Yugoslavia

A brief explanation of the complex 20th-century political history of the former-Yugoslav region: The Kingdom of Serbs, Croats and Slovenes was established in 1918 from the kingdoms of Serbia and Montenegro as well as South-Slavic parts of the Habsburg Empire. It was renamed the Kingdom of Yugoslavia in 1929. Dismembered by Axis Powers in 1941, the occupying forces and their collaborators (Serbian, Croatian, Slovenian etc. quislings) fought a communist-led resistance called *partisans*, under the command of Josip Broz Tito, who finally won and in 1945 established the socialist federalist state.

Socialist Yugoslavia collapsed in a series of armed clashes (Slovenia in 1991, North Macedonia in 2001) and bloody wars (Croatia in 1991–1995, Bosnia-Herzegovina 1992–1995, Kosovo 1998–1999), leaving seven small independent countries in its place, most of them under threat of irredentist movements and policies. Many contemporary right-wing subpolitical groups and movements, including football fans, took names, symbols, and ideological orientations from this troubled history, like *ustasha*, *škripari* (after WWII anti-communist guerrillas), *chetniks*, etc., with which they directly refer to the traumatic episodes from last decades.

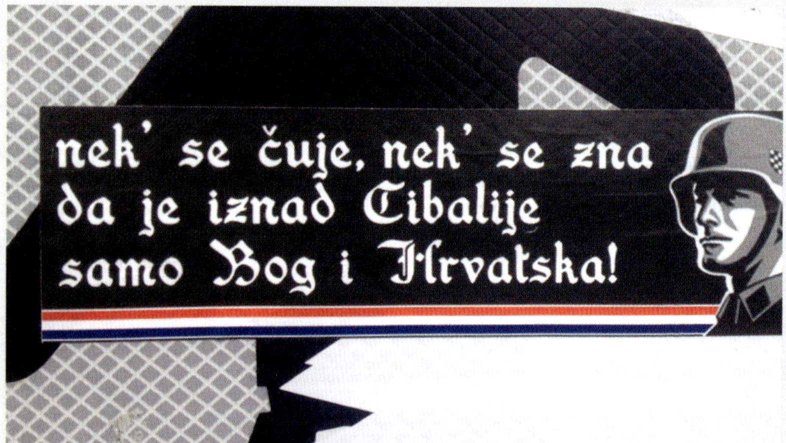

Nek' se čuje, nek' se zna, da je iznad Cibalije samo Bog i Hrvatska! and ustasha soldier (*Let it be heard, let it be known/that there are only God and Croatia above Cibalija!*); by fans of FC Cibalia Vinkovci; sticker; Požega, Croatia; 2016.

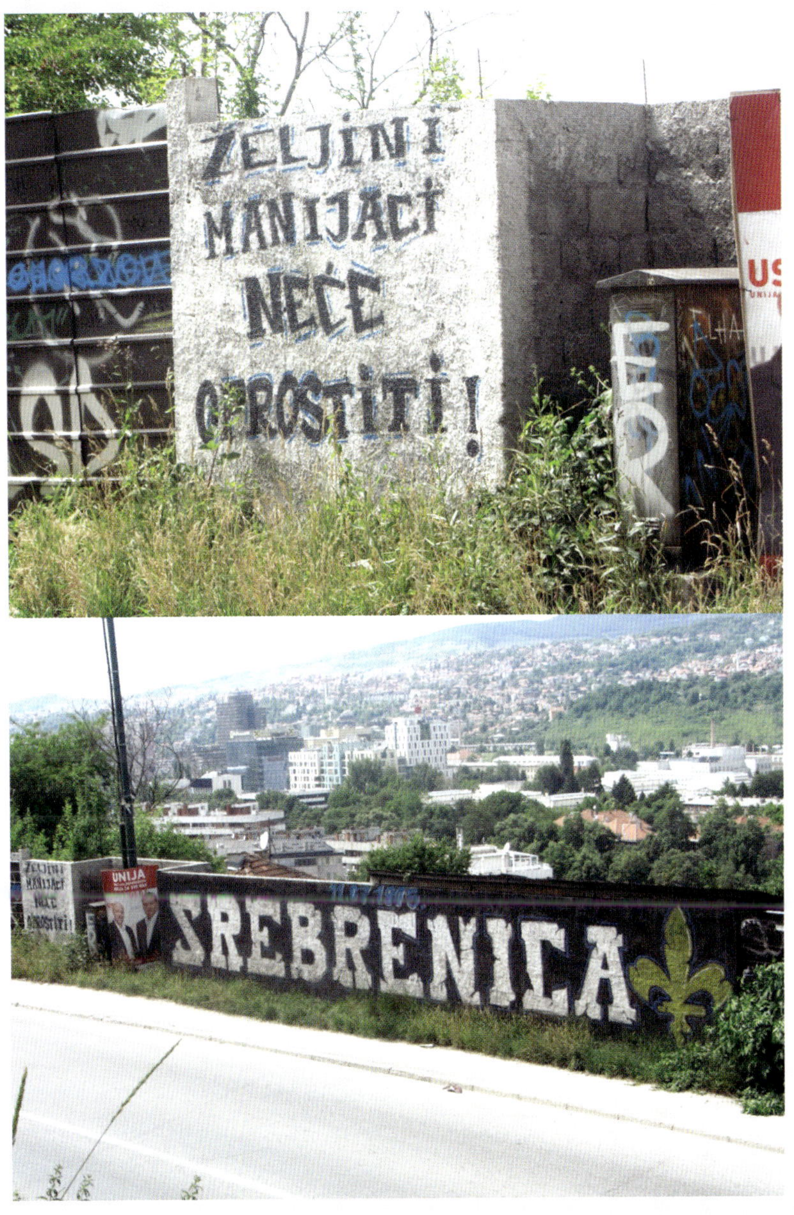

Željini Manijaci neće oprostiti! Srebrenica 11. 07. 1995, the day of the genocide against Bosniaks; (*Maniacs of Željezničar will not forgive!*); by *Manijaci* (*Maniacs*), fans of FC Željezničar Sarajevo; mural; Sarajevo, Bosnia-Herzegovina; 2015.

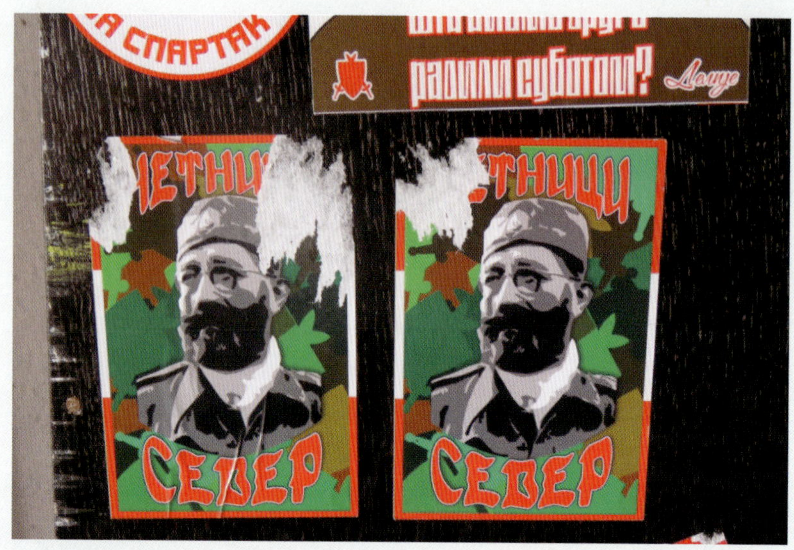

It's worth noting that many of the ex-Yugoslav football teams have existed over one hundred years, changing names through the times under different political regimes and reflecting the new political boundaries of the states they were in. For the beginnings and concise history of Yugoslav football, see Jakovljević (2018).

Above: *Četnici sever* with an image of Draža Mihajlović, leader of the collaborationist chetnik movement in WWII (*Chetniks North*); by *Delije* (*Dukes*), fans of FC Crvena Zvezda, Belgrade; sticker; Belgrade, Serbia; 2016.

Opposite above left to right: Military hat worn by Bosnian Serb officers, including war criminal Ratko Mladić, on a Serbian flag, an hommage to him, and *Zvezda, Serbia, Kosovo, Metohija*, a Serbian nationalist slogan; murals; Marakana Stadium (home of FC Crvena Zvezda), Belgrade, Serbia; 2016 and 2017.

Center left: *Škripari*, Ustasha post-WWII guerrilla, killed by the Yugoslav army; by fans of FC Široki Brijeg; sticker; Mostar, Bosnia-Herzegovina; 2012.

Center right: Ante Gotovina, controversial Croatian army general from the war in Croatia (1991–1995), indicted for war crimes; by *Torcida*, fans of FC Hajduk Split; sticker; Korčula, Croatia; 2011.

Below: *Torcida Never Forget Srebrenica*; by *Torcida*, fans of FC Hajduk Split; stencil; Split, Croatia; 2011.

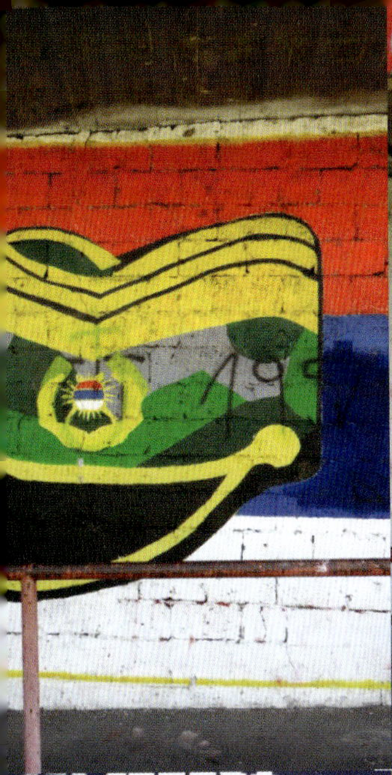

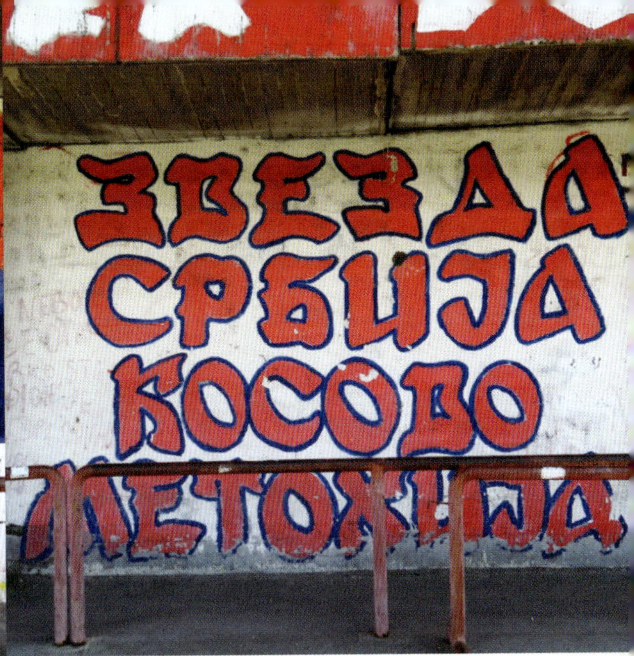

ЗВЕЗДА
СРБИЈА
КОСОВО
МЕТОХИЈА

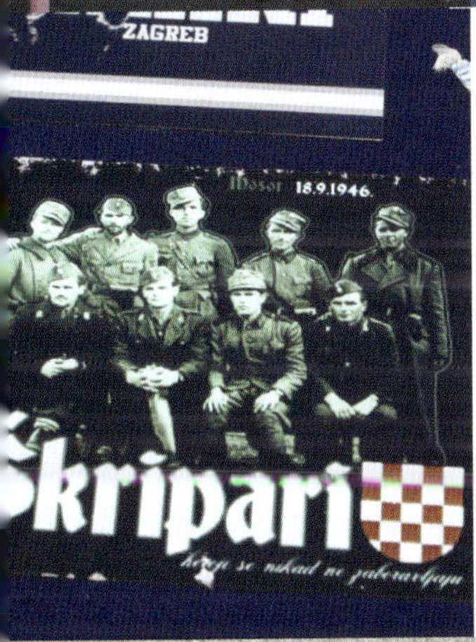

ZAGREB
Vukovar 18.9.1946.
kripari
koje se nikad ne zaboravljaju

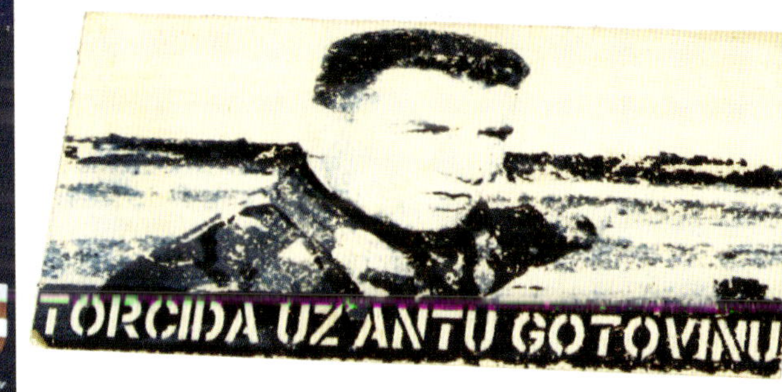
TORCIDA UZ ANTU GOTOVINU

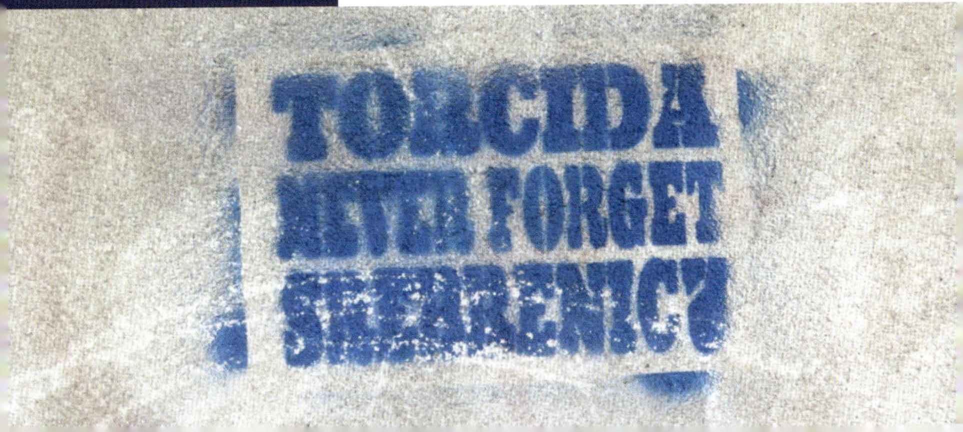

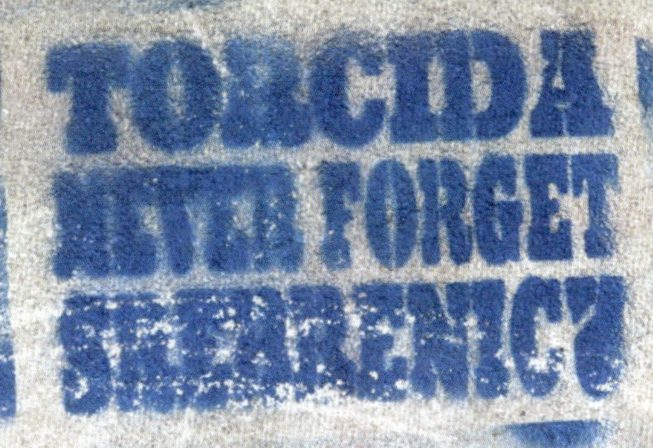
TORCIDA
NEVER FORGET
SREBRENICU

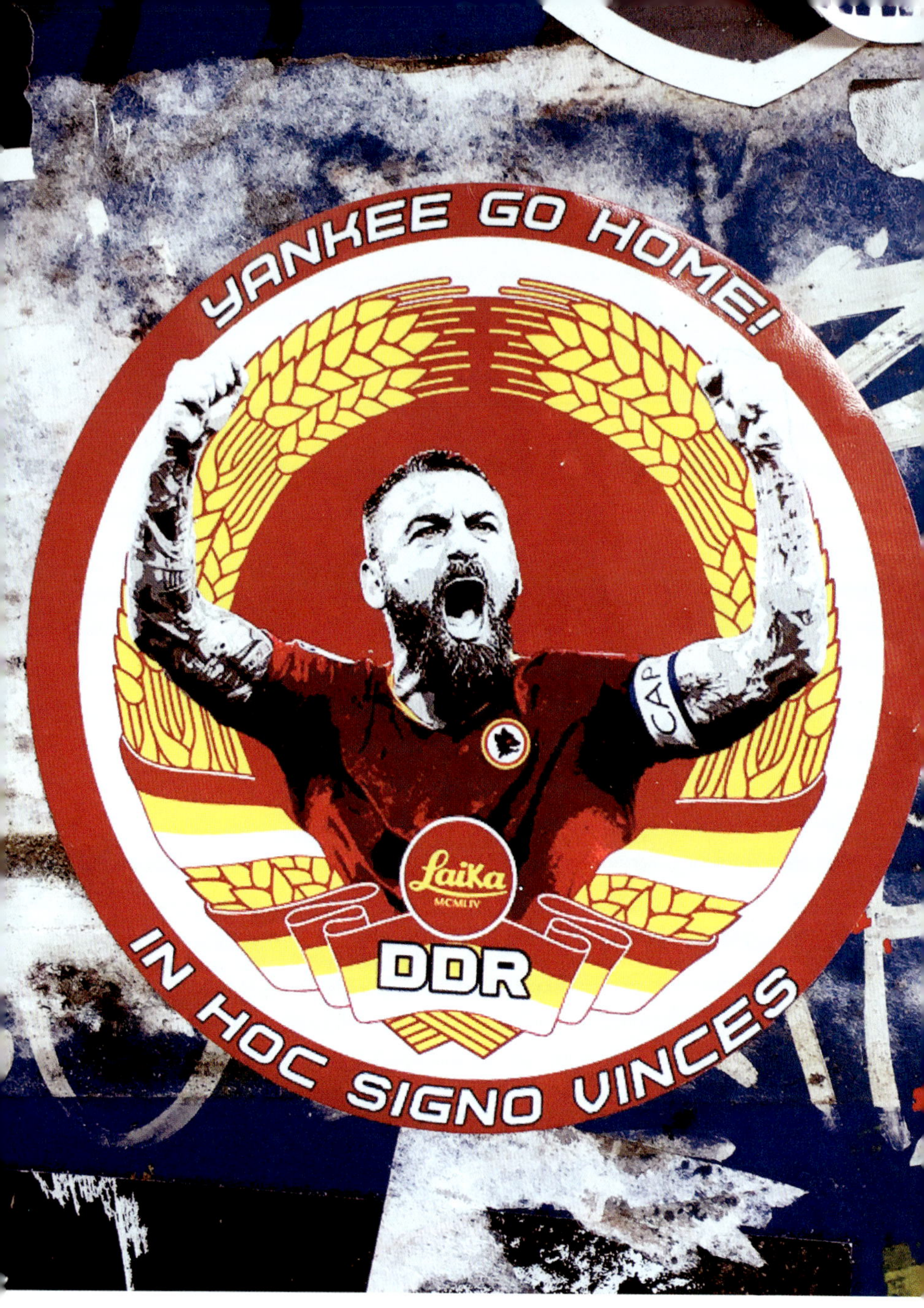

Yankee Go Home! In Hoc Signo Vinces; sticker; Leipzig, Germany; 2011.

Heterogeneity ... Until One Prevails

What an unimaginable production and narrative variety of fan graffiti, stickers, stencils, murals and other forms of illegal public expression! Yet I am simultaneously in awe at all that fails to make an appearance, especially since fans are mostly seen from one perspective and treated, for the most part, one-dimensionally. Instead of conceptual uniformity, homologies, integrity or underlying structure, I find illogical conclusions, incoherent connections, internal contradictions, impossible combinations and incompatibilities on the walls.

It is a veritable "chaosmos," where everyone-everything-everywhere is simultaneously in the game of competing meanings which "coexist, interpenetrate, and change places" (Deleuze, Guattari 2005: 36). Such an amazingly vast diversity of imagery cannot be forced into a common explanatory cadre. A hierarchic interpretation is unproductive, as motifs neither stem from the same source nor are they, to channel Haydn, "variations on a theme." It is pointless to search either for a hidden unity that would fragment and manifest itself in a set of diversities; or for a limited number of common denominators that would somehow explain the differences. Likewise, interpretations must not remain solely on the level of fixed antagonistic oppositions and say, "it is either this or that, no in-betweens." In my concrete example of football-fan graffiti this would mean that they could only be political or apolitical, left- or right-leaning, etc.

No, we have to conclude the exact opposite: final interpretations must at the same time accept their unstoppable diversity and endless connections, even if they seem contradictorily inconsistent looking from afar. This is a dialectic of continuous creation and demolition of the connections between these oppositions, coming from different roots, for their "double-bind" (Vermeulen, Van den Akker 2010: 6), and having *and* in-between at least two mutually exclusive poles that 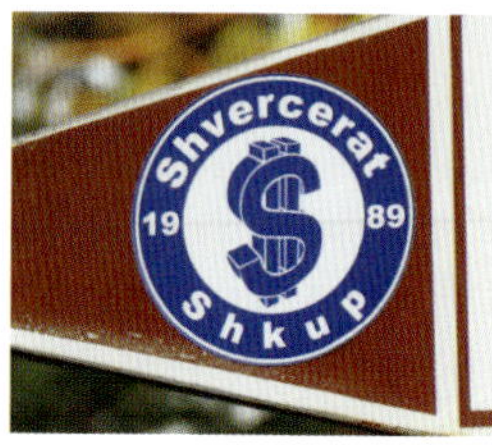 can never come together and join into one. In the essence of fanhood, there must always be an opposing team and opposing fan clubs, and in the antagonisms of such irreductibly plural street creativity, conjunctions *or* and *and yet* are replaced simply by the *and* that connects them in contradiction. To make a concrete example of football-fan graffiti, this means that fans will present themselves as hooligans and town protectors and political and apolitical and rough and polite and this and that, all in a countless string of inconclusive interactions and only seemingly strange concordances.

Therefore, meaning is established through endless anti-genealogical, unexpected, even shocking horizontal connections. Instead of a pyramidal structure typical of hierarchy, there is ramification, where each point meets every other point; one current meaning can only be a short, interim juncture, but in the next moment, it is replaced by another meaning, and then by the next one, and the next one and so forth. Broadly speaking, at any given moment, an unexpected event can "interrupt or deflect the search fortuitously" (Deleuze 1997: 212).

In this contradictory mass of football-fan graffiti themes, it would be wrong to seek fixed meanings, to hope for a single explanation. They do not form

Shvercerat Shkup 1989 (Smugglers Skopje); by *Shvercerat,* Albanian fans of FC Shkupi, Čair district of Skopje; sticker; Skopje, North Macedonia; 2016.

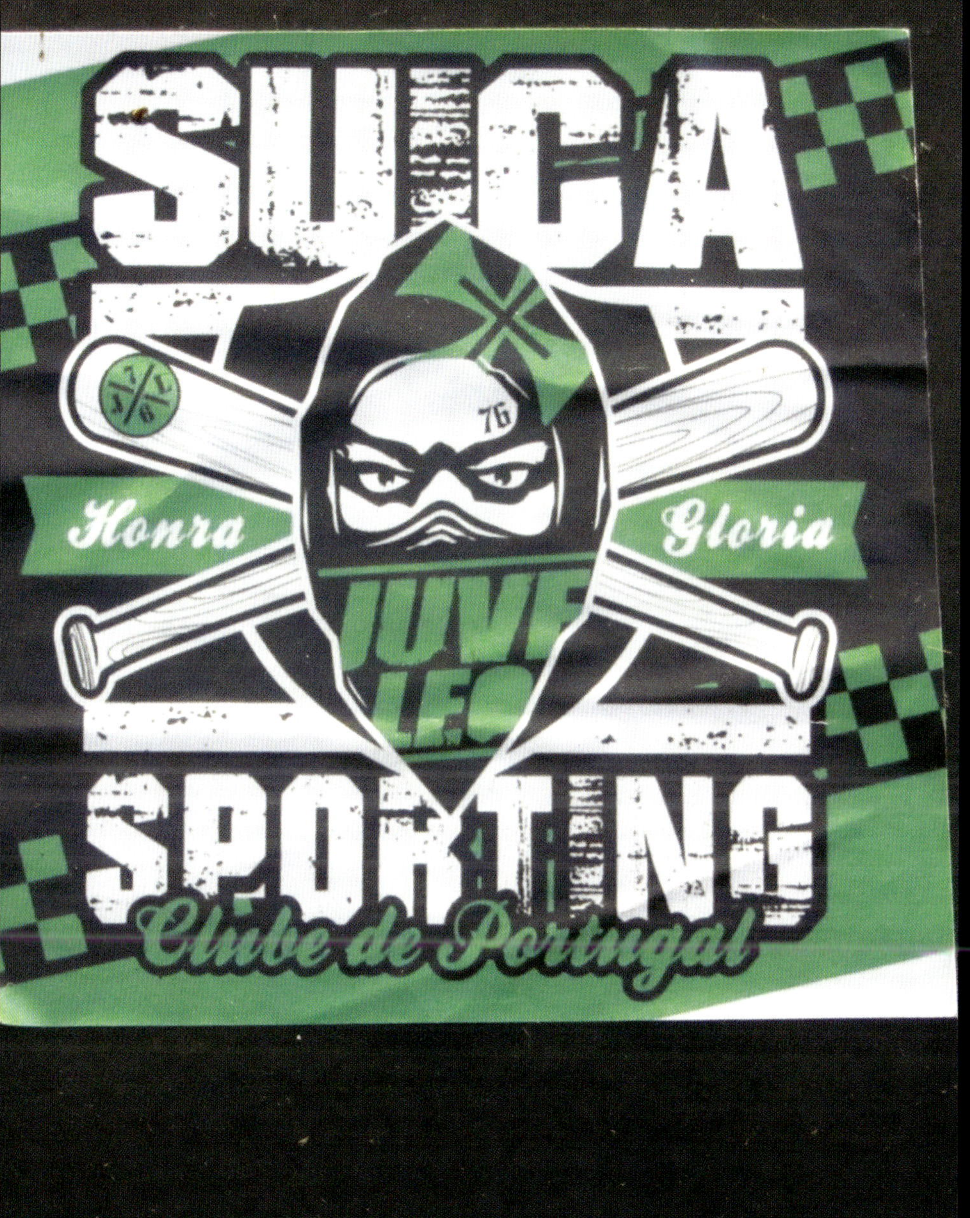

Suíça — Honra, Gloria — Sporting — Clube de Portugal (Switzerland — Honor, Glory — Sporting — Club from Portugal); Swiss fans of FC Sporting Lisbon; sticker; Lausanne, Switzerland; 2016.

exclusive and stable identities. Instead of explaining, these assemblages of meanings and artefacts of meaning-making convince, seduce, and mobilize along simple, but persuasive motifs (community, courage, belonging, identity, history, pop-culture heroes, etc.). They function not despite differences but precisely because of them; not despite identities that change through space and time but, again, because of them. A thesis is not confronted and synthesized with an antithesis but upgraded with another thesis, and then another one, etc., in a nomadic continuity of inconclusive interactions and plural particularities.

This follows the line of thought of critical philosophers Michael Hardt and Antonio Negri around the subject of the *multitude,* which can be applied also to the culture of sport as especially highlighted by football. The multitude is "composed of a set of singularities and by singularity here we mean a social subject whose difference cannot be reduced to sameness, a difference that remains different" and as such it "is not unified but remains plural and multiple" (2004: 99). The initially mentioned cognitive dissonance, provocative nonsenses, or obvious contradictions are not problematic within the multitude: everything "works," but not due to a "preexistent development or perfection but... instead [due to a] global and relative equilibrium" (Deleuze, Guattari 2005: 48). Football-fan graffiti reveal the acentricity of a "new subjectivity" that seems incredibly effortless in linking the extremes, not by canceling them but by living with them; it unites by preserving disunity; it heals the unhealable in such a way that it still leaves the meaning open. This explains why non-white home players are also applauded by the racist home fans; or why nazi imagery and praising Hitler can also be found amongst Slavic fans, even when we know that nazism treated Slavs as *subhumans.*

One explanation for this syncretic ecosystem is that football-supporter culture expresses a radicalized microcosmos of the post-political state that has

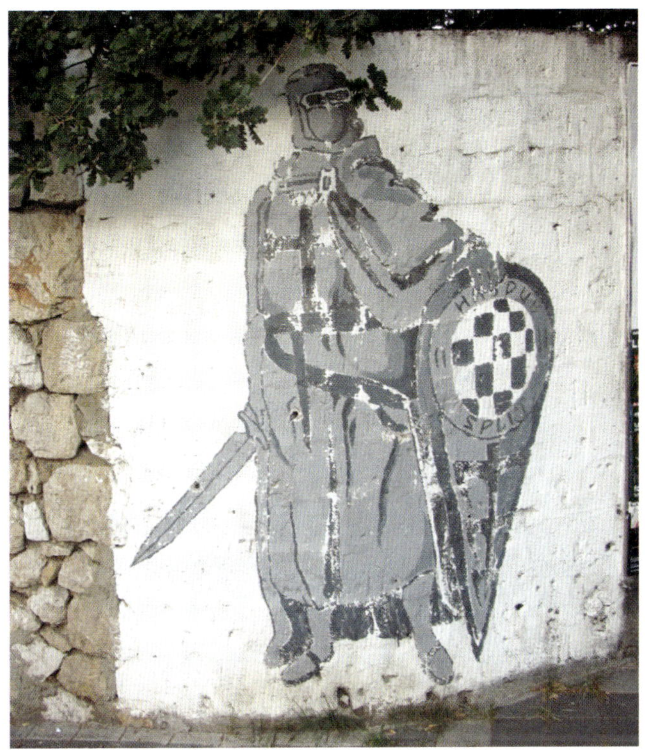

followed the end of the Cold War and collapse of ideological opposites on either side of the Iron Curtain. Real politics "hides" itself in the notions of *civilizational incompatibilities, cultural clashes, economic necessities, differences in lifestyles, technological imperatives, security measures, hygienic regulations,* etc. — in short, it depoliticizes the politics. A new consensus joins the traditional, institutionalized "right" and "left" parties in a common fight against outsiders, the post-national state hides nationalism in the universal human condition, the post-ironic state combines seriousness with jokes, and the post-real combines true and false. And exactly as such, football-fan graffiti seem to tap into the ideological imaginarium of the global macrocosmos

Medieval knight with the sign of FC Hajduk on the shield; by *Torcida,* fans of FC Hajduk Split; mural; Dubrovnik, Croatia; 2015.

of the twenty-first century. Looking at fan graffiti and street art really closely, we can perceive the values and the activity of society as a whole.

Specifically, we must examine its one trait of commonality — the way such an open semiotic system can be and is appropriated by different power structures, which in practice always happens anew and always in specific circumstances. An imposed and enforced unity from the top of the political chain erases the irreducible plurality of *ad-hoc*, even contradictory semiotic alliances. Everything is already here, everything comes in handy, *prêt-à-porter*, ready for (political) use.

This is why we cannot accept the frequently apologized use of extremist rhetoric and symbols in football fandom, including its graffiti and street art, by saying *they don't really mean it* and perceiving over-determined symbols like the Celtic cross, the swastika, or the nazi *Totenkopf* as *merely* fan ornaments, and *monkey chant* simply as a form of cheering. Indicative is the example of Amsterdam Ajax, a club with Jewish roots, and its fans who declare themselves *Super Jews* and fly the Star of David and the Israeli flag. Opposing fans shout *Jews to the gas chambers!* or provoke them with a hand raised in a nazi salute. This is not perceived as "real antisemitism" but is defended as a plain and ordinary fan stance against the opposing team. They fight synonyms with antonyms: if they are A, then we are anti-A, no matter how painful the comparisons are. Fan-based defenders like to refer to the inherent sign polysemy, to the fact that each sign holds many meanings. In principle, this is true: through time, cultural forms begin an independent existence, they separate from their signified. However, not all signs are equally controversial: a firefighter sign or a pharmacy sign or a character from The Simpsons surely do not evoke such an uneasiness as racist or nazi signs do.

Any tries at depoliticizing political signs in football fandom implicitly reveal exactly what they wish to explicitly deny: a symbolic antisemitism, chauvinism, racism, sexism, homophobia, etc., on the ladder of evil that can (again) turn into reality, into praxis. To be even more critical: contemporary Europe is no stranger to loud or subtle, spontaneous or structured racism, xenophobia, chauvinism, sexism, and other exclusivist ideologies and political practices. One cannot use political signs, especially those contaminated with violence and crimes, and pretend to be apolitical. To paraphrase: there is no neutral use of signs and appeals marked by the extremist past (and present!), these are never *just for laughs*, never just a part of the fan jargon, however (un)conscious of this fact the fans — and the rest of the society — are.[10]

The truth is that institutions of power can take such rhizomatic heterogeneity and polysemy, the fact that everything is already present, and turn it into a certain direction. The *they don't mean it seriously* is then changed into something *dead serious*: a free-floating signifier into a determined call for action. Ideology always begins with — a word. Football terraces and the entire fan performance including graffiti have always been a display not only of sports aficionados but also of political agitators.

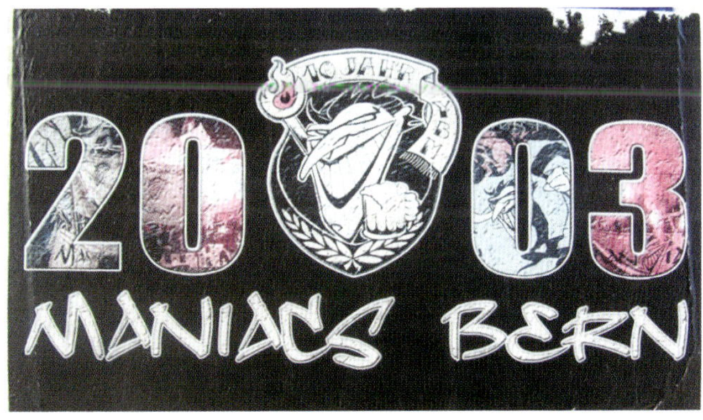

Maniacs Bern — 2003 — 10 Jahre YBM (10th anniversary of Maniacs); by Maniacs, fans of FC Young Boys Bern; sticker; Martigny, Switzerland; 2016.

[10] For several in-depth analyses of the historical roots and present of, on one side, loud, politically explicit right-wing extremism, and on the other side implicit, quiet, subtle, and masked as "apolitical" (the best example is, of course, sports), see MacMaster (2001), Poliakov (1999) and Perry and Schweitzer (2008).

Despite all the current campaigns within (and outside) the football world, racism remains one of the most widespread ideologies — and violent verbal, performative and even physical practices — of football fans, with no indication of decreasing. Recent quantitative, algorithm-based research by the Italian scholars Marco Caselli, Paolo Falco and Gianpiero Mattera, accomplished during the COVID-19 lockdown in Italy, efficiently proved that "the performance of African players improves significantly when supporters are no longer at the stadium" (Caselli, Falco, Mattera 2021: 8, 9) because they are not targeted with racist insults, chants, booing, gestures, etc., and that "racial harassment harms performance" (Ibid., 15).

Since the '90s, initiatives such as Kick it Out or Football Against Racism in Europe (FARE) have been among those who draw attention to this fact. On the local level, amateur football in Italy is promoted by leftist groups like *La resistente — Atleti socialisti* (*Socialist athletes*), having an old-style ball and red star on their stickers (see page 8). A similar initiative in Slovenia is called *Brcnimo rasizem* (*Let's kick out racism*) with an annual tournament which is at the same time also a left-wing political manifestation (as evinced by their poster).

When wars began in ex-Yugoslavia, it became clear how thin the line between organized fan groups and paramilitary groups is; how marginal discourses of football fans quickly grow into dominant political discourses and, sadly, also praxes. Where the first inter-ethnic violence erupted on football fields, the first *volunteers* left the terraces to go to the front (Čolović 1996, 2011: 109–133; Vrcan 2003, Sindbæk 2013: 1017, Djordjević 2015). Regretfully, these actions also remain alive today as extremist groups will often recruit members amongst football fans. And this is when football becomes quite literally what people call it: *more than just a game.*

Opposite: *Brcnimo rasizem* (*Let's kick out racism*); poster; Ljubljana, Slovenia; 2020.

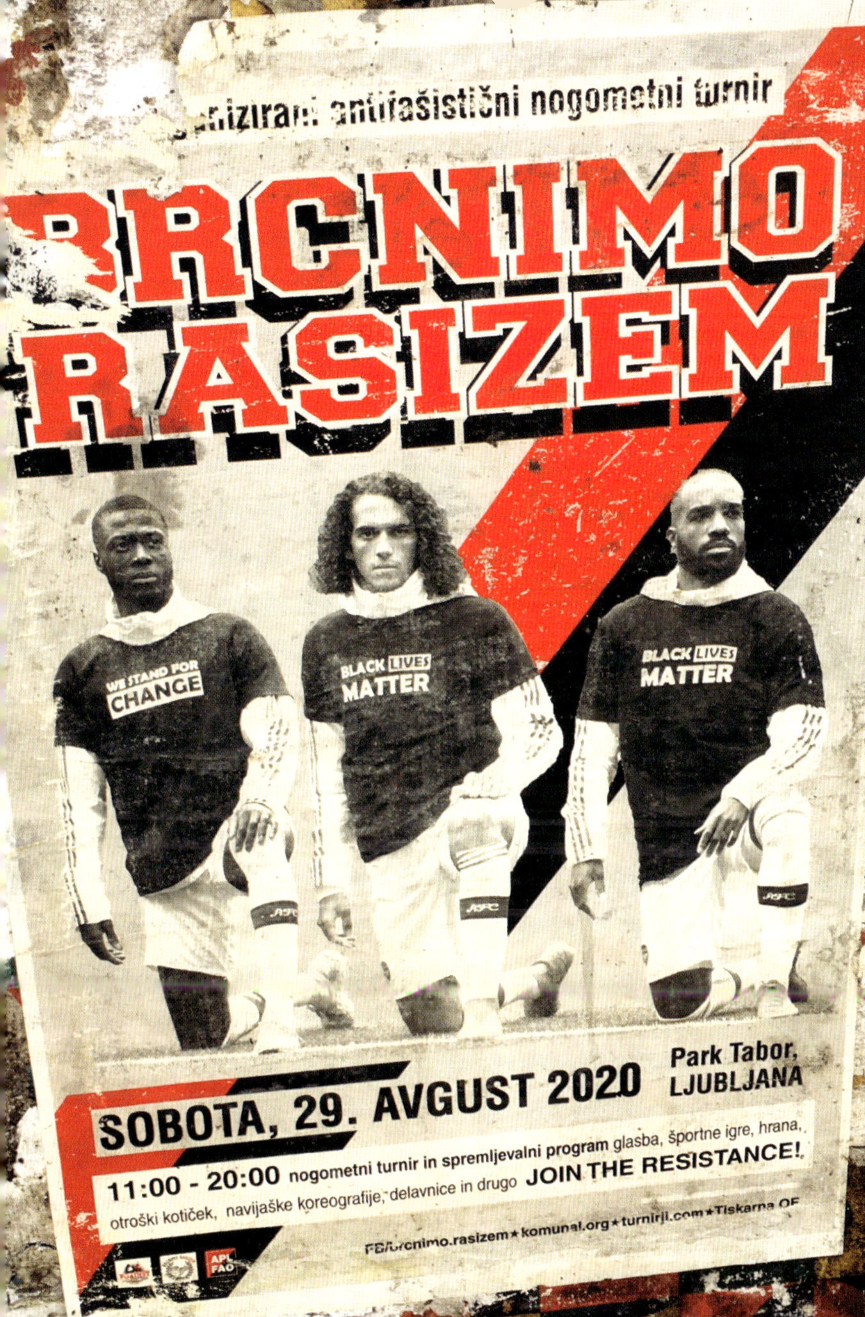
organiziran antifašistični nogometni turnir
BRCNIMO RASIZEM
WE STAND FOR CHANGE
BLACK LIVES MATTER
BLACK LIVES MATTER
SOBOTA, 29. AVGUST 2020
Park Tabor, LJUBLJANA
11:00 - 20:00 nogometni turnir in spremljevalni program glasba, športne igre, hrana,
otroški kotiček, navijaške koreografije, delavnice in drugo JOIN THE RESISTANCE!
FB/brcnimo.rasizem ★ komunal.org ★ turnirji.com ★ Tiskarna OF

Ultras on screen

The explosive mixture of football fanhood, ethno-nationalism and right-wing radicalism is the topic of the Serbian coming-of-age/crime drama *Skinning* (*Šišanje*), showing the transformation of a troubled teenager into a racist-skinhead football fan (dir. Stevan Filipović, 2010). The earlier Italian drama *Ultra* (*Ultrà*) vividly depicts brawls between fans of FC Juventus and FC Roma (dir. Ricky Tognazzi, 1991). Most recently, an Italian coming of age drama is now streaming on Netflix, *Ultras* (dir. Francesco Lettieri, 2020); the trailer opens with graffiti on a police station: *Tutta colpa della disoccupazione* (*Everything's the fault of unemployment*).

There are several films on English fans, notably among them *Firm* (dir. Nick Love, 2009) and *Green Street Hooligans* (dir. Lexi Alexander, 2005). A Croatian action-comedy, *ZG80* is about the clashes of Dinamo's *Bad Blue Boys* and Crvena Zvezda's *Delije* at the derby in Belgrade in 1989 (dir. Igor Šeregi, 2016).

The parallel lives of three Italian *tifosi* — *juventino*, *internista* and *milanista*, all of them portrayed by Diego Abatantuono — are depicted on a much lighter note in *Eccezzziunale... veramente* (dir. Carlo Vanzina, 1982). Its success paved the way for similar comedies, *Tifosi* (dir. Neli Parenti, 1999) and the sequel *Really SSSupercool: Chapter Two* (*Eccezzziunale veramente — Capitolo secondo... me*, dir. Carlo Vanzina, 2006).

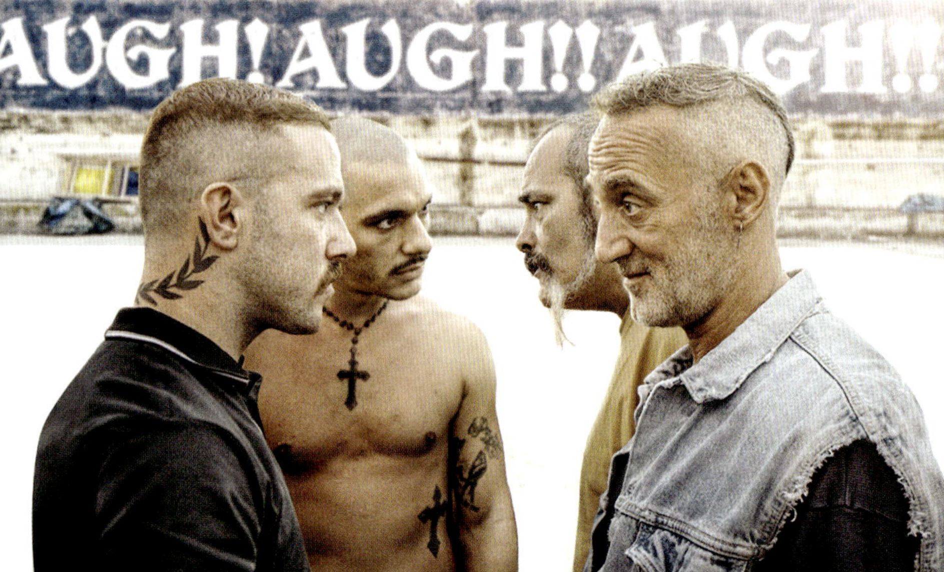

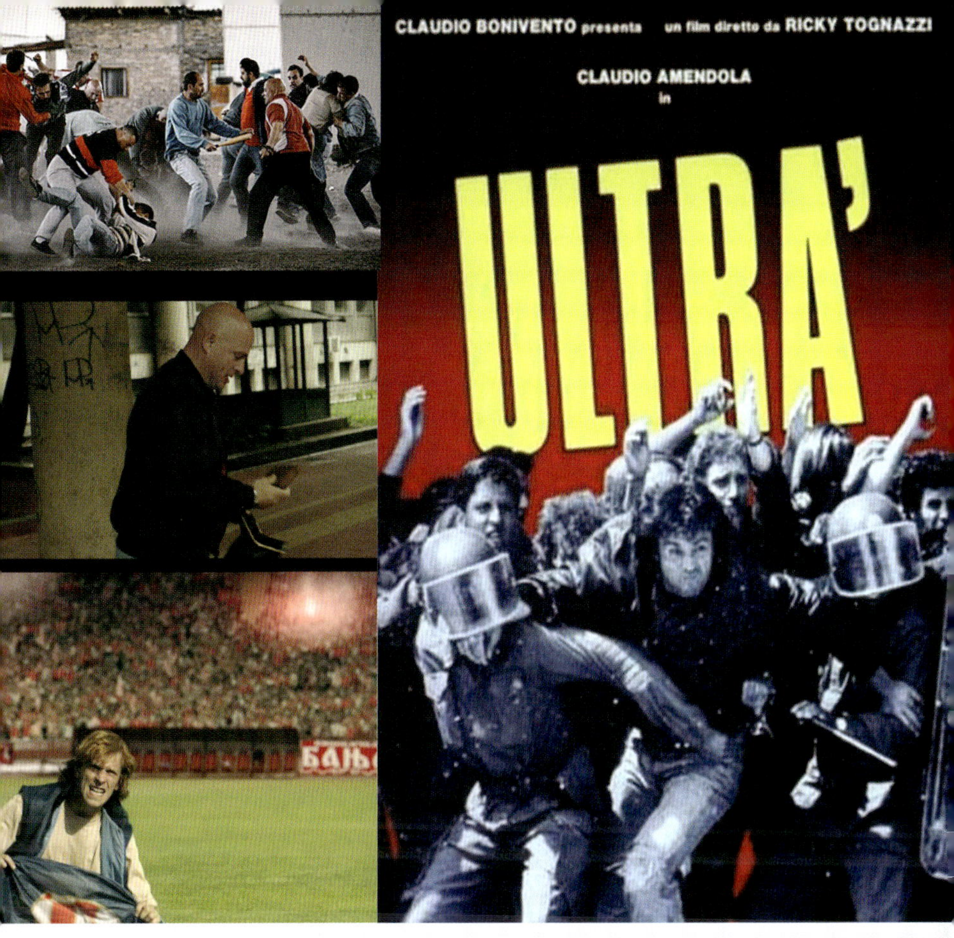

These movies vividly depict football-fans' lifestyles, values, ideological orientations and (often subpolitical and criminal) activities, relations towards others in the "outer world" and especially towards fans of other clubs, as well as their organization, attractive audio (chants, anthems, songs, cheering, salutes) and visual elements, like choreographies, banners, flags, and their design in general, as well as ways in which they decorate their apartments or rooms, cars, bicycles etc., then also gestures, marches, dress-codes, haircuts, tattoos, their street creativity, etc. Among the latter, graffiti and street art play the central role, appearing in most of the sequences and creating authentic *mise-en-scène* of their meeting points, "headquarters," bars, *their streets,* and stadiums.

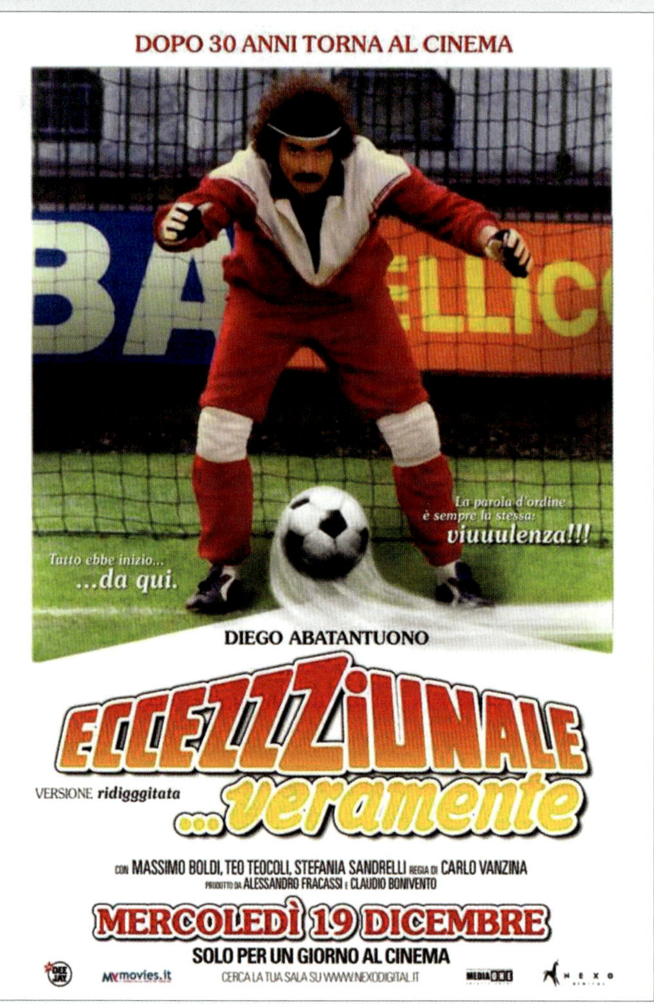

Previous pages, left to right: Publicity film-still from *Ultras*, directed by Francesco Lettieri. Italy: 2020. Distributed by Netflix.

Publicity film-stills from *ZG80*, directed by Igor Šeregi. Croatia: 2016. Distributed by 2i Film.

Poster for *Ultra* (*Ultrà*), directed by Ricky Tognazzi. Italy: 1991. Distributed by Turner Classic Movies.

These pages: Posters for *Eccezzziunale... veramente* and *Eccezzziunale... veramente (Capitolo Secondo... me)*, directed by Carlo Vanzina. Italy: 1982 and 2006. Distributed on DVD and by Rai — Radiotelevisione Italiana Spa.

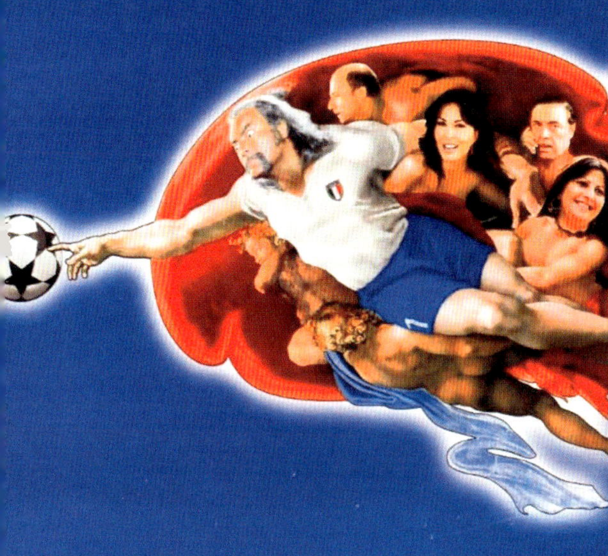

ALESSANDRO FRACASSI presenta una produzione MEDIA ONE in collaborazione con RAI CINEMA

DIEGO
ABATANTUONO

ECCEZZZiUNALE
veramente
CAPITOLO SECONDO...ME

un film di CARLO VANZINA

CARLO BUCCIROSSO   UGO CONTI   MAURO DI FRANCESCO
LUIGI MARIA BURRUANO   TONY SPERANDEO
con NINO FRASSICA nel ruolo di Turi con la partecipazione di ANNA MARIA BARBERA
con la partecipazione di SABRINA FERILLI

sceneggiatura di DIEGO ABATANTUONO   CARLO VANZINA   ENRICO VANZINA
prodotto da ALESSANDRO FRACASSI   regia di CARLO VANZINA

www.01distribution.ir

III. WRITERS SPEAKING: SLOVENIAN FOOTBALL——-FANS TALK ABOUT THEIR GRAFFITI

Small football environments, those on the margins of corporate football and far away from big business and global media coverage, also present an extremely interesting field of research. Football experts — enthusiasts both as researchers and as fans — show numerous examples and cases of the complex relations between football fandom, ideological orientations, political affiliations, class and ethnic identities. O'Connor (2021) convincingly compares such cases on the troubled edges of the ex-Soviet Union (feuds between Armenia and Azerbaijan about the Armenian enclave Nagoro-Karabakh, between Georgia and Russia about Abkhazia and South Ossetia, between Romania and Russia about Moldova and Transnistria, and between Ukraine and Russia about the Donbass), as well as between Serbia and Kosovo. In each of these, separatism and centralism, resistance and repression, old historical wounds and new geostrategic ambitions, domination and rebellion were transferred also to sports, in particular to football — and even more, to the football-fan scene. Montague (2020) goes even wider, covering — along with aforementioned factors — scenic examples from both Americas, from the European football "heartland" of Germany and Italy, from conflict areas of Kosovo, Northern Macedonia, Turkey and Donbass, to as far as Indonesia. In England, "fascist infiltration of football hooligan firms is nothing new" — for example, National Front "put a lot of resources into recruiting activists from the terraces" (Smith, Smith, Ward 2010: 7). In Bulgaria, anti-Muslim and anti-Roma attacks were co-organized and accomplished by football fans (Gueorguieva, Goncharova, Karakusheva 2021: 157, 158).

As I connect all these broader determinants with fandom, it's also important to consider the viewpoint of those football fans who actually create graffiti.

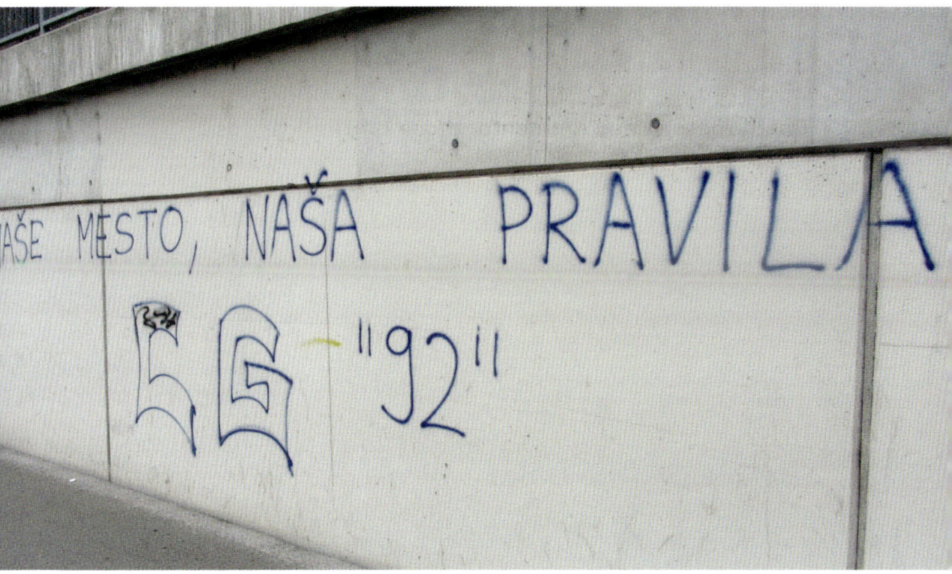

Naše mesto, naša pravila — CG "92" (*Our town, our rules — Celjski grofje* [*Dukes of Celje*], established in 1992); by *Celjski Grofje,* fans of FC Celje; graffiti; Celje, Slovenia; 2014.

What is their way of viewing the world — in their words, in their images and colors, with their graffiti and with their stickers? What happens when "terrace-wars" turn to the walls and become "graffiti-wars" or "cross-out wars"?

In the research of both graffitiing and fandom, not many people ask the protagonists about who they are and what they are doing, what their values are, what they want or do not want. My intention was to listen to them, ask them who holds the spray can, the sticker or the stencil, why, and how do they do it — all while I was reflecting their reflections, checking their claims, and putting them into a wider theoretical, historical, and comparative context. I decided to conduct my research (throughout the second half of the last decade) in my home country of Slovenia, which has not-extensive, but still very vibrant, organized and competitive foot-ball-fan groups.[11]

In performing both emic (from the inside) and etic (observational) ethnographic research from the site of the graffiti itself, I used comparisons, did participant observation at football matches, read media reports on them and browsed their web pages. In other detailed writing, I have compared the results of both main anal-ysis methods — testimonies from nine different fan groups plus close observers of the Slovenian *tifoscene*, as well as the semiotic meanings of their wall visuals. For our purposes here, I will focus on a summary of this case study to reveal (mis)matches and (in)con-sistencies between what fans had to say about their graffiti and the graffiti itself.

Since the topic was delicate, I was only able to reach fans through a "chain of trust": one of the observers directed me to the first fan, then that fan suggested another, etc. On several occasions, the interviewee himself took charge at the end of the interview and called my next potential target while I was still pres-ent. I promised them anonymity, we met on their "turf,"

[11] For the ethnic, social and political history of football on present-day Slovenian territory, see Dobovšek (2019). He considers contemporary Slovenian football as "being on the periphery (except few exceptions) does not achieve significant results, but instead it trains players for rich foreign clubs" (111).

and they were also asked to bring (or send) photos of their fan graffiti and street art or their stickers. Some came with other regalia and many showed me their fan tattoos. They found it great that finally somebody would write down *their truth about themselves*, as they emphasized on several occasions. I was sincere and non-judgmental, which of course, helped. Their explanations could become very emotional, much unlike their public image as tough guys. Any mistrust had been waved away merely because I had been referred to them by their co-fans for which they felt — as I will explain later — respectful rivalry, even if involved in inter-club feuds. Often, before or after the interviews, fans would lead me through parts of the town that they had spray-painted or stickered, if not, they would at least point me in the right direction.

Fans are typically not well versed in creating *nice graffiti*, as they put it. They admit to not being *true*, subcultural *graffiti artists* — if a need arises for a

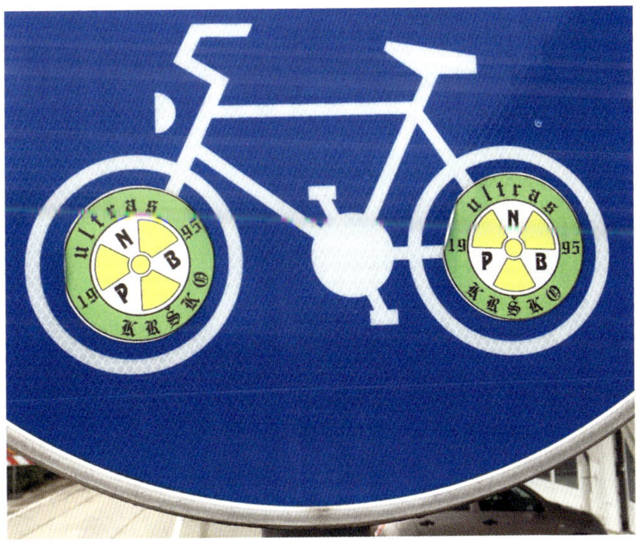

Ultras Krško NPB 1995; by *Nuclear Power Boys*, fans of FC Krško; sticker; Krško, Slovenia; 2021.

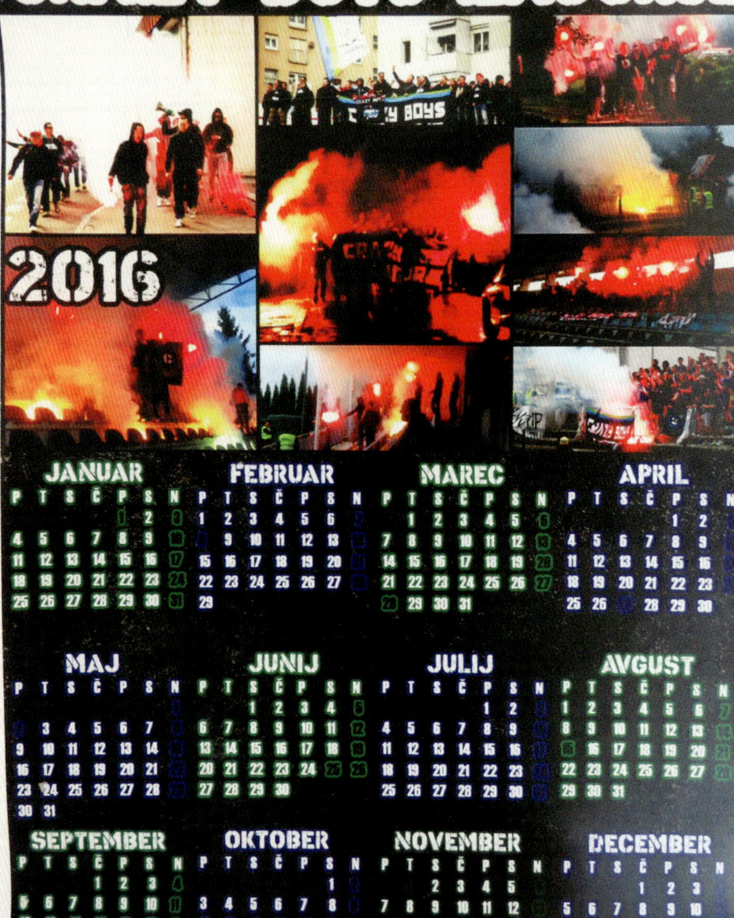

CRAZY BOYS ZAGORJE
2016
JANUAR
P T S Č P S N
FEBRUAR
P T S Č P S N
MAREC
P T S Č P S N
APRIL
P T S Č P S N
MAJ
P T S Č P S N
JUNIJ
P T S Č P S N
JULIJ
P T S Č P S N
AVGUST
P T S Č P S N
SEPTEMBER
P T S Č P S N
OKTOBER
P T S Č P S N
NOVEMBER
P T S Č P S N
DECEMBER
P T S Č P S N

special graffiti or mural, they outsource it; only one of them was an actual graffiti writer. Fans follow a simple imperative: to repeat *ad infinitum*; the more stickers, graffiti and stencils wherever, the better! Following "night actions" of *decorating* in hometowns, the graffiti are checked and evaluated by the fan-group leadership (older, more experienced formal or informal "commanders," *capos* or *capotifosi*, to use globalized Italian ultras' slang). These activities exemplify their sense of *belonging* to the club, their team, their town. Their graffiti and street art express bravery, solidarity, masculinity and outsiderness. One of the interviewees expressed himself especially explicitly, saying that their answers *to the devaluated world are what can today be seen as a tad traditional, reactionary values: fidelity, belonging, solid identity.*

In this context, two of their anti-globalist values appear interesting. First, they almost do not watch global football: their stickers and stencils prove their opposition to, as they call it, *modern football*, as it is true that *cash plays the game, not footballers*. Instead, they prefer local football, their home footballers, some of whom are almost amateurs. Similarly, they are against UEFA and FIFA because of their over-commercialization and turning football into a global spectacle. *You cannot watch football from your couch*, was a recurring phrase — you

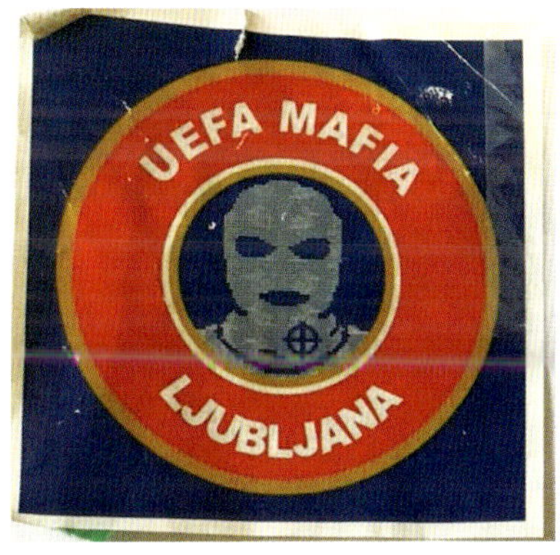

Opposite: Calendar for the year 2016 by *Crazy Boys*, fans of FC Zagorje; Zagorje, Slovenia; 2016.

Above: *UEFA Mafia — Ljubljana*, Celtic cross; by an unidentified ultras group; Ljubljana, Slovenia; 2015.

watch it loudly, standing on the terraces (usually on the parts with cheap tickets, behind the goals — in global ultras' language, in *curve*). Secondly, more than national identity, they underlined *local-patriotism*: they practically never attend Slovenian national team matches, and if they do, it is definitely not organized with their fan group because they would clash with other groups. This is another anchor that holds them in their local, town environment, and was also confirmed by the observers. However, they seem to find no problem in applying those globally recognized signs and symbols of fans that include the ACAB abbreviation, an old ball, old cleats, the Celtic cross, the RAF roundel, Union Jack, a pint of beer, a laurel wreath[12] and so on. One of the interviewees confided to me that *everybody does it, and it's getting a bit annoying.*

For the most part, their self-image and presentation revolves around their subcultural standards of what is *cool* and *beautiful*, mixed with the histories of their cities and towns and the legacies of their particular clubs — for example, when they were founded, their

[12] On the one hand, this is a sign of the club's/group's *everlasting glory*. On the other, it is a logo of a popular casual wear brand Fred Perry.

14 — Celtic cross — 88 — G.D. — Celtic cross — Y.C. (14 = white suprem-acists' "sacred words," 88 = Heil Hitler, Green Dragons, Youth Crew); by fans of FC Olimpija Ljubljana; graffiti; Ljubljana, Slovenia; 2017.

coats of arms, etc. Every interviewee underlined how important graffiti aesthetics is — they do not like *kids who only scribble* on walls. But it is the content that is, in the end, more important. They proudly display official years of establishing their group, e.g., (19)88, (19)89, (19)91, (19)92. However, an abbreviated version of the birth-year of *Green Dragons,* 88, is also a code name for *Heil Hitler!* (H is the eighth letter in the English alphabet), therefore an established neo-nazi sign.[13]

They combine *holy coats of arms*, colors, anonymous characters and other symbols of their towns/quarters/clubs/fan groups: a *Viole* sticker, in — of course — the color violet, for example, shows the image of a skinhead holding a beer and a chain, and a Celtic cross in the background. Some of them also display names of the fan sub-groups (various youth sections, e.g., *Frontline Youth*, *Baby Crew*, *The New Garde* or *Youth Crew*). Often their graffiti and stickers feature pop-cultural icons of likeable bullies, drunks or lamers à la Homer Simpson (and his drinking buddy Barney

[13] As 18 is also code for *Adolf Hitler,* or sometimes just 8 for *Hitler.*

Baby Crew GD 88 (one of the sections of *Green Dragons,* 88 stands for the year of their creation/Nazi code for *Heil Hitler!*); by *Green Dragons,* fans of FC Olimpija Ljubljana; graffiti (fasciofont); Ljubljana, Slovenia; 2021.

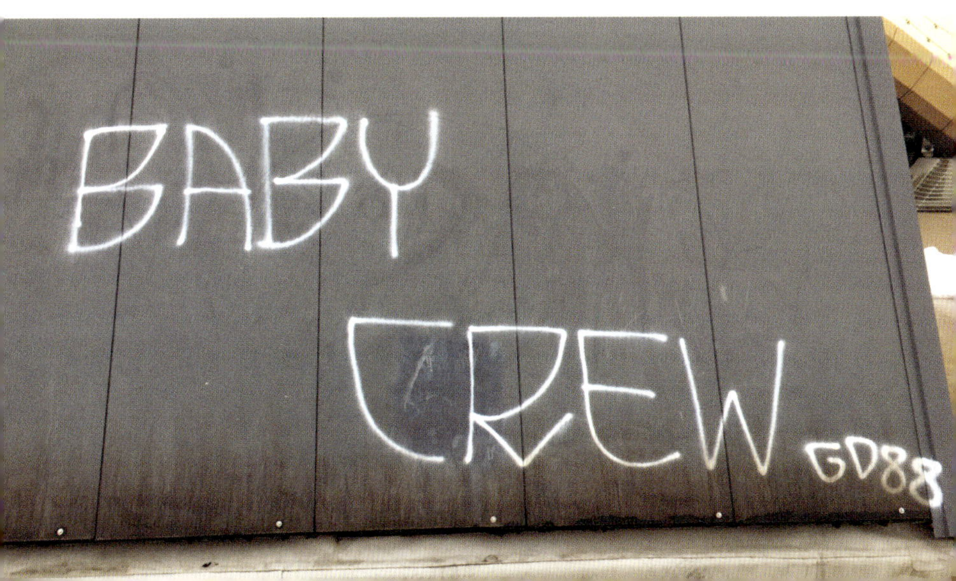

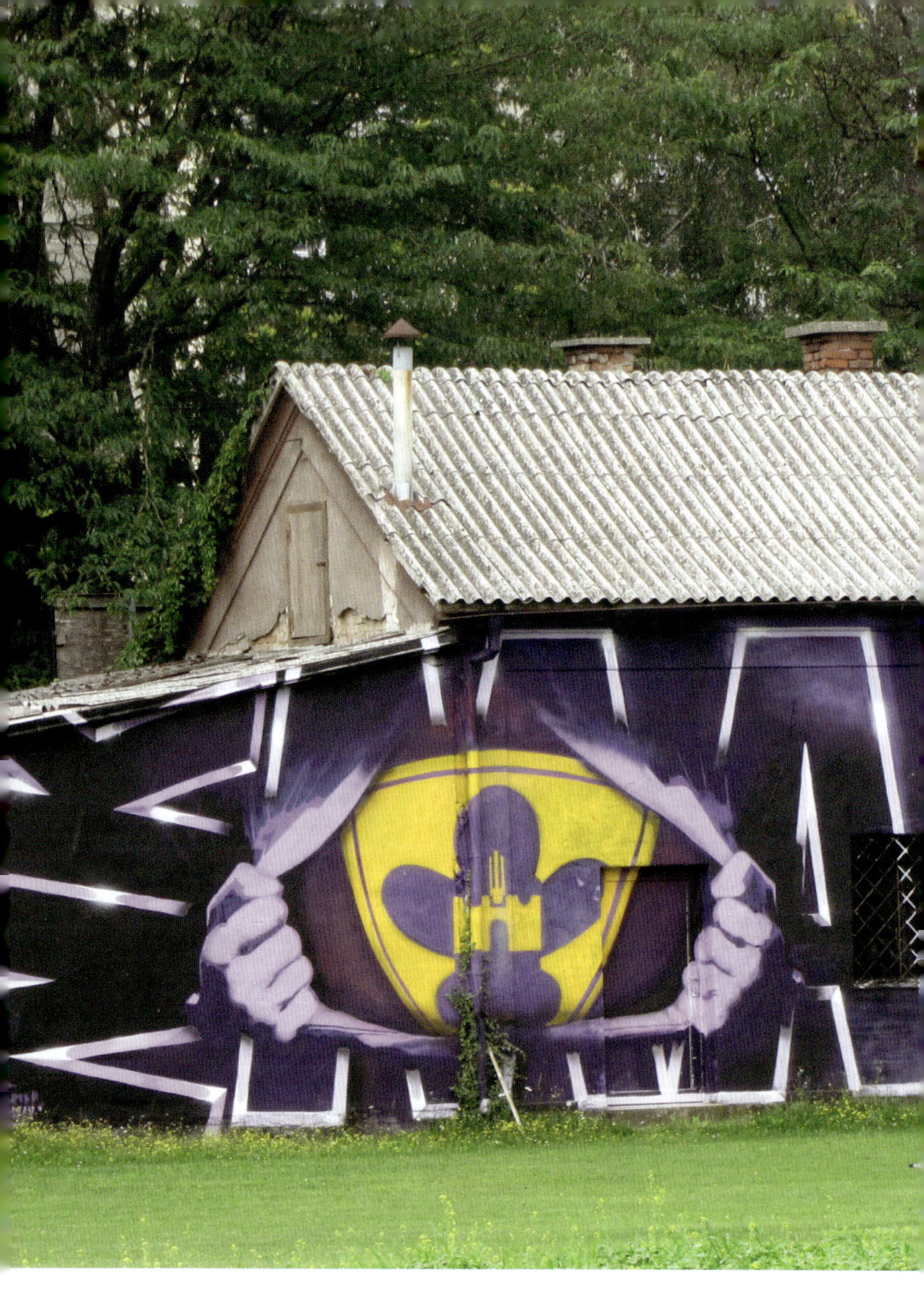

Maribor; by *Viole*, fans of FC Maribor; mural; Maribor, Slovenia; 2014.

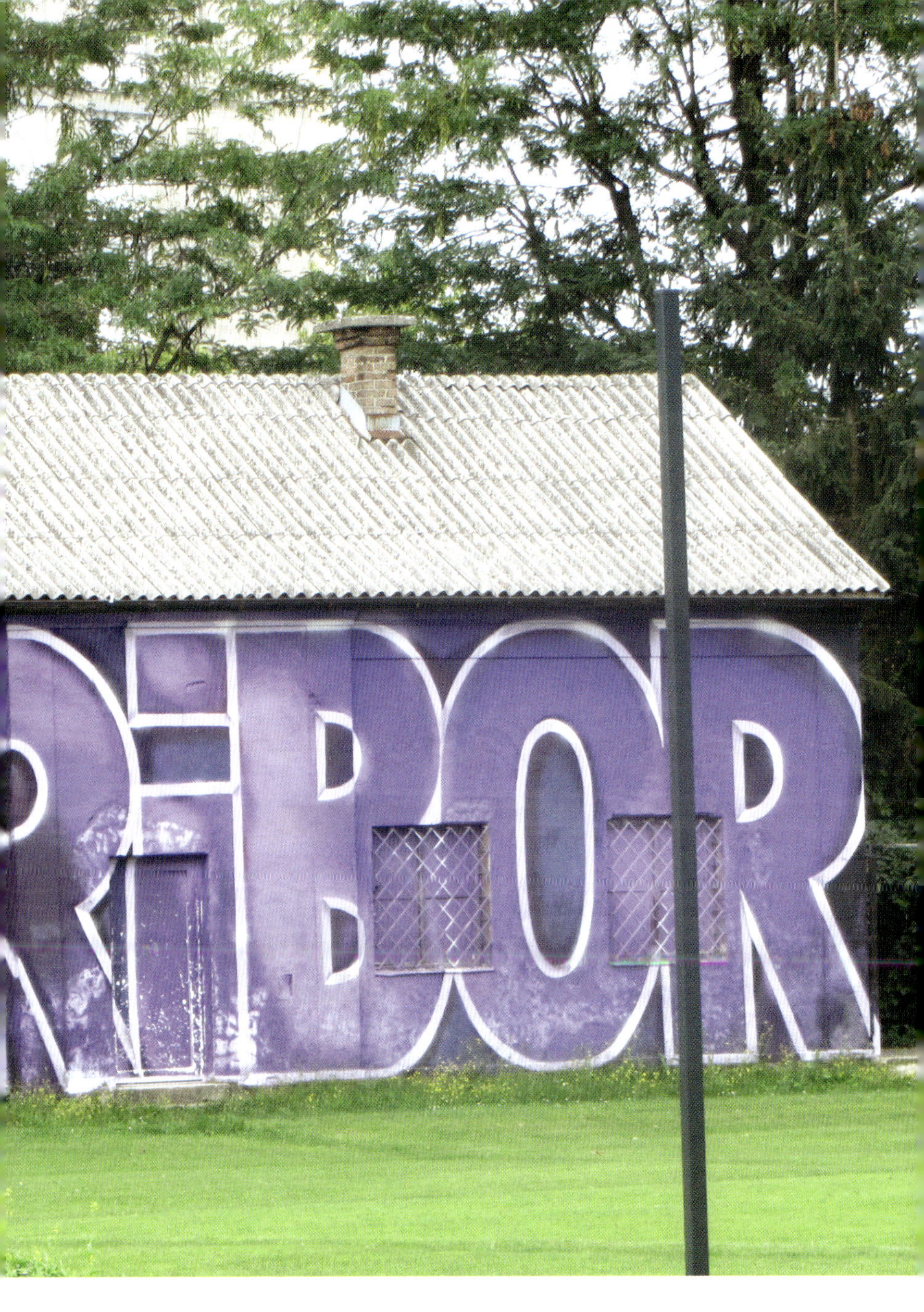

Gumble), Hägar the Horrible, Beavis and Butt-Head or Andy Capp. Some will pick more resolute characters for these metonymic illustrations, for example The Joker, Robert De Niro from *Taxi Driver* (dir. Martin Scorsese, 1976) or the masked face from the cover of Kasabian's debut album (2004).

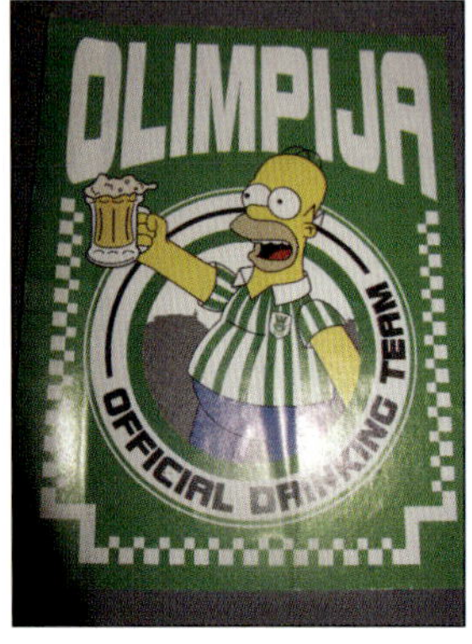

Slovenian football fans say they promote themselves more than they attack others (though in graffiti battles for turf they vehemently cross out each other's stickers and stencils). Furthermore, they often affirmed not seeing opposing fans as enemies but rather as competitors with whom they share common fan values and lifestyle even though they root for different clubs. This is also why they *respect* each other — as they explicitly stated on several occasions — and work in solidarity with others when they clash with the law. The Ljubljana *Dragons* supported the persecution of the *Animals*, the Sofia-based, notoriously extreme right-wing fan group of CSKA (featuring a large swastika on their stickers) (see page 85).

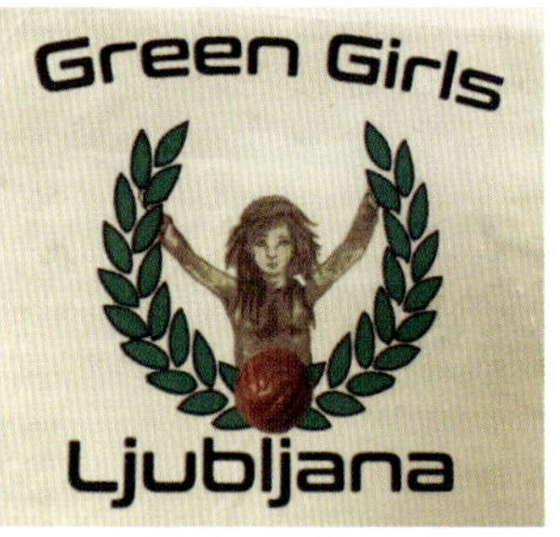

They have other enemies: journalists or media in general, police officers, and in some cases club management and owners (which at times results in boycotting

Above: *Olimpija — Official drinking team*; by *Green Dragons,* fans of FC Olimpija Ljubljana; sticker; Domžale, Slovenia; 2014.

Below: *Green Girls Ljubljana*; part of the *Green Dragons* fan group, FC Olimpija Ljubljana; sticker; Ljubljana, Slovenia; 2020.

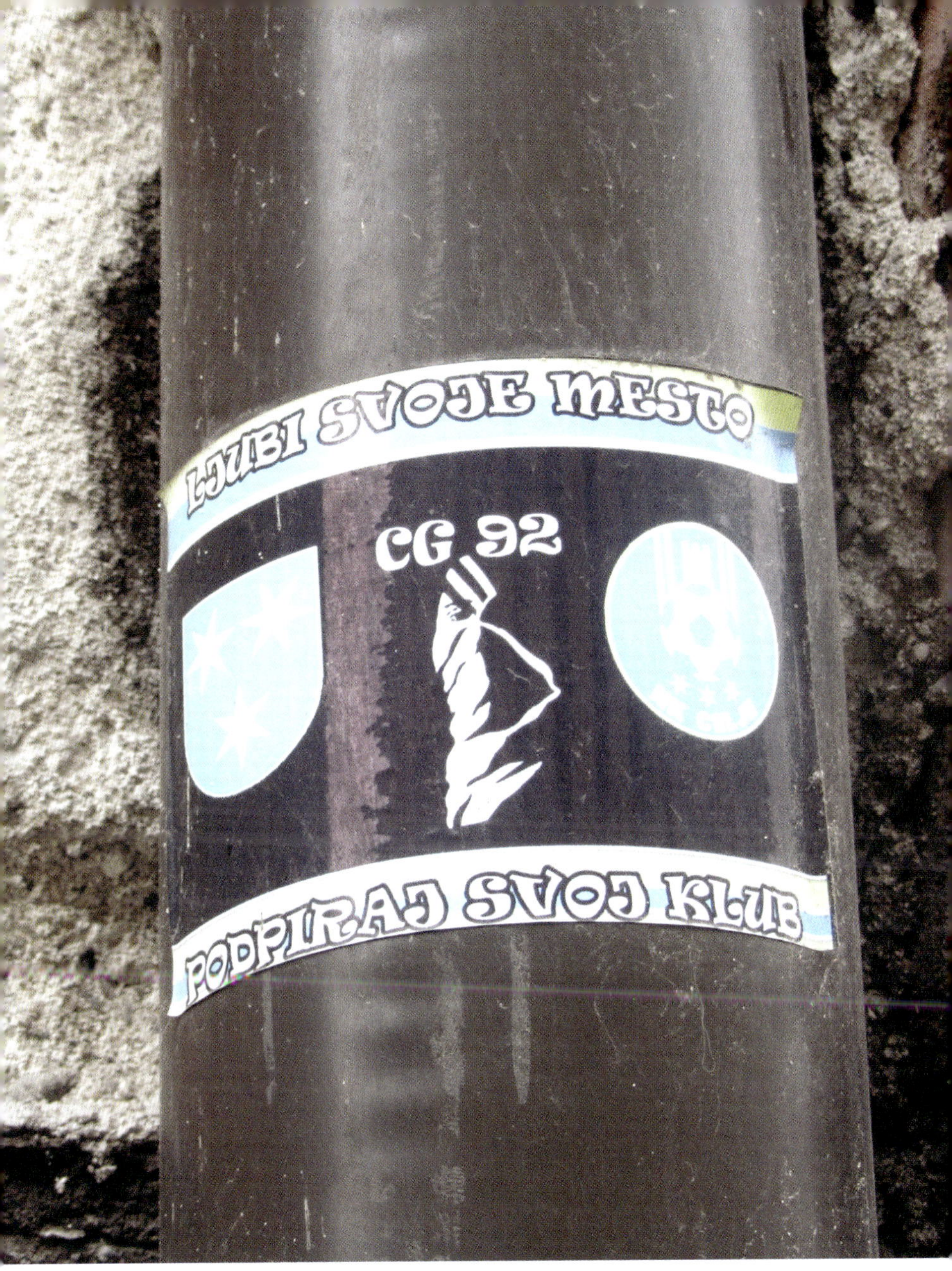

Ljubi svoje mesto, podpiraj svoj klub — GC 92 — NK Celje (Love your city, support your club — Celjski grofje /Dukes of Celje/ — FC Celje); by *Celjski grofje (Dukes of Celje)*, fans of FC Celje; sticker; Celje, Slovenia; 2016.

matches until their demands to change certain people are met). Their voluntary outsidership results in enjoyment of the self-important mysteriousness at the border between the hidden and the public, *hiding in the light*, as the iconic subcultural author Dick Hebdige entitled one of his studies (1989). His colleague Phil Thornton establishes how "hardcore followers of any subculture react negatively to mainstream media exposure, as it infringes upon their sense of ownership and the feeling of elitism and uniqueness" (2012, 114). They are proud of their *No one likes us, we don't care* attitude, as AFC Ajax fans claim on their sticker (see pages 122–123). While true that the Slovenian public maintains a prevailing negative attitude toward football-fan

TBNG — ND Gorica 1947 — Hägar the Horrible (Terror Boys — Sport Club Gorica, established in 1947); by *Terror Boys,* fans of FC Gorica; mural; Nova Gorica, Slovenia; 2020.

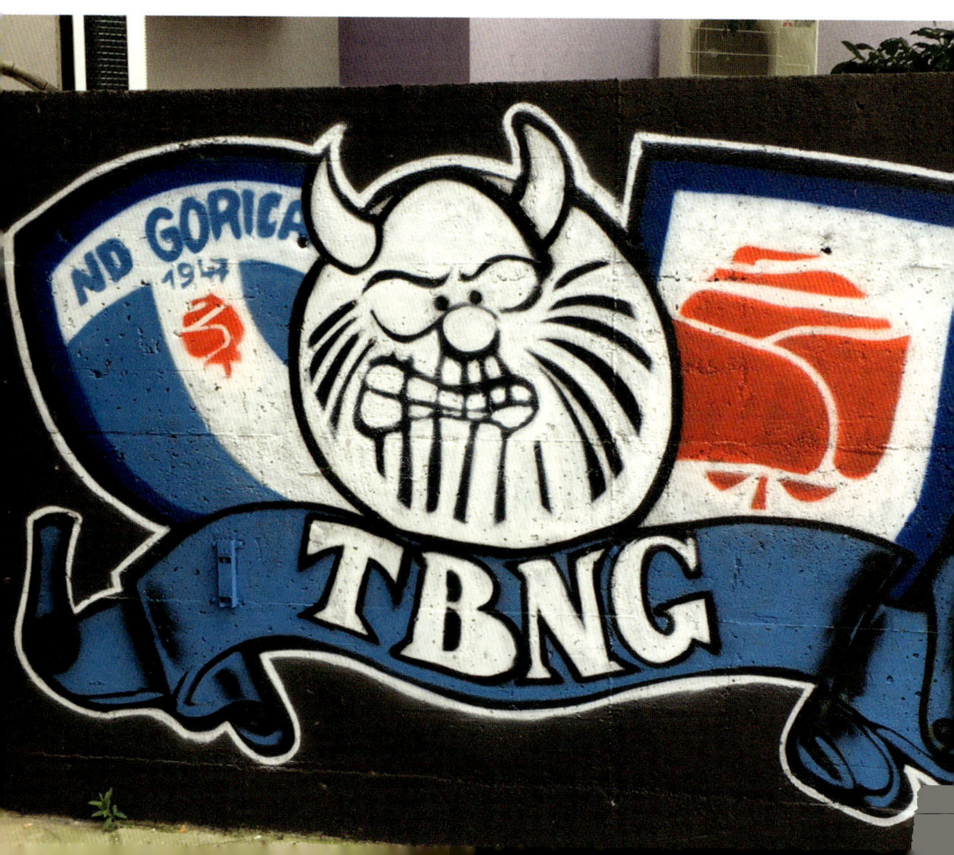

graffiti, the moral panic is not unlike the fear that erupted when other subcultures (ravers, metalheads, punkers, first rockers, mods, etc.) began establishing.

The trickiest area of fan subculture relates to their political and national beliefs. Everybody explicitly assured me that political beliefs influenced neither their cheering (in the words of one: *There's no politics on the terraces!*, in the words of another: *Give your head, heart, voice for the club!*) nor their graffitiing. Football is what is supposed to count, whereas politics is a matter of each individual not the group as a whole. Nevertheless, as a majority they agree that their groups act politically heterogeneously and are more right- than left-leaning.

I got some bad ideas in my head — Celjski grofje (Dukes of Celje); by *Celjski grofje*, fans of FC Celje; sticker; Trojane, Slovenia; 2015.

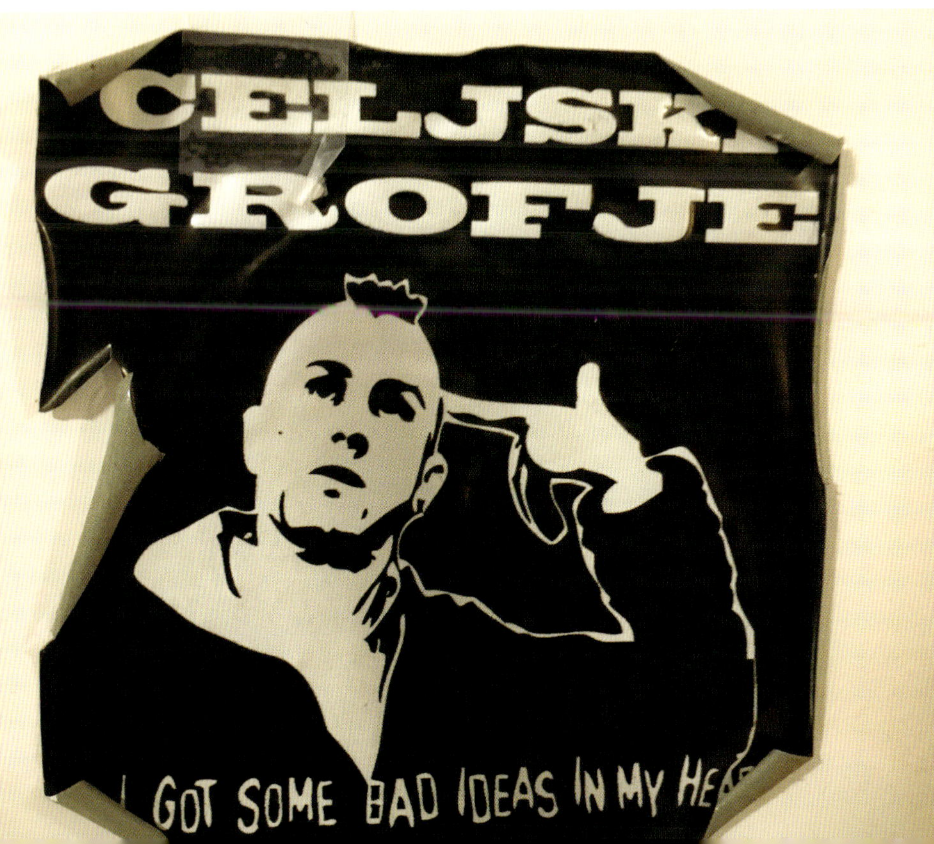

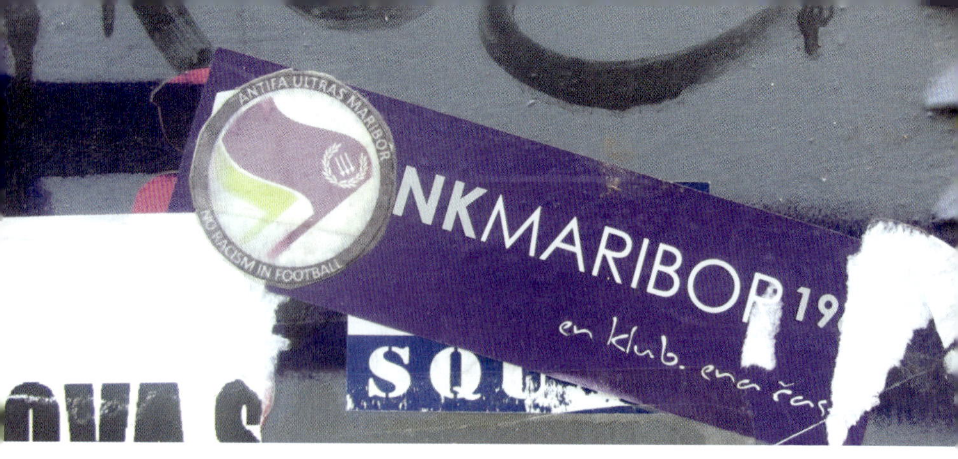

It is interesting to note that on many occasions, predominantly before elections, some of them were approached by representatives of right-wing parties (the Slovenian National Party, Slovenian People's Party; presidential candidate Lojze Peterle, Maribor mayor Andrej Fištravec and others were seen parading in their club's/fan group's scarves). One of the observers noted that the scope of this activity is nevertheless smaller than in some other countries.

Observers expressed a higher level of criticism about the politics of football-fan subculture: in the '90s, it was more apolitical, while later it grew to be more right-wing. This is a typical trend that Montague (2020: 207) noticed also in Germany, Italy, in southern and eastern Europe: "ultras had moved rightward, towards ultranationalism and sometimes outright neo-fascism." Observers emphasized the strong connection between the *Green Dragons* and *Viole* and the extreme-right groups (extreme nationalists, neo-nazis, usually masked in the generic casual look sported by fans) — in short, with a witty phrase of Smith, Smith, and Ward (2010: 20), the "fash mob." They are very *efficient in recruiting youngsters; for example, in high schools.* Stickers of the far-right and nationalist

Antifa ultras Maribor — No racism in football — NK Maribor — En klub, ena čast — antifa sign (FC Maribor — One club, one honour); by the antifa branch of Viole, fans of FC Maribor; sticker; Maribor, Slovenia; 2015.

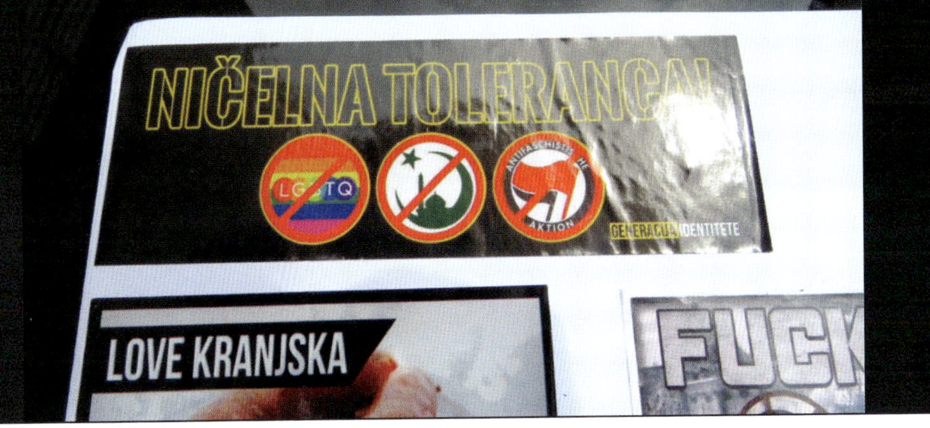

Identitarian Movement (*Generacija identitete*), which I found on the stadium in Ljubljana, combines boxing gloves and books with their symbol and a football-fan prop, a megaphone.

Observers believe the first, the *Dragons*, to be more extremist in their political beliefs than *Violas* who nonetheless are a certain political actor in their town due to the high number of its members. In the Maribor protests of fall 2012–winter 2013, however, *Viole* took

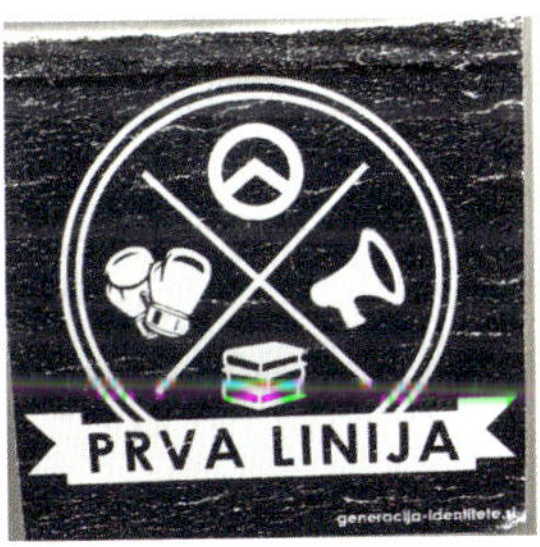

a stand with the protesters against the then mayor and against police violence but were later excluded from the activities organized by the uprising groups, according to two observers.

Two stickers by the Slovenian branch of *Generation Identity*, a pan-European extreme-right political movement in different European countries. Above: *Ničelna toleranca — Generacija identitete* (*Zero tolerance — Generation Identity* with crossed out LGBTQ sign and flag, Muslim symbol, and antifascist sign and symbol); Portorož, Slovenia; 2021. Below: *Prva linija* (*Frontline*); Žalec, Slovenia; 2020.

Following page: *No one likes us, we don't care — A.F.C. Ajax — Heldhaftig, Vastberaden, Barmhartig* (motto of Amsterdam — *Valiant, Steadfast, Compassionate*); by fans of FC Ajax Amsterdam; sticker; Amsterdam, Netherlands; 2012.

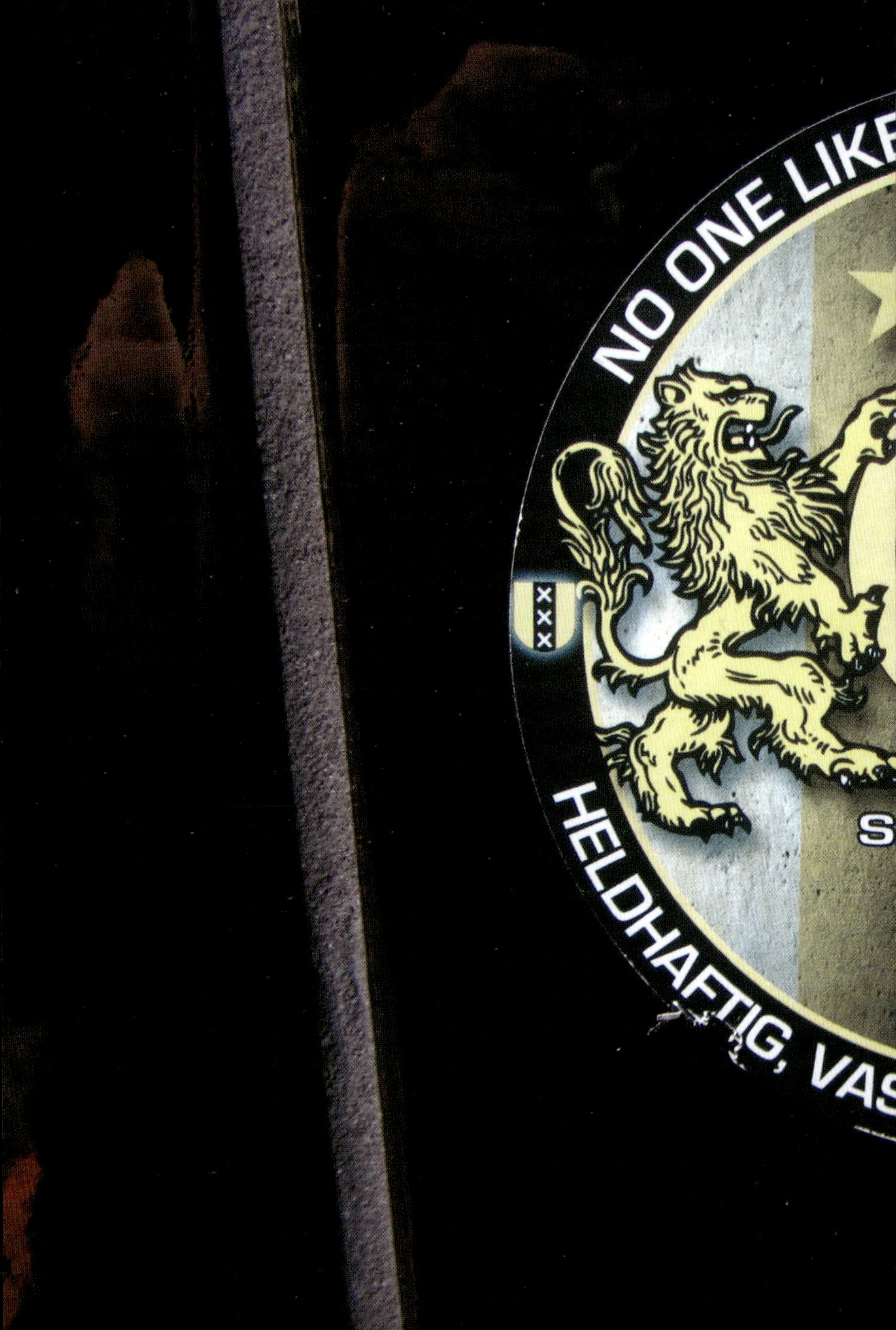

NO ONE LIKE
HELDHAFTIG, VAS

S, WE DON'T CARE

.C.AJAX

TERDAM

E 1900

rschehelden.nl

ERADEN, BARMHARTIG

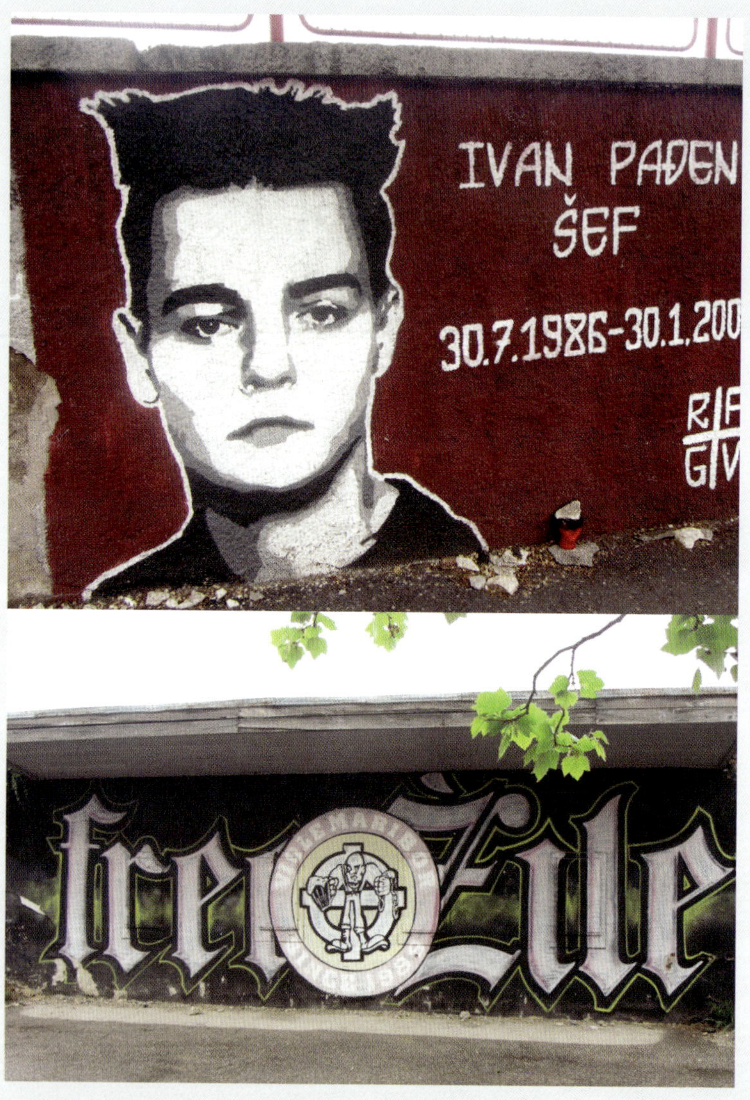

Above: *Ivan Pađen "Šef"*; by *Red Fuckers*, fans of FC Orijent Rijeka, for a deceased member of their club; mural using the classical *fasciofont* letters; Rijeka, Croatia; 2015.

Below: *Free Žile — Viole Maribor — since 1989*; support for Marko Živko "Žile," member of *Viole*, fans of FC Maribor, imprisoned for stabbing one of their rivals *Green Dragons*'s supporters in 2011; mural; Maribor, Slovenia; 2015.

Fan commemorations and support of other fans

Football fans show their solidarity with their imprisoned comrades or those who have died in different ways. In a particularly dramatic example, I was finding stencils and stickers calling for

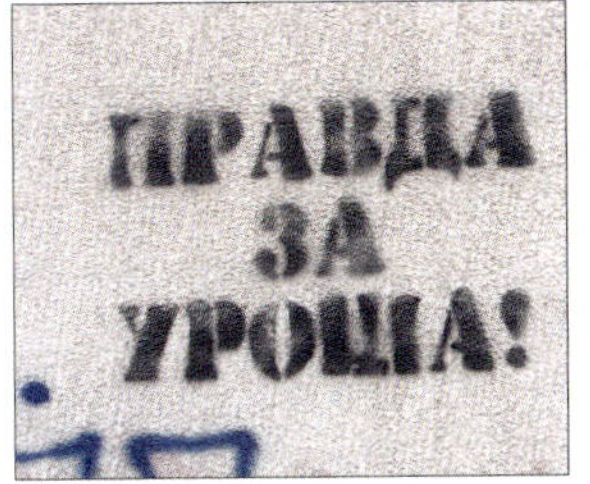

justice for Uroš in other parts of the Balkans as well as in Slovenia, but also in a few places in Europe. I took photos of stencils and stickers in his support even in Amsterdam. The imprisoned *Delije* fan Uroš Mišić severely injured a police officer in 2007 by trying to push a burning torch into his mouth.

Graffiti, stencils, stickers and even simple posters all over Bosnia-Herzegovina are calling for *truth for Vedran*, Vedran Puljić, member of *Horde zla* (*Hords of Evil*, fans of FC Sarajevo), shot before the game against FC Široki Brijeg in 2009.

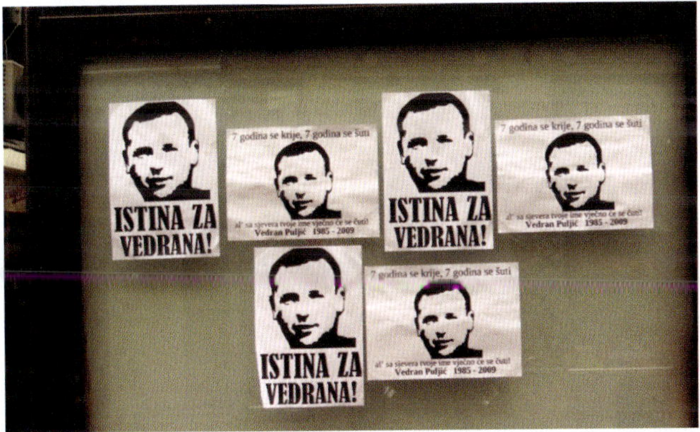

Above: *Pravda za Uroša!* (*Justice for Uroš*); by *Delije* (*Dukes*), fans of FC Crvena Zvezda Belgrade, for an imprisoned member of their club; Belgrade, Serbia; stencil; 2015.

Below: *Istina za Vedrana!* (*Truth for Vedran!*); by *Horde zla* (*Hords of Evil*), fans of FC Sarajevo, for a member of their club who was killed; posters; Sarajevo, Bosnia-Herzegovina; 2016.

Following page: *Justice for Uroš*; sticker; Amsterdam, The Netherlands; 2012.

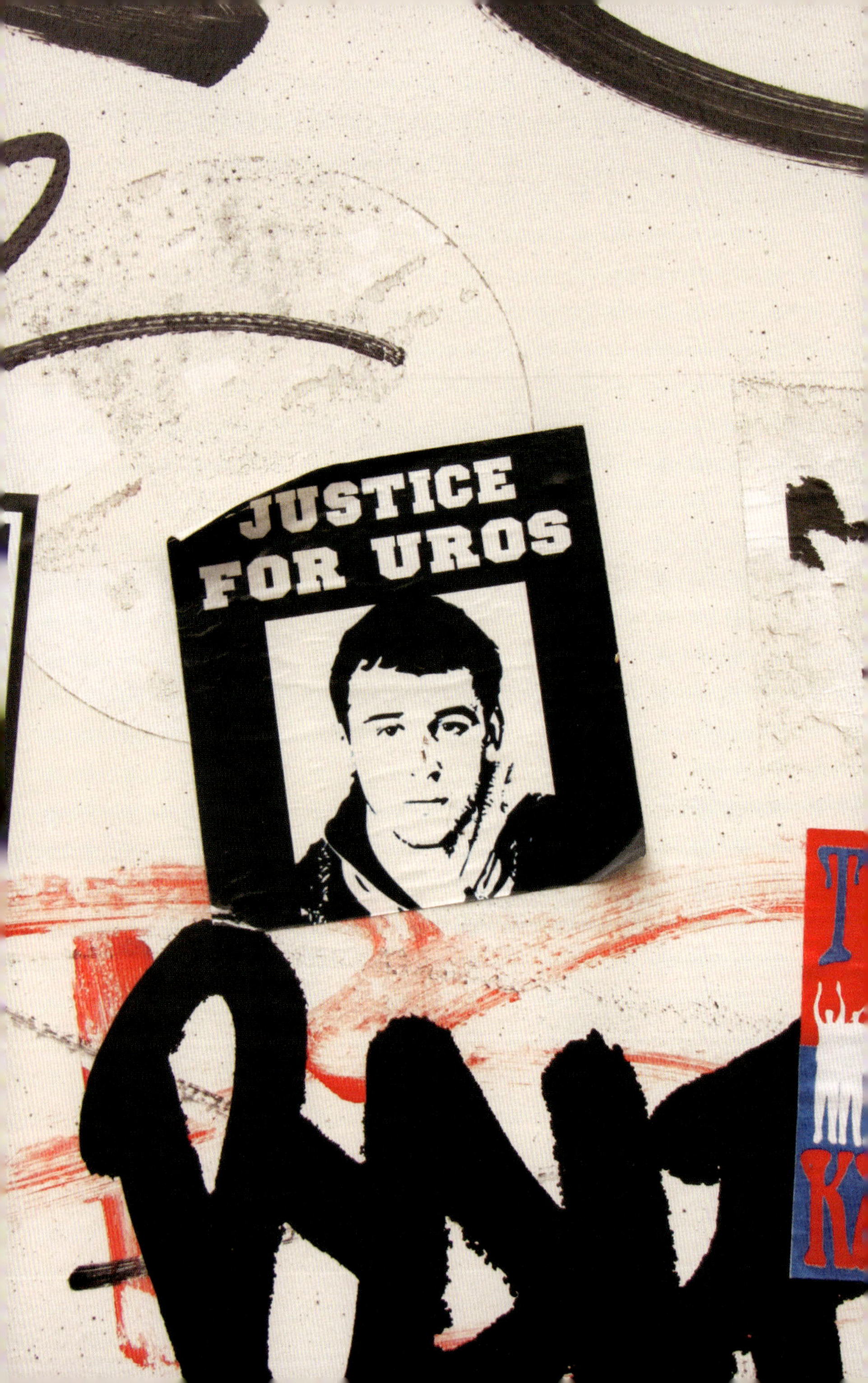

JUSTICE FOR UROS

Football-fandom and the extreme right

Here and on the following pages, I touch upon another delicate topic — the complex set of relations between ultras culture and neo-fascist, chauvinist, racist, patriarchal, etc. ideologies, and the way football-fan groups interface with extreme-right political parties and movements.

Of course, Slovenian football fans are *far from all being nazis*, as one of the observers pointed out — yet they continue to accept and tolerate those among them that express such extremist views and hold onto extremist iconography. Were they really apolitical, as they declare themselves, their management would eliminate this. As for now, their lack of action and response means nothing but silent agreement.

In the last few decades one important but maybe obscure symbol to people outside Slovenia has become a classic example of Hobsbawmiam "invented tradition" and an undisputed symbol of Slovenian extreme nationalists. From mainstream politicians like Zmago Jeliničič or Janez Janša to different subpolitical groups and football fans, the black *Caranthanian panther* can be seen. The panther was historically part of a coat-of-ams of different noble families that ruled Slovenian lands during the Middle Ages. Recently it also became part of the symbolic imagery of some units of the Slovenian Army and Police, yet these two institutions have never complained when extremists have employed it as theirs.

Equally disturbing, observers confirmed that a majority of young, newly recruited fans see the *Celtic cross* only as a common fan symbol. Many of them are not aware that it is a hidden neo-nazi sign, used globally by extreme-right subpolitical groups. Other images

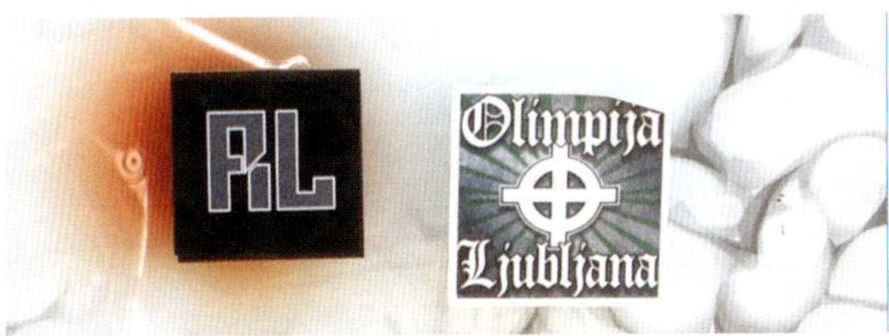

RL and *Olimpija Ljubljana* (*Radical Ljubljana* and Celtic cross); a sticker by *Radical Ljubljana* and a sticker by *Green Dragons*, fans of FC Olimpija Ljubljana; Ljubljana, Slovenia; 2016.

have also infiltrated the fan clubs to the point of *kids* not recognizing — or not wanting to recognize — their historicity. For example, the image of Hitler, nazi army-unit insignia, the SS logo

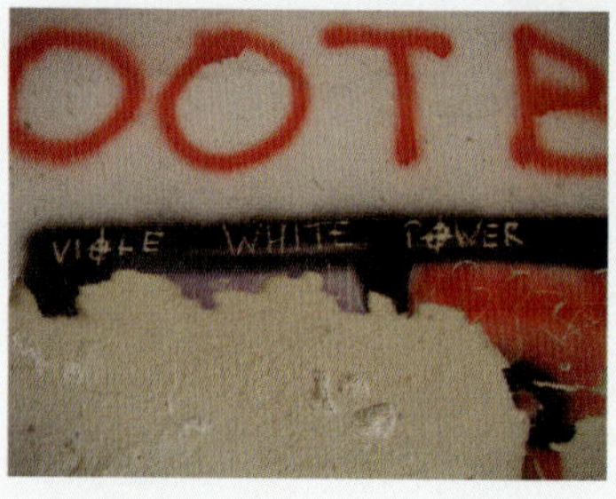

(so called /double/ sig rune, calling for "victory," "sieg"), swastikas, or the *Slavic sun*, which is actually a double swastika (called *kolovrat*) and means spinning wheel, or *little sun*, and which is now becoming popular among different Slavic neo-traditionalist and neo-nazi groups, demanding racial purity of Slavs, etc. Disturbingly we also find *Blood & Honour* symbolism like Gothic script, neo-nazi signs, *Totenkopf*, references to *Combat 18*, neo-nazi terrorist groups, etc.

Cyphers and codes are also important: beside *88*, which was explained before (meaning *Heil Hitler*) there are also *18* (for *Adolf Hitler*, 1 is code for *A* and 8 for *H*), *WP-WW* (which stands for *White Power — World Wide*), *C18* or *318* (for *Combat 18* group), *28* (*Blood and Honour*), *RL* for *Radical Ljubljana* (a new pan-Slavic, chauvinist sub-political group in Slovenia, connected with similar ones in other Slavic countries), and of course a sad white-power classic,

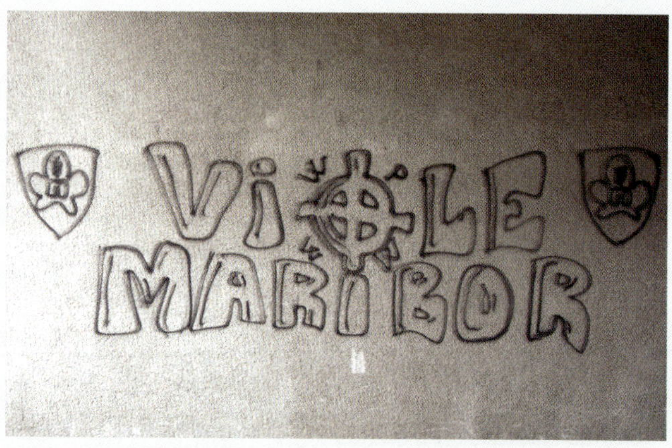

Above: *Viole White power*; by *Viole*, fans of FC Maribor; scratchiti; Maribor, Slovenia; 2011.

Below: *Viole Maribor* with Celtic cross; by *Viole*, fans of FC Maribor; graffiti; Maribor, Slovenia; 2011.

128

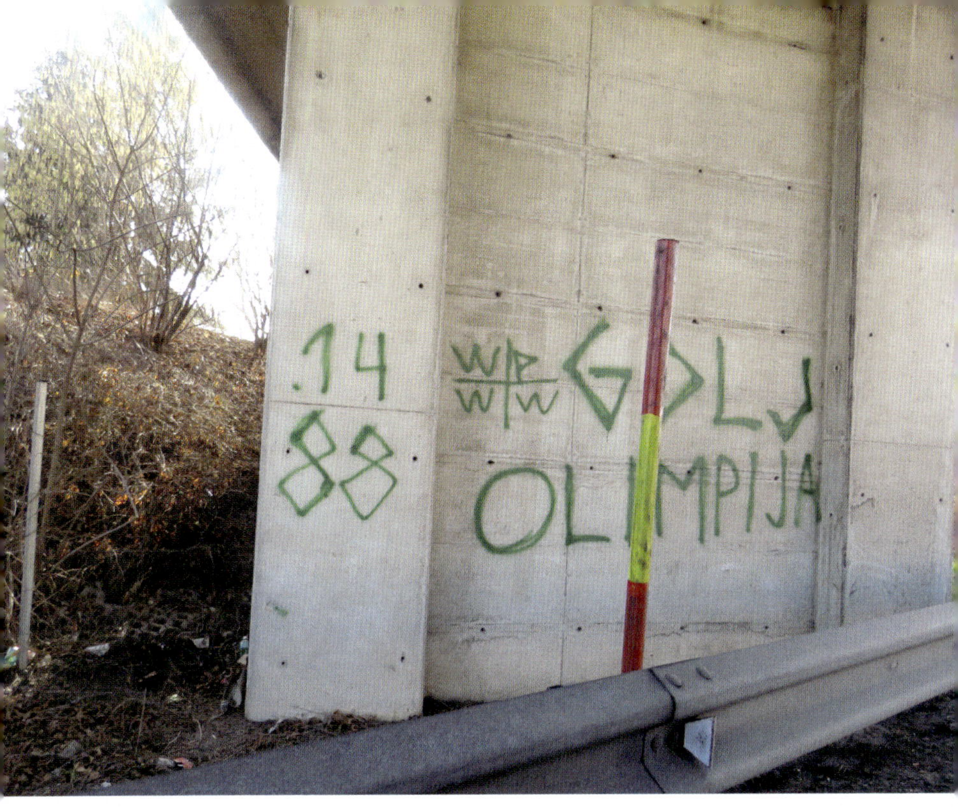

14, meaning *We must secure the existence of our people and a future for white children*, coined by American white supremacist David Lane and popularized in the 1990s. Sometimes they are combined, like *14/88* in what becomes a joint racist and neo-nazi code.

In the case of the *Green Dragons*, as remarked one of the observers, neo-nazis infiltrated the club after a dire period when the team fell into the Slovenian Fifth Football League. But among the fans I talked to, there were no comments regarding it being connected to the white supremacy fan subgroup called *Capital Riot Crew* (from the early 2010s). And in the case of the *Viole*, nobody evoked their former leader who was also the leader of *Hervardi* (*Hervards*), an extreme nationalist and militant group.

14 88 WPWW GD LJ Olimpija (neo-nazi, white supremacist cyphers including WPWW, standing for "White Power World Wide," *Green Dragons, Ljubljana*); by *Green Dragons*, fans of FC Olimpija Ljubljana; graffiti; Brezovica, Slovenia; 2016.

Unlike those by fan groups of Serbian or Croatian football clubs living in Slovenia — which my interviewees claim to be nationalist — Slovenian fans consider themselves to be ethnically heterogenous. But this was disproved by the observers: they pointed out racist and chauvinist outbursts of Slovenian fans on the terraces and elsewhere (e.g., *monkey chants* directed at non-white or Balkan players, shouting *gypsy, gypsies*, etc.). Also, there are clear political affiliations: *Delije* support the *Greater Serbia* and connections with Russia, they demand Kosovo be returned to Serbia; *Grobari* make similar claims; *Torcida* leans toward nazis and ustasha symbolism and ideas; such iconography can also be seen with the *Bad Blue Boys*; *Lešinari hate Bosnia*, etc.

Given that fan graffiti often feature extreme right-wing political symbols — the Celtic cross, *Caranthanian panther*, Gothic script, swastikas, the numbers 88 and 18, images of Hitler, etc. — I was interested in fans' attitude towards them.

Fans answered in five different ways. Firstly, that it all depends on individual understanding: *kids* only treat them as fan symbols while the right-leaning fans see their politicality. Secondly, they regarded the panther to be an old Slovenian symbol and as such justifiable, whereas the swastika and the Celtic cross were not. Thirdly, they said they use none of those political symbols, only local ones — as the fan structure is also politically and ethnically heterogenous. Fourthly, they individualized such behavior (*it is a work of individual members, not the group as a whole*). And lastly, they avoided giving clear answers despite the fact that some of their members unambiguously showed nazi political persuasion, also via graffiti. Fans wrote this off as a *mere provocation*, nothing more than a *joke*. One interesting answer came from a fan and an observer: fans will not use such symbols because they are nazis but expressly and exclusively to oppose existing values. Even when they disagreed with what the symbols stand for, it was more important to show their contradiction to others.

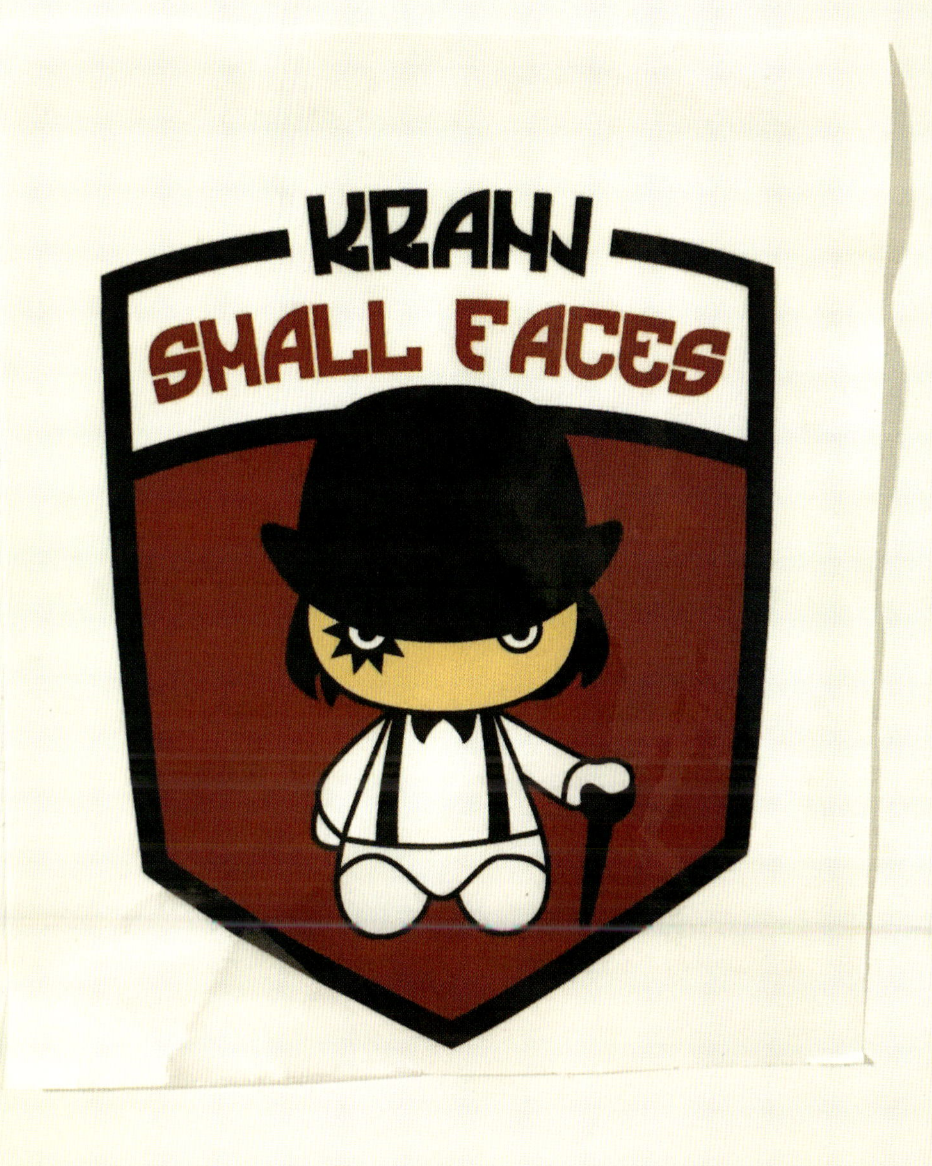

Small Faces Kranj with a cartoon of the villain from *Clockwork Orange* (dir. Stanley Kubrick, 1971); by *Small Faces*, fans of FC Triglav Kranj; sticker; Kranj, Slovenia; 2014.

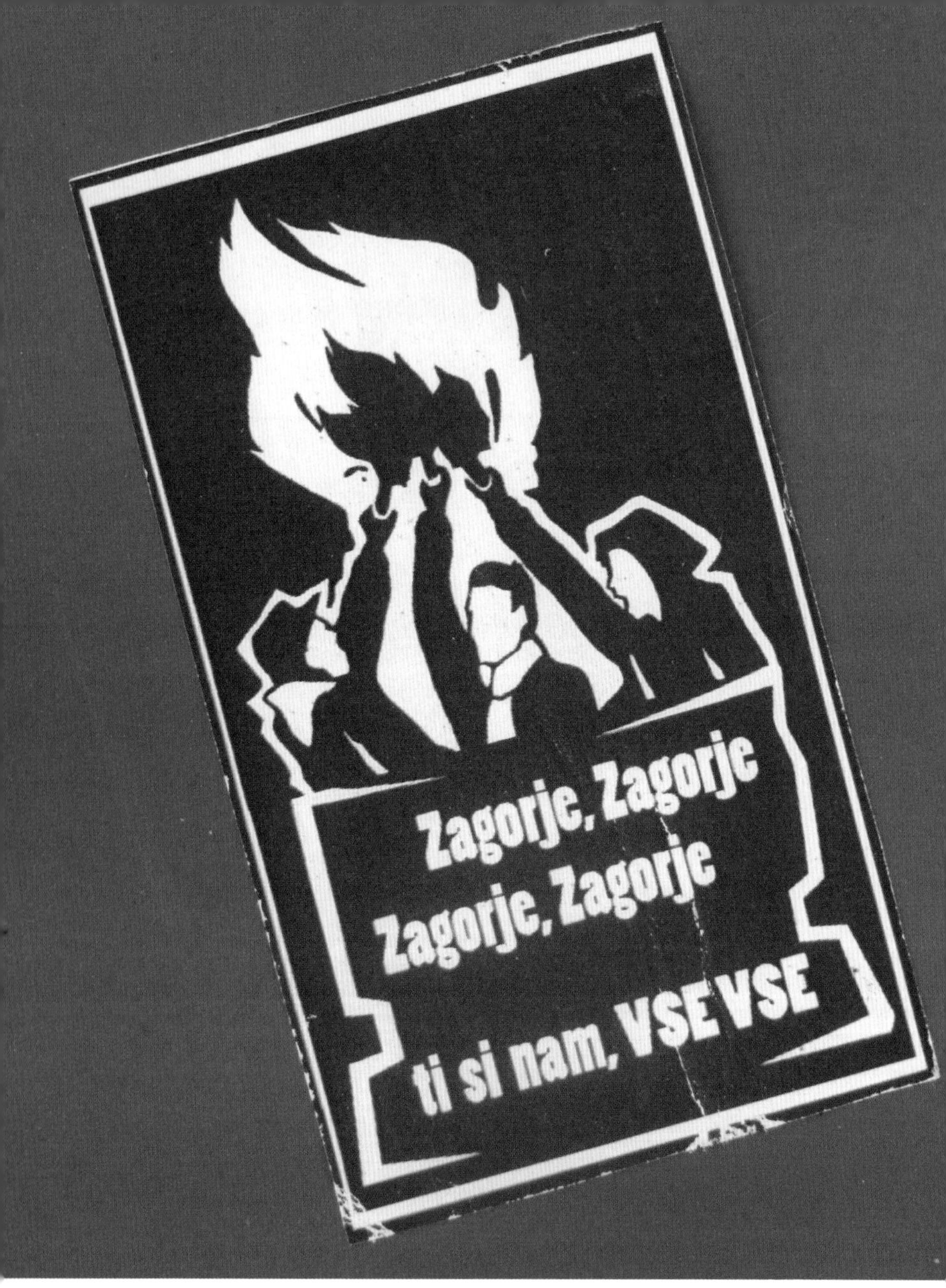

Zagorje, Zagorje — Zagorje, Zagorje — ti si nam VSE VSE (Zagorje, Zagorje — Zagorje, Zagorje — you mean EVERYTHING, EVERYTHING to us); by *Crazy Boys*, fans of FC Zagorje; sticker; Zagorje, Slovenia; 2014.

I was listed by Slovenian football fans the numerous activities of theirs that *never make it into the news*: blood donations, clothes collections for the homeless and the poor, cleaning and maintaining sports grounds,

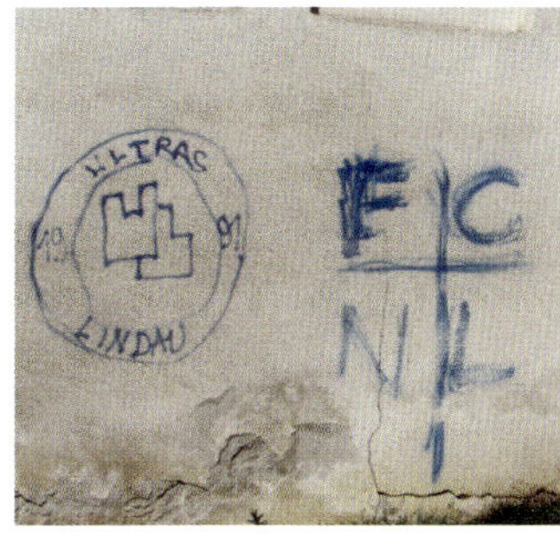

donations for any imprisoned (opposing) fans, etc. They see themselves the victims, in a sense, of poor public perceptions, whereby the term *mob* was used more than once. Journalists were described as *clueless, uninformed, insulting, catastrophic, generalizing, inciting, sensationalist, two-faced,* and *scandal-seeking* (*more people get hurt at village fetes than at football matches!*, one fan claimed resolutely).[14] Several interviewees also emphasized that unlike the rest of Europe (in Russia, Poland, England, the Netherlands, Greece and Italy, for example), there were never any serious or tragic fan riots in Slovenia. Fans are also never linked with organized crime; they do not deal drugs or control illegal businesses. This stands in contrast to those better organized and bigger football-fan groups in other parts of

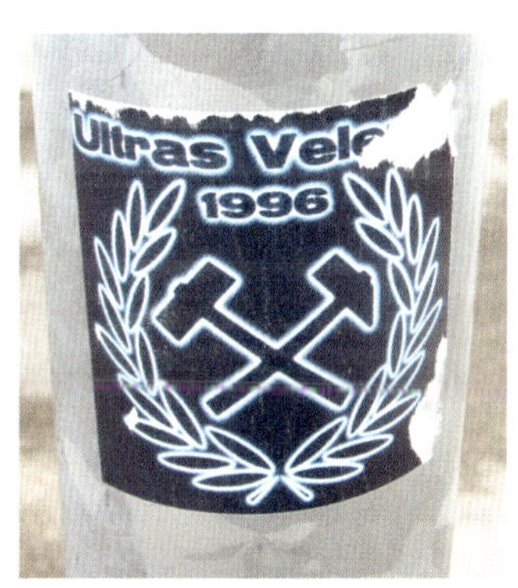

the Balkans who are much more engaged in such activities and have strong connections with high politics.[15]

Above: *Ultras Lindau 1991 — FC NL* (*FC Nafta Lendava/Lendva*); by *Gorgone,* fans of FC Lendava; graffiti; Lendava/Lendva, Slovenia; 2012.

Below: *Ultras Velenje 1996*; by *Knapi* (colloquial name for *Miners*), fans of FC Rudar Velenje; sticker; Velenje, Slovenia; 2014.

Graffiti and stickers are used as a means of communicating with the opposing fans, or rather as means of provoking or agitating them. As for appeals to violence (*Kill, kill the Styrian/Frog! 101% anti-Frog* by the *Viole*; while *Green Dragons* has a similar sticker, *Gruppo Antiviola* or *Hools Ljubljana 101 % Antiviola* graffiti with crosses added to the O's, making them Celtic crosses; and *Anti-Gorgone Crew* by the *Black Gringos*)[16] in graffiti as well as in chants, one fan understands them only as a fan performance, as a *ritual and not real violence*, expressed only on walls and in cheers. *We don't really mean it*, says another.

In the end, it took me by surprise how similar everyone's answers were. I had heard many stories from other sources that were fairly different from those I learned from the fans: there were, for example, anti-gay incidents, anti-immigrant and anti-Roma statements, banners (the most infamous being the long anti-refugee *Viole* banner during the peak of the *migrant crisis* in November 2015), actions and so forth. But fans would often catch themselves in contradictions: they would, for example, claim not to be nationalist/racist while mentioning nationalist/racist outbreaks. On the other hand, some fans exhibited a high degree of individual and social (self)reflection: they believe fandom to be a revolt against an existing way of life, a distrust of any authority and a rejection of commercialization, a questioning of the repression that the others silently tolerate, and an alternative developing of collectivity and solidarity amongst the fans and in the face of atomization and alienation of people in contemporary societies. All this is nicely shown in the sticker of supporters of FC Rapid Wien: a sneaker proudly stands over a broken police helmet with 1312 on the front, with clear message: *Against state authority* (see page 57). Their marginal position comes not from fate but out of choice or, as one fan was happy to assert: *We live our own way and not like the other ninety percent who don't concern us*. Anti-everything: a typical case of subcultural exclusivism.

[16] *Styrian* stands for *Viole* fans, and *Frog* is directed at *Green Dragons*: people from Ljubljana are ridiculed as frogs because of the nearby marshes.

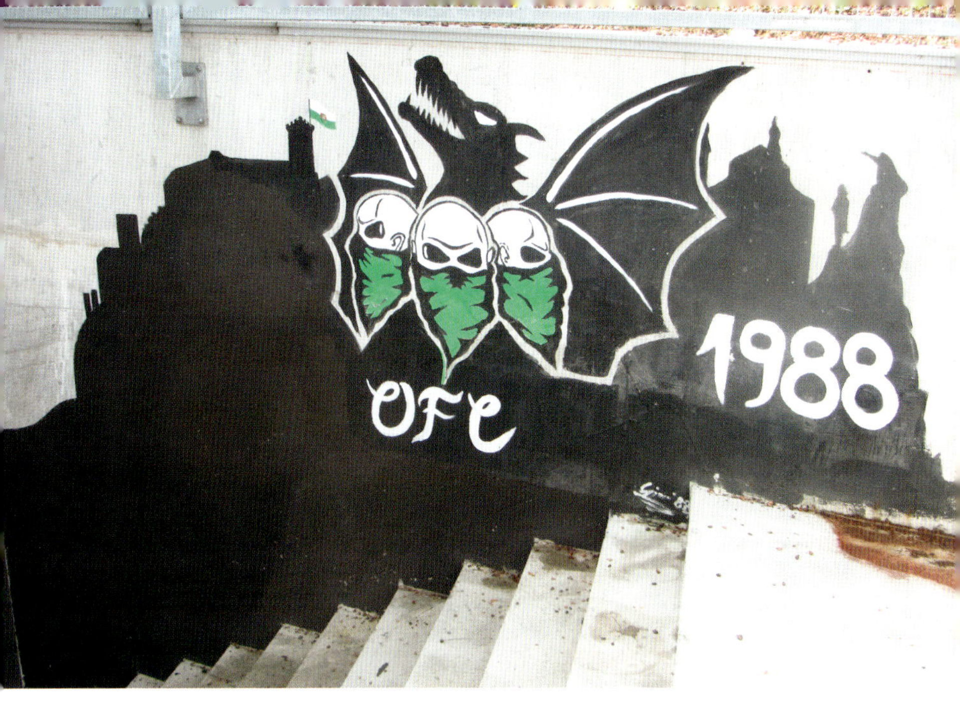

[7] In their press
release, the club
management
wrote that
(ahem!) *these
were motorcycle
helmets available
for sale anywhere
online and worn by
Drivers of classic
bikes…*

I found the largest discrepancy between fans' answers and their graffiti, stickers and stencils in terms of whether politics influence them, with their relationship towards extreme right-wing symbols. Affinity towards the extreme right can also be seen on the scandalous official FC Maribor poster — just to be clear, this is a club not a fan poster! — from May 2015 promoting the *Battle for Styria* (a match between the Styrian clubs Maribor and Celje) and depicting Maribor players with nazi *Stahlhelm* helmets from WWII.[17] It therefore comes as no surprise that the walls of Maribor boast violet swastikas or abbreviations *SLO*, with a cross over the O, and club initials. And finally, their graffiti reflect no daily party politics or Slovenian external policies; the same goes for gender or class issues. There is also almost no left-wing symbolism or rhetoric: a few exceptions would include two *Viole* stickers (*Antifa Ultras Maribor* and *No Racism in*

OFC (Olimpija Football Club) 1988, by *Green Dragons,* fans of FC Olimpija Ljubljana; mural; Ljubljana, Slovenia; 2018.

Football) and one by the FC Nafta Lendava foreign fans with *Love Nafta — Hate fascism — Smash homophobia* (see page 154). On the other hand, they also break with their own ethnic exclusivity; for example, *Green Dragons* took sides with their long-time club janitor of Bosniak descent who was in dispute with the new club management, and showed their support in various ways, also with a mural and banners.

In terms of rejecting the media and the police, apart from an occasional *Fuck the media* sprayed in club colors, there are very few graffiti or stickers that would problematize how the media paint a negative fan picture. However, those against the police appear in large quantities: not just the clichéd *ACAB* but also appeals to stop *violence against the fans*, explanations that *Pyrotechnics is not a crime!* (see page 18), rejections of the Anti-hooligan Law, etc. On a *Dragons*' sticker, a pig in a police uniform finds out that *We fucked your wives!*

In conclusion, just to be clear, I have absolutely no intention of making excuses for fans' activities and opinions, to defend them from frequent albeit not always completely legitimate criticism, or to speak in their stead. Quite the opposite: with these pages, I simply wish to "give a voice" to fans holding spray cans and stickers, and compare it to their wall legacy. As several of their statements and views do not match their graffiti, stickers, murals, and stencils, the combination of these research methods proves its validity.

Fans' verbal expression needs to be understood as complementary and supplementary to their visual expression — no matter how contradictory this may

Jebali smo vaše žene (*We fucked your wives*); by *Green Dragons,* fans of FC Olimpija Ljubljana; sticker; Ljubljana, Slovenia; 2019.

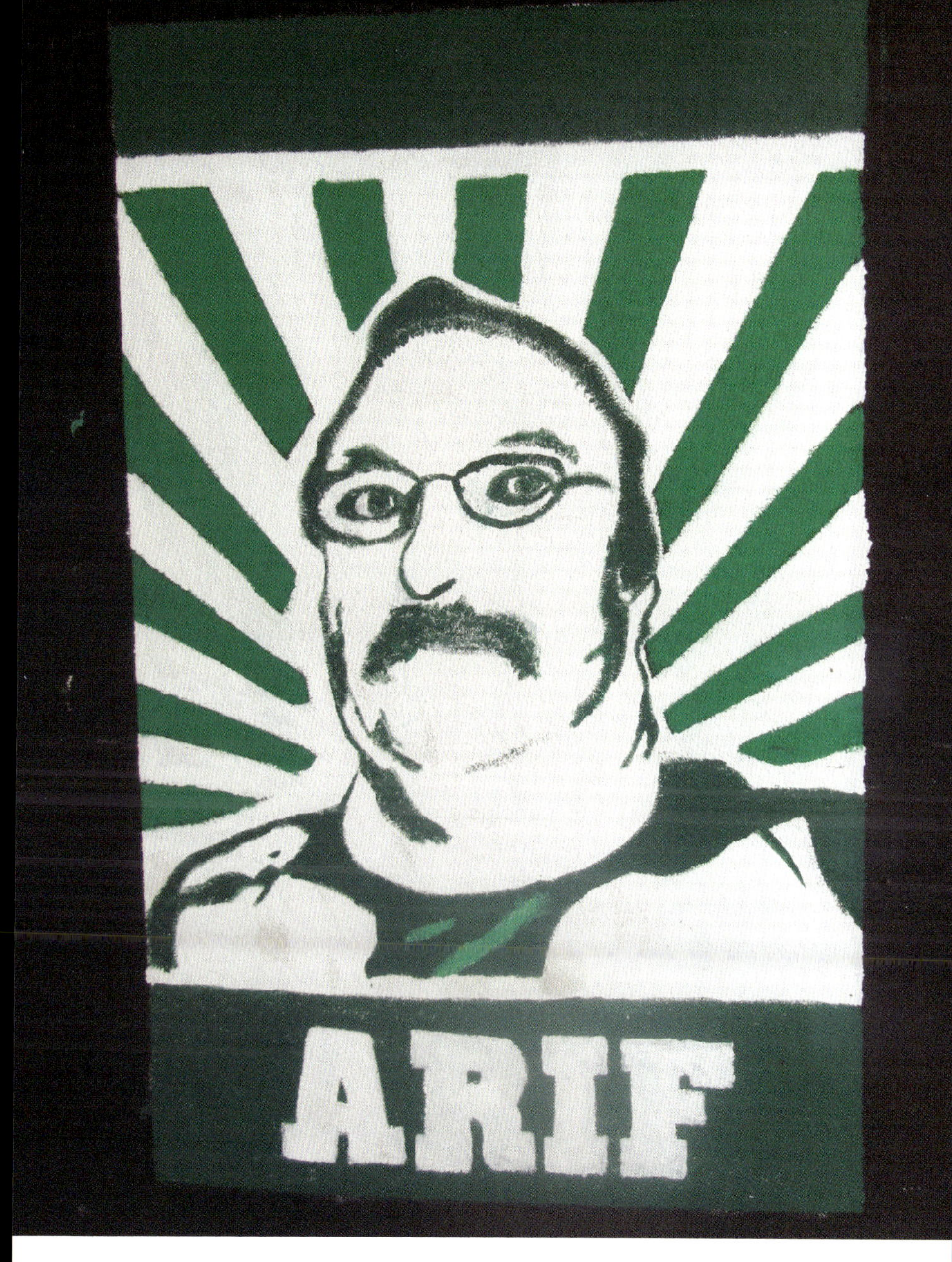

Arif (name of FC Olimpija's long time janitor of Bosniak origins); by *Green Dragons*, fans of FC Olimpija Ljubljana; mural; Ljubljana, Slovenia; 2014.

seem. We simply find ourselves in the metamodernist spirit of oscillating between opposite poles. In Montague's words (2020: 332):

Fans are, despite their heterogeneity and competitiveness towards other fans, united in their perception of themselves as parts of the same subculture, parts of an "urban tribe." Their outsider stance comes of free will, their ghettoization is exclusive — yet they complain when the media (the ideological state apparatus) describe them as such, and when the police (the repressive state apparatus) treat them as such.

This entails fans' symbolic positioning. What both the Slovenian interviewees' statements and their graffiti language show is that their "absolute enemies" are the media, the police and the state with their restrictive measures, and the international organizations UEFA and FIFA — other fans are merely "friendly enemies" (or "frenemies"), as they share a common subcultural belonging and values. While fans show antagonism to the former, they show agonism to the latter in the same way cultural theorist Chantal Mouffe imagined it ("*antagonism* is struggle between enemies, while *agonism* is struggle between adversaries" 2000: 102, 103). These fans are therefore discursively constructed through a conflictual consensus with other fans on the one hand, and through a value-based dissensus with the institutions of the existing, unstoppably pluralized global society on the other.

This also gives rise to the third contradicting dynamic that can be "saved" with the metamodern *and.* Slovenian fans oppose *modern football*, reject the globalization, commercialization, tycoonization and spectacularization of football — but without all these, their clubs would play in inter-municipal leagues instead of national or European ones. The terraces and the walls scream xenophobia, racism and nazism — but there are many non-white and/or foreign players running on the fields. As far as content, technique and aesthetics go, Slovenian fans' graffiti, stickers, stencils, etc., are strikingly similar to those from other parts of fan Europe; the names of fan groups also sound very global, internationalist, as a majority of them are in English. On the other hand, as Polish anthropologist Roch Sulima (2005: 87) points out, "sport rituals, similar to rituals of youth music, create relatively the most intensive and emotionally the most engaged series of graffiti in the urbanscape: these graffiti are becoming the most important bearers of local identity, and of even more deeply motivated *territorial identity*." Slovenian football fans swear to belong in

*Mi smo tisti na katere so vas starši opozarjali — GD — Celtic cross — RU (We are the ones your parents warned you against — Green Dragons — Rudnik /*part of Ljubljana); by *Green Dragons,* fans of FC Olimpija Ljubljana; graffiti; Ljubljana, Slovenia; 2018.

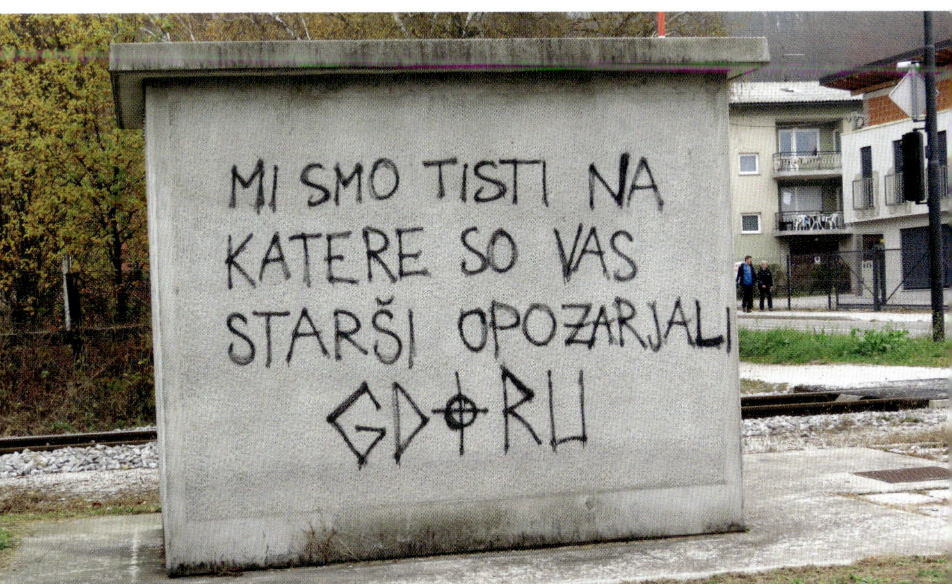

a local environment, which points to the traditional Slovenian decentralization, strong localism or regionalism, "homeliness" (Žižek 1987: 9–46), in Italian known as *campanilismo*, and last but not least, the recency of a unified Slovenian national ideology. The majority of clubs are named after towns or places[18] and geographical sites[19] — they, according to researcher and chronicler of Slovenian football Tim Dobovšek (2019: 110) — "represent an entire local area and should, for its organic unity, act in its interest." Clubs with independent names are in the minority,[20] while there are a few more bearing sponsors' names.[21]

At this point, Slovenian football-fan visual ideology meets the one that is predominant in Slovenian society today with its "jargon of authenticity" (Adorno 1973) and the concrete praxes this jargon entails. "Grudges" between Maribor and Ljubljana, intolerance to all

[18] Domžale, Maribor, Koper, Celje, Gorica, Izola, Zavrč, Krško, Radomlje, etc.

[19] Krka, Mura, Triglav, etc.

[20] Olimpija, Rudar.

[21] Tabor Sežana, Kalcer Radomlje, Nafta Lendava, Primorje Ajdovščina, Aluminij Kidričevo, Bravo Ljubljana, etc.

Celje, naše mesto — CG 92 (Celje, our city — Celjski grofje 1992); by *Celjski grofje*, fans of FC Celje; inscription; Celje, Slovenia; 2014.

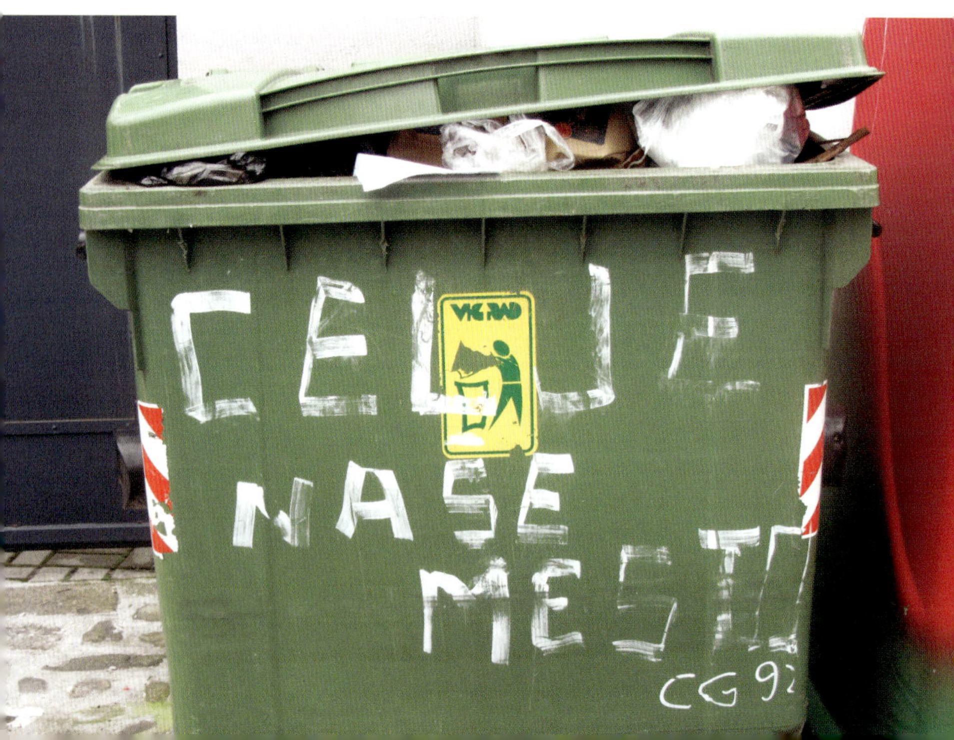

[2] The last U.S. ambassador in the Socialist Federalist Republic of Yugoslavia, Warren Zimmermann called Slovenian nationalism "Garbo nationalism": it has pretty face, but it is still nationalism.

Others of Slovenian society, normalization of right-wing extremism, "Garbo nationalism,"[22] Balkan-phobia, etc. — this all sounds very familiar. Fan graffiti and sticker artists do not have to look far for inspiration. There is no loud schism between the ideology and praxis of one and the others, there is a silent agreement. A certain concern that is typical for the relationship of the Slovenian media, and cultural and political mainstream towards fans is more of a consequence of ideological closeness than opposition. To the protagonists of this mainstream, fans represent their "bad consciousness" rather than adversaries, and their *wildness* makes them easy targets for projecting all that is also ever so present in the political center. Fan graffiti and street art hold the mirror to contemporary Slovenian society which tries to avoid it with all of its might — so that it may never recognize itself.

Ribari Izola (*Fishermen Izola*); by fans of FC Izola; mural; Jagodje, Slovenia; 2021.

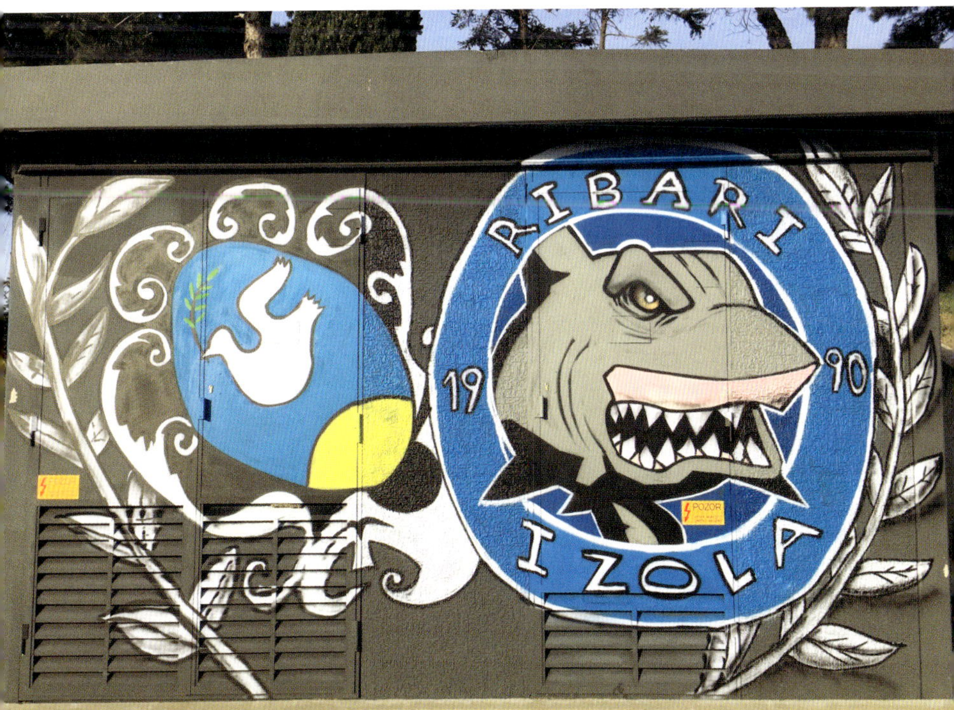

IV. CONCLUSION

Let's return — after this excursion into the picturesque and rough world of football-fan graffiti and street art — to a central question of graffiti studies: What is the actual social power of graffiti, what influence — if there is any to begin with — do they have on the social reality around them? Additionally, how do these vivid examples and insightful cases of football-fan graffiti and street art frame relations between arts/aesthetics, politics/ideology and fan subculture/sub-politics? The understanding of graffiti and street art oscillates between cynical rejection on the one side (it is a "permitted rebellion," an "aesthetization of the status quo," a "new hegemonic speech," etc.) and the acknowledgment of their emancipatory potentials on the other.

The domestication of graffitiing in the world of established art and the fragmentation of its totality are targets of well-grounded criticism. Once incorporated into the art mainstream, this now already ex-street culture provokes mostly critical reactions. In this scenario, graffiti is degenerating, repeating the fate of avantgardes, neo-avantgardes and youth subcultures, which rejected and destroyed the existing art only to end or self-destruct in the very same. Another *never* in the series of the never-said nevers: in 1986, the futuristic *revolution* ended with the *Futurism and Futurisms* retrospective in Palazzo Grassi in that same Venice that Marinetti along with his aesthetic revolutionaries in their 1910 manifesto threatened to destroy. *Authentic* punk attire is sold in Zara and H&M, while *rad* skateboards with three-digit price tags can be bought in skateboard boutiques next door. In their "Have a Nice Day" video (2005), Bon Jovi teach how to do and disseminate street art; *Liberation*, the new Christina Aguilera album, *Available June 15*, was advertised throughout New York by (deliberately) negligent stencils in 2018; as one of the street art icons, Obey (Shepard Fairey) created an acclaimed *Barack Obama Hope poster,* in actual fact, a stylized stencil, for the U.S. presidential election in 2008. *Fee, not free* is a street phrase I picked up during my field work that succinctly sums up this situation.

"Every work of art is an uncommitted crime," concludes Adorno pessimistically (2005: 111). If affirmative culture "procures political acquiescence by presenting false resolutions of conflict and artificial harmonies in the aesthetic sphere" (Wolff 1994: 89), the specific graffitiscape of Slovenian football fans surfaces the societal tensions in the undercurrent of the Slovenian

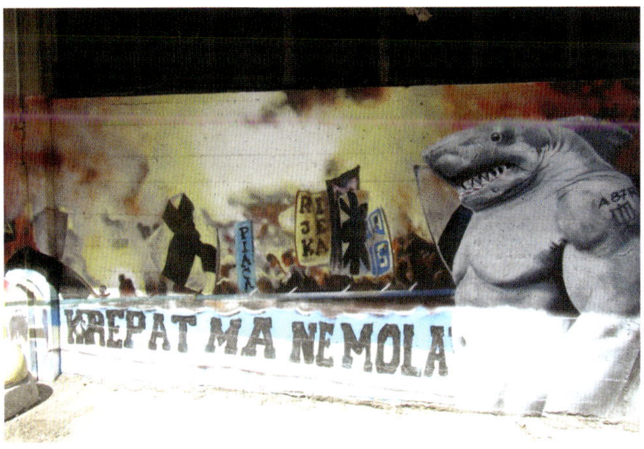

Krepat ma ne molat (*Rather to die than to give up,* written in local slang); by *Armada,* fans of FC Rijeka; mural; Rijeka, Croatia; 2015.

EVERY
WORK
OF ART
IS AN
UNCOM
MITTED
CRIME

cultural imaginary. We can now expand this case study to see how it is a microcosm for the metamodern dynamics in all of European football.

The basic mistake, the *original sin* of the larger part of graffiti studies so far has been their depoliticization: graffiti are considered nothing more than pictograms or urban ornaments. Books on graffiti, those lavish and expensive ones published in large formats, never even mention *political graffiti* as a concept or include them in the selection! We would browse them in vain if we wanted to find spray-painted ridicules or praise of politicians, pacifistic and emancipatory appeals, nationalistic maxims or fan chants. An academic depoliticization of graffitiing chooses various strategies. In the first place, they are explained as nothing more than a youth game, tomfoolery, showing off and recklessness of young people with cans of paint. Some go as far as calling their authors "kids," not even "youngsters" or "adolescents": "kids write graffiti because it's fun," claim Chalfant and Prigoff (1987: 7). Quite literally, graffiti are understood as "just kidding." Secondly, they are perceived as a sporting test, if we read Daichendt (2017: 7): "distinctly different from the traditional art world, where technical skill seems not to apply, street art has always seemed more akin to sport."

However, the most efficient decomposition of graffiti politically through academic reception reduces them to mere aesthetics or design, placing them exclusively into the art world.[23] In this sense, the scientific discourse on graffitiing presents a graver danger for graffiti than the unappreciated authorities out there that keep sending anti-graffiti squads, snitches, painters and cleaners to fix them: it translates criticism into aesthetics, transgression into trend, political messages into cultural praxes, social outsiders with spray cans into romantic rebels without a cause. It literally does what Hadjinicolaou (1978: 4–6) had always been reproaching existing art history, namely that it is "one of the last outposts of reactionary thought."

[3] Reynolds, for example, writes that "as a designer and photographer [he] found special interest in the graphics and design of the graffiti." (1975: no page)

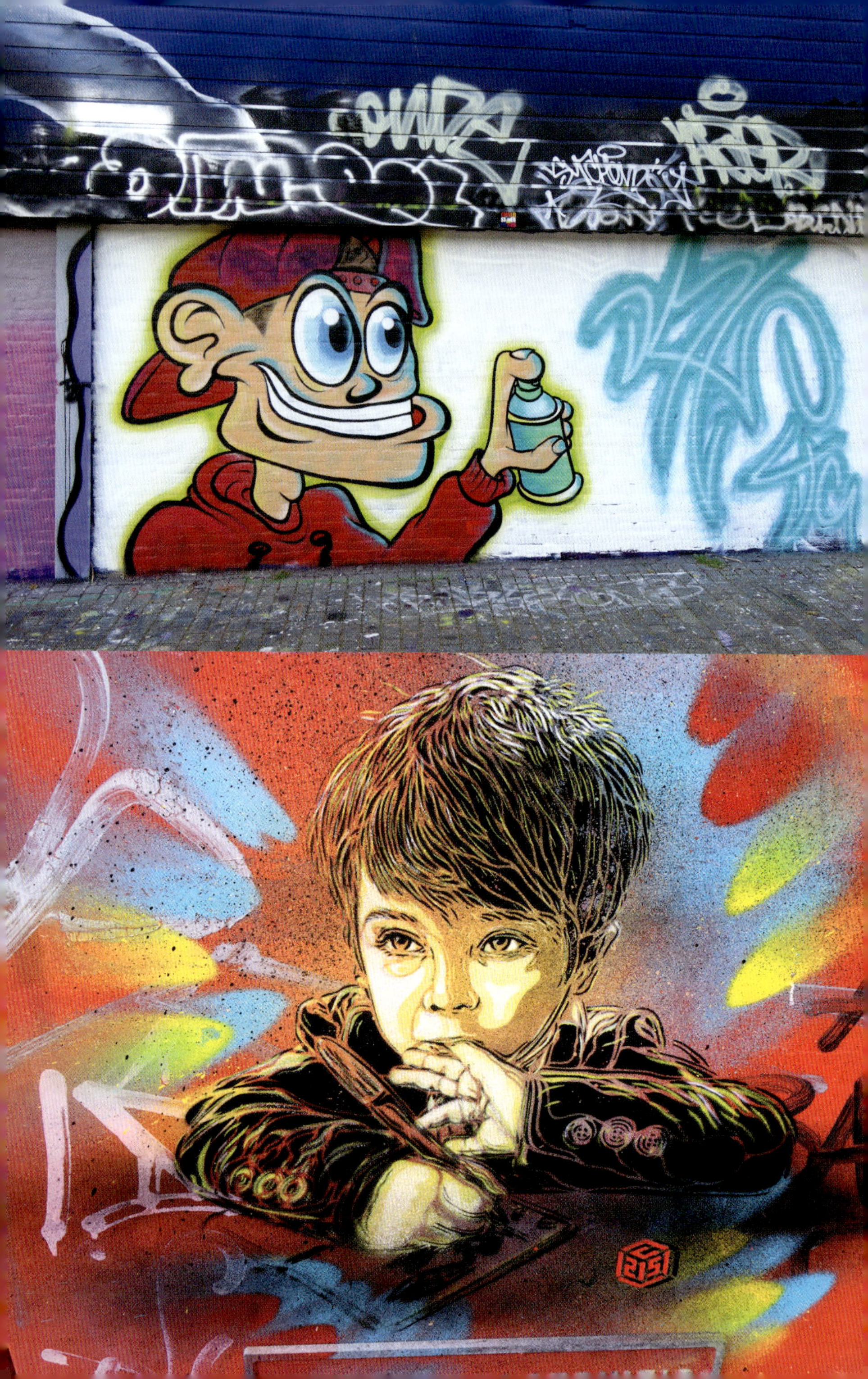

I completely agree with all of the criticisms of graffitiing and street art mentioned: the degeneration of the original idea, compensation, depoliticization and reduction to mere aesthetics. However, as these cases prove, there are many more aspects they fail to consider. Do not get me wrong: I would hate to force reality by searching for direct politicality in graffiti subculture as a whole. Graffiti are, of course, also adolescent showing-off, an adrenalin rush and, however hard it is to accept it, pure aesthetic artwork. This, however, fails to explain the entirety of the graffiti and street art production, far from it.

As suggested by the graffiti included here, city walls carry politics and not art as the conventional and institutionalized form of creativity. While dominant ideologies create false dilemmas as to whether a graffiti pertains to art or to politics, to aesthetics or to ideology, is it something beautiful or is it vandalism, and strive to separate one from the other, I take this symptomatic *or* and change it into *and*. Graffiti and street art are politics *and* art, ideology *and* aesthetics, visual intervention *and* political praxis,

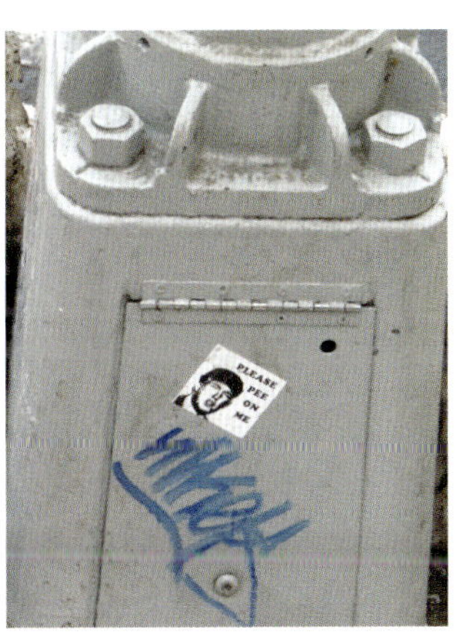

beauty *and* vandalism. A graffiti pertains to art, as long as I understand that "art is the negative knowledge of the actual world" (Adorno 2002: 160). Its value lies not (only) in itself but in the position it adopts and in the consequences that result from it: it is valuable if it encourages people to think and inspires them to act.[24]

Opposite above: Graffiti; Rotterdam, The Netherlands; 2019.

Opposite below: Different street-art techniques; Genova, Italy; 2020.

Above: *Please pee on me (Donald Trump)*; sticker; New York, USA; 2017.

The active-critical involvement of graffiti and street art lies not only in their explicit political statement, i.e., in the fact that they clearly express a political message, but also in the mere pre-discursive gesture of their

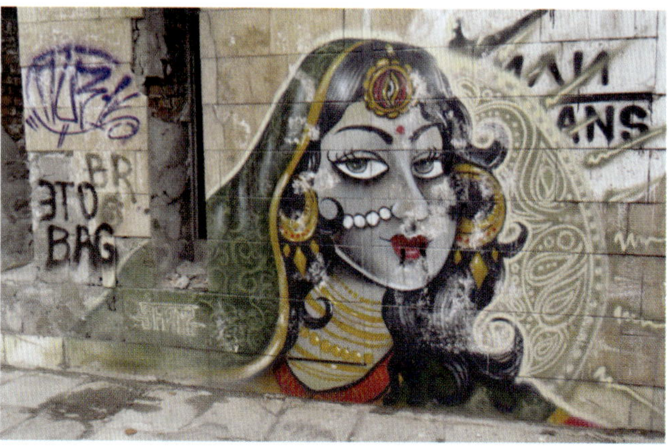

creation and autonomous existence. The single act of appearing on the street without permission represents a radical aesthetic and political action: graffiti are by definition images of dissent. The subversiveness of graffiti also lies in their public nature, their street char-acter, in a direct sense as a political address. Rancière claims that "if there exists a connection between art and politics, it should be cast in terms of dissensus, the very kernel of the aesthetic regime: artworks can produce effects of dissensus precisely because they neither give lessons nor have any destination" (2010: 140).[25] Their politicality lies in their autonomy, that is in the "emancipation of aesthetic," and in their "useful-ness," that is in the "aesthetic of emancipation."

In both senses, a graffiti is a radical act, as it disrupts an overly clean wall with something that should not be there. It is a "material disturbance," an interruption of empty walls, buildings and the city behind them: either as an implicit empathy (in the form of a subcultural graffiti with its subtle, enchanted poetics, which moves the viewers into a new aesthetics), or as an explicit reflection (in the form of a direct political graffiti, which

25 Charles Baudelaire claimed much the same: "I sin-cerely believe that the best criticism is the criticism that is entertaining and poetic; not a cold analytical type of criticism, which, claim-ing to explain everything, is devoid of hatred and love, and deliberately rids itself of any trace of feeling.'

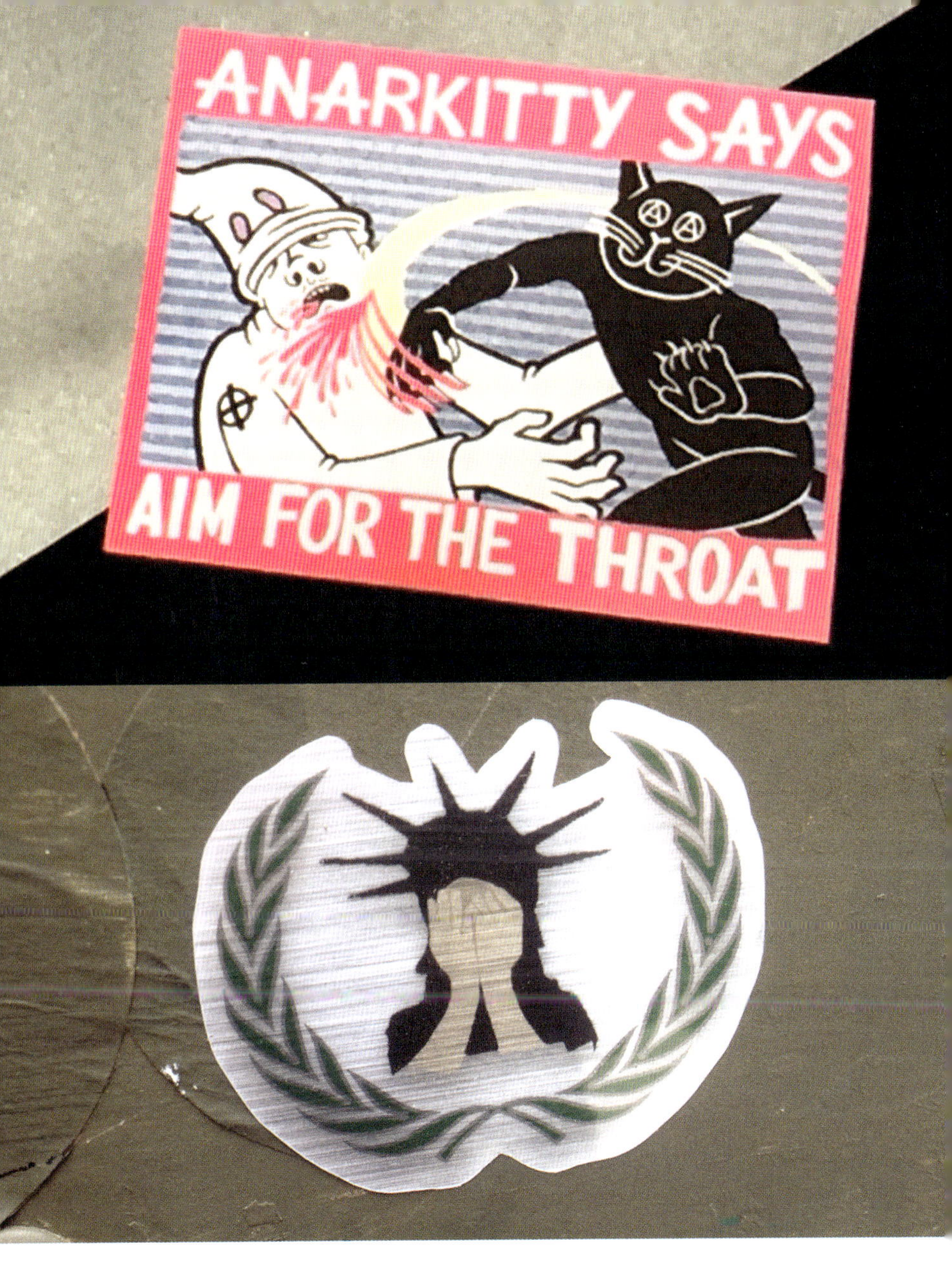

Opposite: Mural; Bishkek, Kyrgyzstan; 2017.

Above: *Anarkitty Says — Aim for the Throat*; sticker; New Haven, CT, USA; 2020.

Below: Sticker; New York, USA; 2018.

149

screams in order to wake up viewers so they understand a real situation). It irritates in a quite Bakhtinian way, *carnivalesquely*: by shocking, directly, with the images of an upside-down world, wittily and playfully, yet at the same time seriously and consistently. Graffitiing moves one step ahead of the auto-destructive art concept by the neo-avant-garde artist Gustav Metzger: it is destruction in the moment of creation — and simultaneously creation in the moment of destruction.[26]

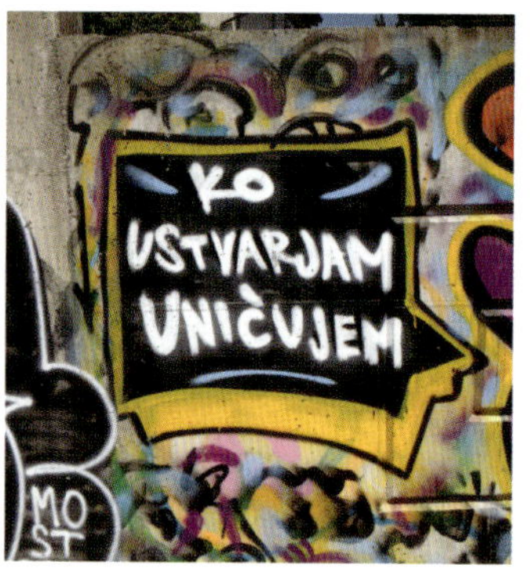

This entirely Brechtian intervention or "alienation-effect" states that art is constantly destroying aesthetic illusion and imagined social totality by critically reminding us of the "naked world" out there, by bringing the viewer back into reality, by sobering the viewer with reality. It achieves this by "producing astonishment rather than empathy," as Benjamin (2007: 150) describes Brecht's epic theater, by using irony to make pathos fall.[27]

A graffiti is a visible sign of discord within a social, cultural, aesthetic, political or, indeed, any kind of consensus. The mere act of it — not just its content! — represents the first step in disagreeing with the existing as it attacks what is most sacred in classist society: private property and, if possible, its most exposed guarantors (e.g., banks, police stations, churches, supermarkets, headquarters of political-parties). With or without words, it communicates that it does not acknowledge aesthetic or social authorities.

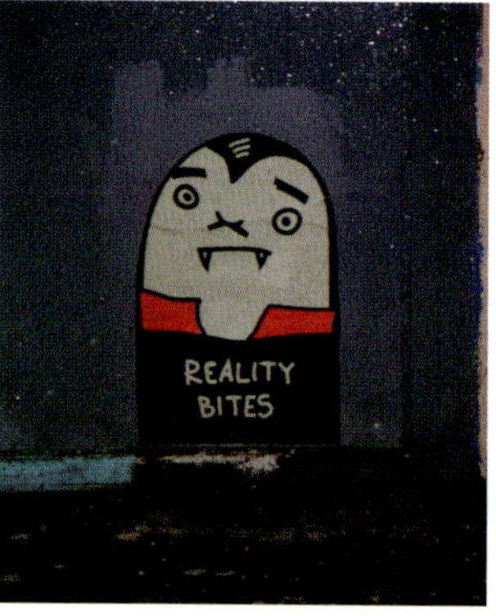

[26] Expressed in a Nova Gorica graffiti, *When I create I destroy* (2018).

[27] In graffiti language *Reality bites,* as states a Budapest paste-up through the image of a stylized Dracula (2011).

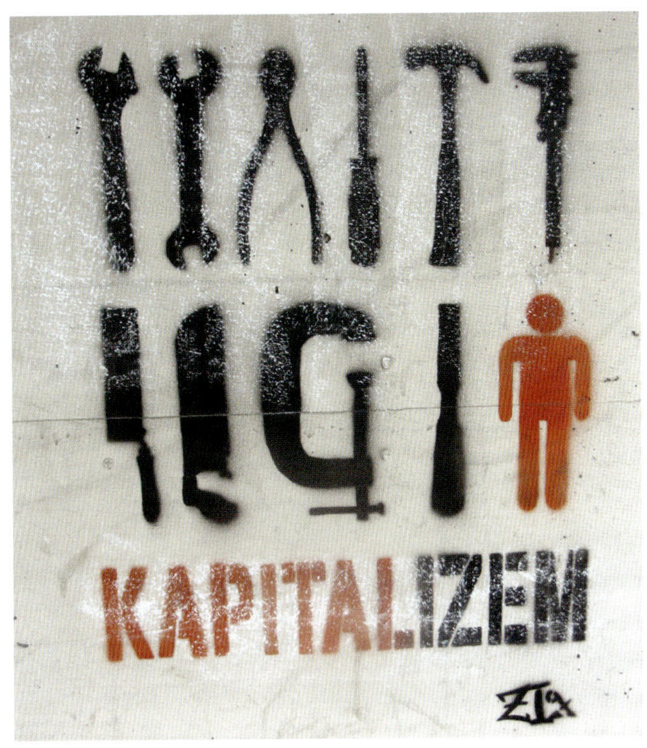

In its dissensus, however, it does acknowledge a variety of other things: "profane" creativity, participation, public engagement, bottom-up democracy, alternative, materiality. Creativity and self-initiative are restored and returned home to everyday life from where they were violently pushed into enclosed spaces at the beginning of the modern age. Creativity redeems itself by going back to the streets, back to the people in an avant-garde or, to be more precise, constructivist manner of "bringing art into real life" as did Vladimir Tatlin, Vladimir Mayakovsky or El Lissitzky. Out of "sacred spaces," away from trendy elitism!

Opposite above: *Ko ustvarjam uničujem* (*When I create I destroy*); graffiti; Nova Gorica, Slovenia; 2018.

Opposite below: *Reality bites*; paste-up; Budapest, Hungary; 2011.

Above: *Kapitalizem* (*Capitalism*); stencil; Celje, Slovenia; 2014.

Furthermore, the subversiveness of this production lies in the "return of the repressed," of the analog and material into this extremely digitalized world that we know today.

Graffiti scream that there are still walls out there: walls that need to be spray-painted and walls that need to be demolished. As if they followed Brecht's maxim of "don't start from the good old things but the bad new ones" (Benjamin 1977: 121), graffiti carries progressive 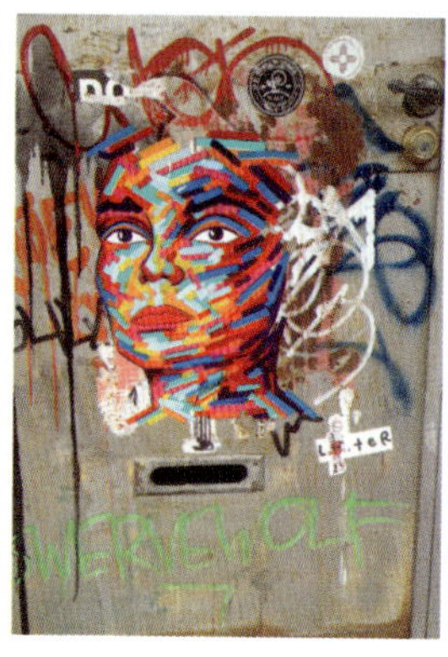 and transformative potentials within itself though these are never automatic guarantees for its subversiveness: we have to be extremely careful not to be naïvely optimistic. The included examples show how graffiti construct and reflect political divisions and unities — especially in the contemporary Balkan and Central European transition "from socialism to feudalism," as Verdery sarcastically foresaw (1996: 204–228), or to an open, fair and inclusive society. They are spray-painted as much by left-wingers as by right-wingers, by progressive as by conservative individuals, by those with "red hangover" (Ghodsee 2017) as by those with new ideas, by libertarians as much as by autocrats, by the intolerant or racist as much as by proponents of social change, by members of different subcultures as much as by advocates of the *status quo*, by the political opposition as much as by the ruling majority. It depends on each example whether they are the weapon of resistance or a weapon of authority, insurgency or conformity, i.e., whether they are usurped by the powers of emancipation or the institutions of domination.

All of these contradictions of football-fans' graffiti and street art were symptomatically summarized by fans' turbulent reactions after England lost the finals

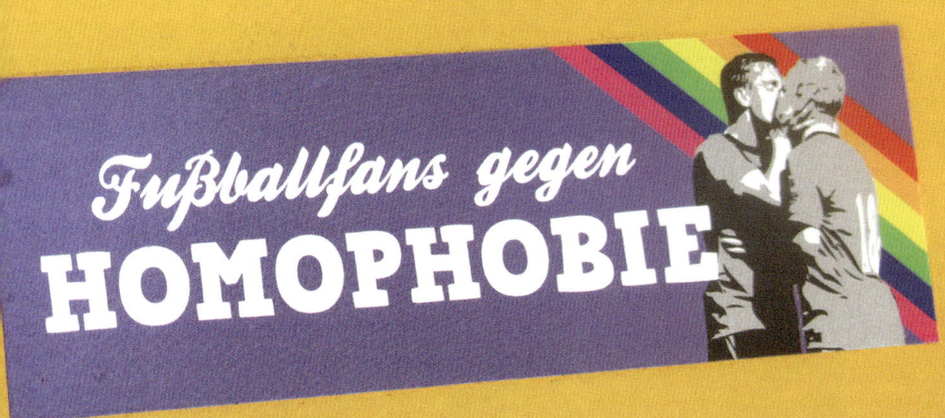

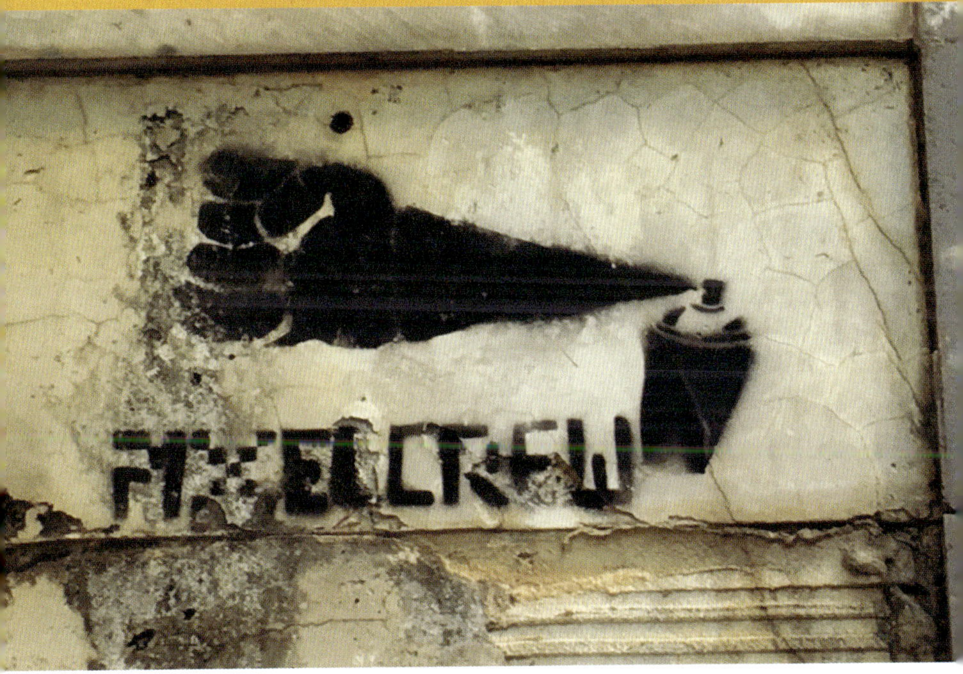

Opposite: Graffiti; New York, USA; 2018.

Above: *Fußballfans gegen Homophobie (Football fans against homophobia)*; by unidentified football fans; sticker; Innsbruck, Austria; 2013.

Below: *Pixelcrew*; stencil; Durrës, Albania; 2019.

of the European Championship 2020 in July 2021. All three English players that missed their shots in the penalty shootout were Black. A famous mural dedicated to the striker Marcus Rashford in his hometown of Manchester was immediately defaced with abusive

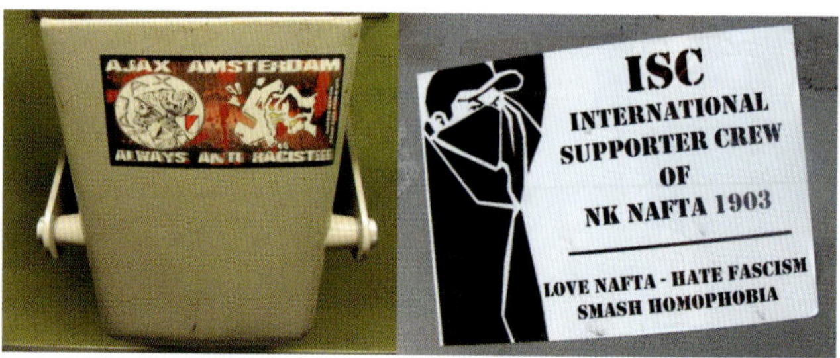

graffiti, drawings and inscriptions (simultaneously with the avalanche of racist expletives on social media). This symbolic pogrom provoked another group of football fans — and the football public in general — who stepped up and defended the players by all means, covering up the vandalized section of the mural with notes, English flags and stickers in his/their support (calling, for example, Rashford *Hero* or *Role Model* or *Brother*, the three of them *Three Kings*, asking them to *Keep going*! and thanking them, and referring in their critical calls to the Black Lives Matter movement). The local writer, Akse P19, who did that piece very soon repainted it to its original monochrome state.

Graffiti and street art remain a "litmus paper" of the social condition, its reflection, critique and compensation. They proudly and boldly display aesthetic dissensus (subcultural graffiti) or political dissensus with the mainstream discourses and practices, complementing them. Turbulent political circumstances stimulate, by definition, strong street responses — both in terms

Above left: *Ajax Amsterdam always anti-racist*; by fans of FC Ajax Amsterdam; sticker; Utrecht, The Netherlands; 2015.

Above right: *ISC, International supporter crew of NK Nafta 1903 — Love Nafta — Hate fascism — Smash homophobia*; by *Gorgone*, fans of FC Nafta Lendava; sticker; Lendava/Lendva, Slovenia; 2014.

of radicalizing their content and in their quantity. Although I'm frequently living in or traveling through New York, one of world's Meccas of graffiti and street art subculture, I've never seen as much political graffiti as I did in the days around January 20, 2017, during the time of Donald Trump's inauguration. The city was literally covered with graffiti, stickers, posters, installations, paste-ups, murals, chalk-art and sidewalk-art pieces, fueling the anti-Trump sentiment and complementing the other forms of protest (the Women's March on Washington, mass demonstrations in New York and other American cities, internet activism, etc.). The brutal killing of George Floyd incited graffiti and street-art responses all over the world with messages like *Justice for George Floyd* or repeating his last words, *I can't breathe*. The same happened with the Black Lives Matter and #MeToo campaigns. Feminist graffiti like *I don't want flowers, I want revolution* or *Long live*

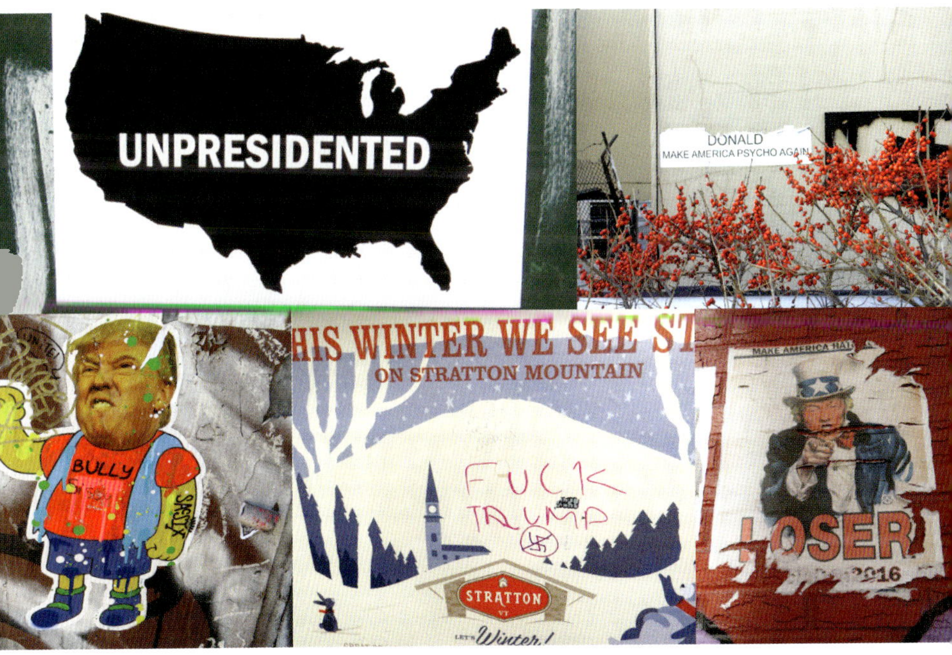

Various anti-Trump stickers, inscriptions, graffiti and wheat-paste posters; New York, USA; 2017.

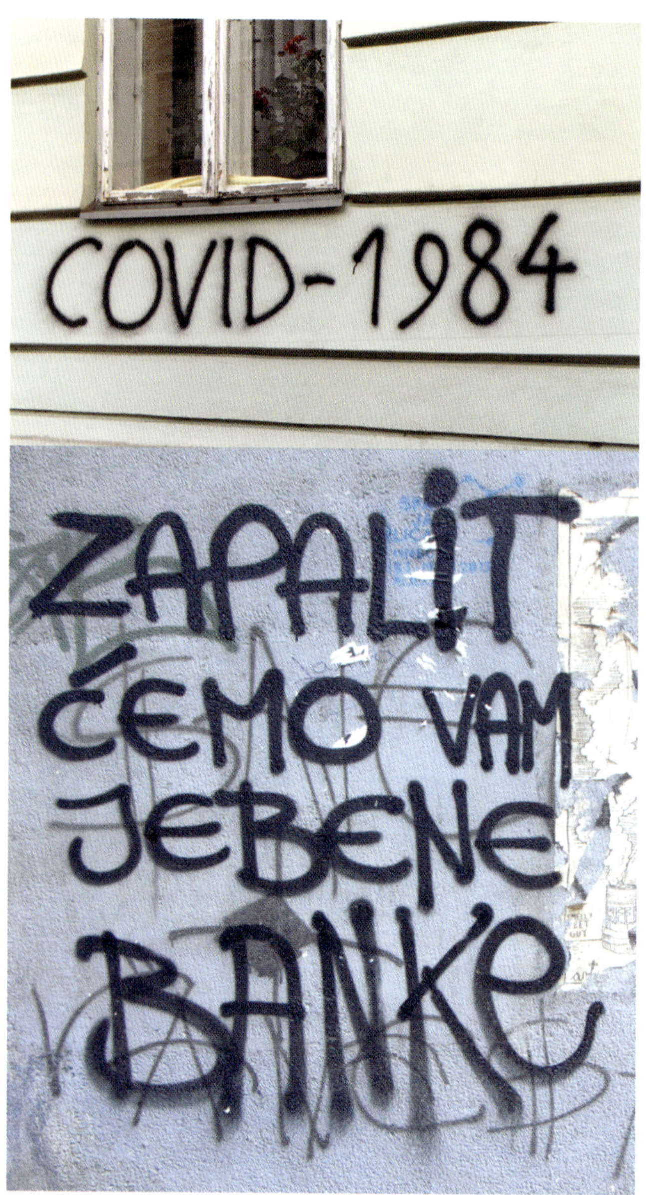

Above: *Covid-1984*; graffiti; Ljubljana, Slovenia; 2020.

Below: *Zapalit ćemo vam jebene banke* (*We'll set fire to your fucking banks!*); graffiti; Rijeka, Croatia; 2015.

Women's Day or *Women's Day is not enough* are mushrooming around March 8, as do pro- and anti-LBGTQ+ graffiti before Gay Pride events (from *All loves are equal, I don't need /Gay/ pride to walk around the city* or *No to transphobia — Transform yourself!* to adamantly against *Let's stop the LGBT revolution* or one that could be read from either side as a welcoming invitation to come out of the closet or a threat, *We are waiting for you*).

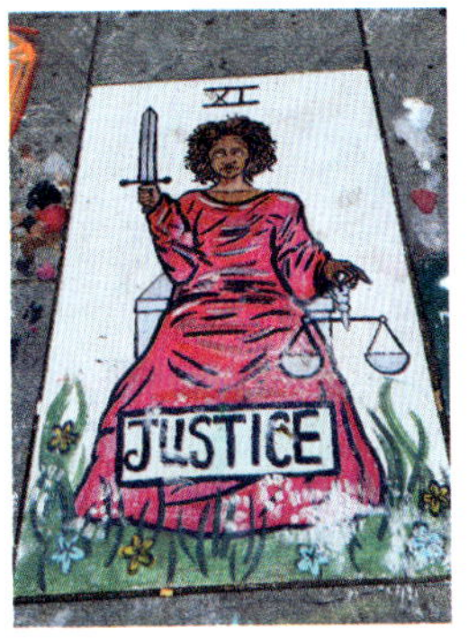

Political graffiti and stickers are preserving some cities' traditional political orientation: in the case of left-leaning Rijeka in Croatia (*Eat the rich, don't eat shit; Anti-system — For the culture of resistance and solidarity; We'll set fire to your fucking banks;* joined with number of anarchy and antifa signs in different techniques) or Genova (*Genova is antifascist; Fight fear — Destroy fascism; - /less to/ military, + /more/ hospitals*), they definitely prevail over the right-wing ones. The Covid-19 pandemic also stimulated activists with spray-cans, criticizing measures of governments and recognizing them (*Covid-1984, Fascism under the mask of corona* or *State is the real virus*). Political graffiti and street art are still in harsh competition with other media — traditional, electronic or digital — an important way to construct and reflect the social reality around us. If someone is not sure about something, if s/he wants to know more or searches for an alternative explanation, then I suggest looking to the walls of the surrounding city. The truth is out there, waiting to be seen.

Above: *Lady Justice (Tarot card XI)*; sidewalk drawing; New York, USA; 2020. Photo courtesy Seph Rodney.

Following page: *Uniti contro la repressione — Working class — Genoa CFC 1893 — I caruggi 1988* (*United against the repression — Working class — FC Genoa 1893 — I caruggi 1988* [local activist organization in Genova]); by fans of FC Genova; sticker; Genova, Italy; 2020.

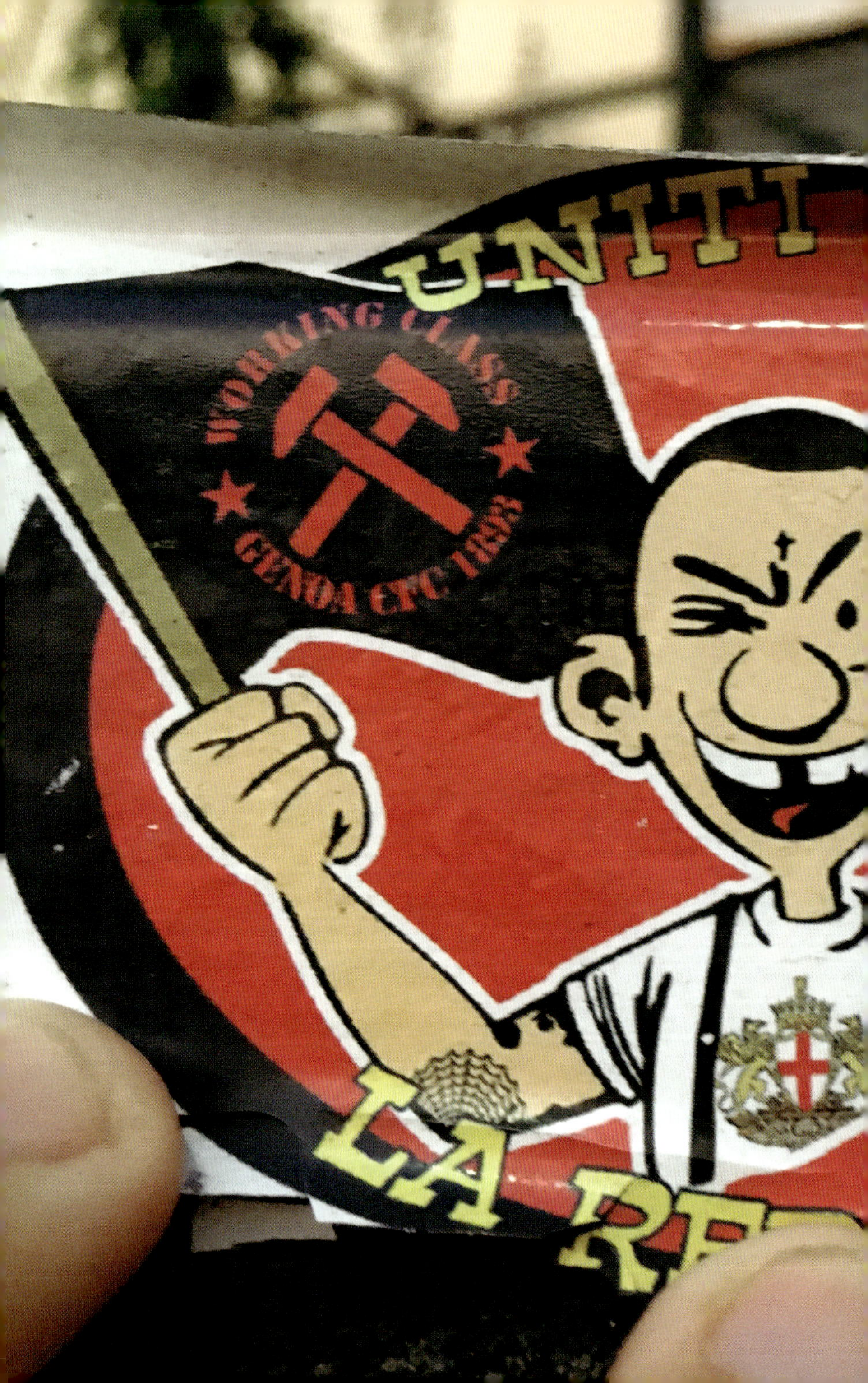

UNITI
WORKING CLASS
GENOA CFC 1893
LA RE

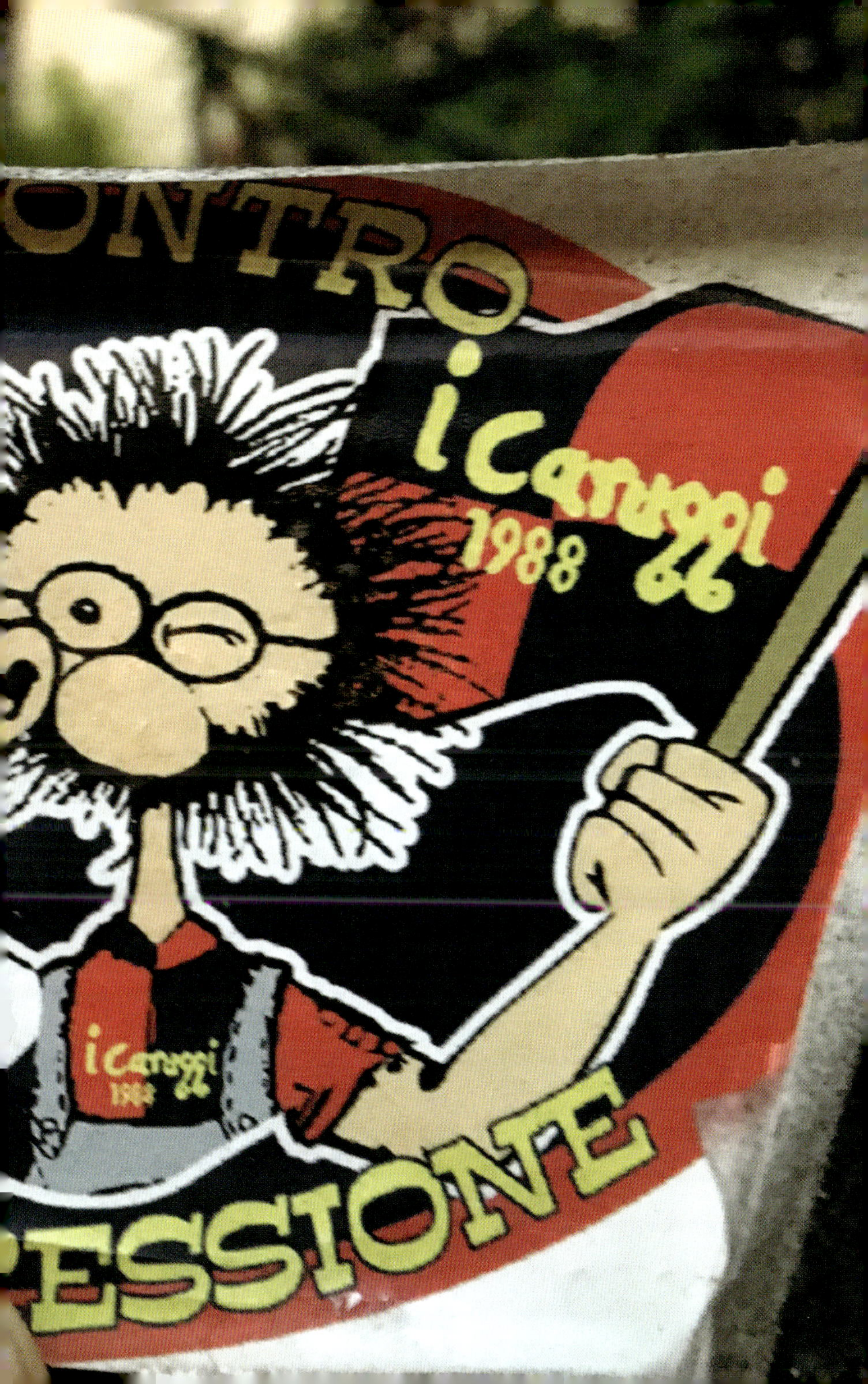
ONTRO
i Caruggi
1988
i Caruggi
1988
ESSIONE

APPENDIX: THE NEW ULTRAS' LETTERS

By Tauras Stalnionis

I remember my middle school days, when I discovered a crumbled piece of paper with a strange alphabet. It was circulating in school for some time, passing from pocket to pocket, from class to class, copied endlessly by inexperienced hands distorting the original and slowly mutating with every new copy. It was an elaborate '70s style graffiti font, and I drew my name in it. The idea of a unique typographic identity, which represents a mysterious global underground movement, sounds so exciting. By getting access to those letters, you enter the community. You become a part of an idea. From now on, there are us and all the others. To have an alphabet is not the same as having only a symbol or a list of fixed slogans. By having a typeface, you can express your own message, which is automatically approved by the whole group because you speak in their (our) voice. This is how I felt.

Now, I try to imagine how a football fan must feel. An easy way to be seen as part of the culture is to use a typeface called Ultras Liberi. With its recognizable and strong letters, nobody can doubt where the message is coming from. A text in Ultras Liberi becomes a part of the ideology, and your action becomes part of the movement. Aesthetics weaponizes the message and empowers you to turn heads. This might sound inspiring, however, the meaning of that movement, at least judging from its visual representation, remains an open question. This vaguery is because ULTRAS LIBERI letters, just like it's history, aren't precisely drawn. Just like the Austrian ART NOUVEAU (art movement) and the French ORDRE NOUVEAU (a far-right magazine), from RATA & NEGRA to BENITO MUSSOLINI, Ultras Liberi has been an exercise in collective collaboration, which openly recognizes the soft power of design even if the current version of it obviously lacks simple design skills.

The widely spread use of Ultras Liberi manifests a willingness to adopt it as a tool for *branded* visual language, but its current form poses some important challenges. First of all, the characters of the typeface aren't united; they vary in style and design logic, amalgamating different ideas and making it difficult for fans to remember exactly how certain letters look. Unfortunately, if they cannot remember, they cannot write them. This is clearly visible in letters like 𝗦 and 𝗠 (M), as well as 𝗗, 𝗔 and 𝗩 (V). Even if the intention of joining straight and curved lines is clear, most

times you see a graffiti in Ultras Liberi, these characters will be more or less modified compared with the original.

Furthermore, there is a clear ambition to achieve a dramatic, aggressive, and somehow monumental effect. The problem, though, is in proportions and stability of some of the important characters. Generally, the letters are relatively squished to be tall and narrow, which makes them appear much less serious than the sharp angles and strong occasional serifs would prefer to be perceived. The most frequently used character in most of the Latin alphabet-based languages — therefore the most important letter, 𝗘 — is swinging on its rounded base and harshly contrasts with overly monolithic 𝗛, 𝗞 and 𝗧.

Ultras Liberi invests heavily in aggressive, asymmetric sharpness like 𝗔, 𝗗, 𝗩 and 𝗝, which at first achieve its goal but at the same time create holes in words, making some letters appear in clusters, breaking phrases apart. On top of that, some characters, like 𝗗 (D), 𝗩 (V), 𝗝 (J), 𝗥 (R) and 𝗠 (M) are not clear enough, making the impression of stuttering even stronger.

Reading such aesthetically strong letters is not only an intellectual, but also a visual experience. The medium of printed or written letters is not a neutral representation of information (as attempted with Helvetica), but a message in and of itself. It brings readers from the sphere of the intellectual mind into that of the eye, subconsciously triggering bodily responses. In his essay "Eye and Mind," Maurice Merleau-Ponty describes the perception of aesthetic experience as fundamentally different from the intellectual one, making it impossible to use the methods of one to describe the other. The aesthetics of the Ultras Liberi typeface leave traces of the writer's tone of speaking, and in

2002 Ultras Liberi; by *Ultras L'emkachkhines*, fans of FC Esperance Tunisia; mural; location/date unknown; via Facebook.

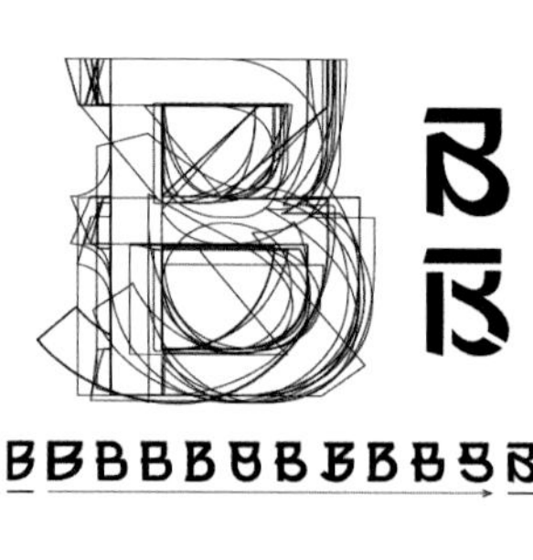
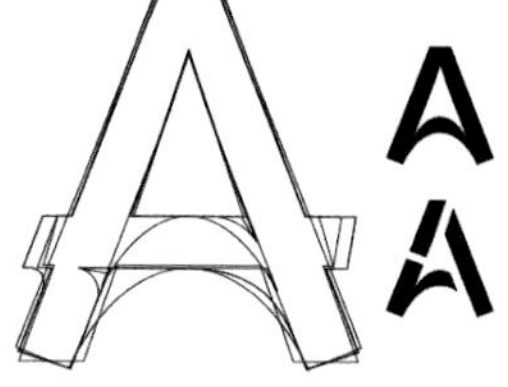
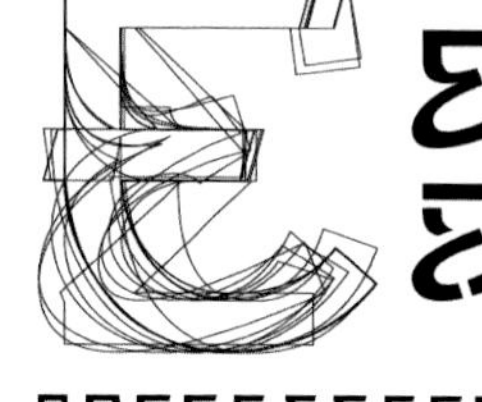
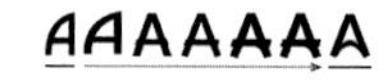
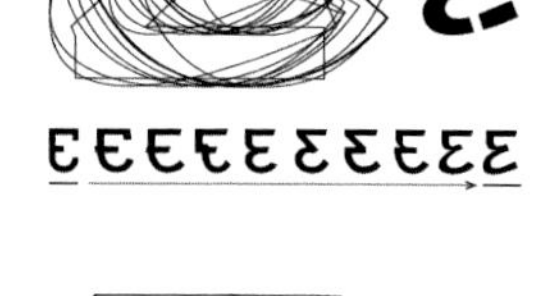
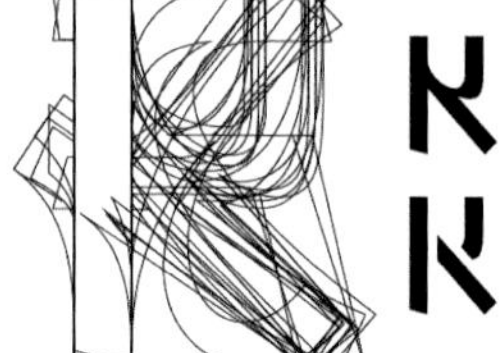
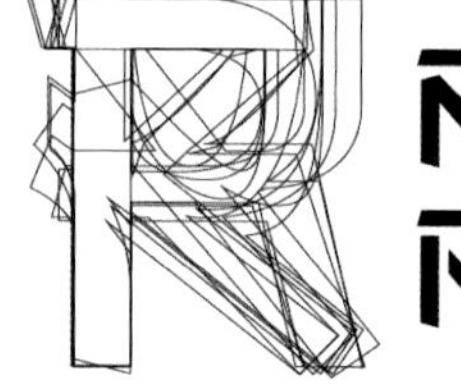
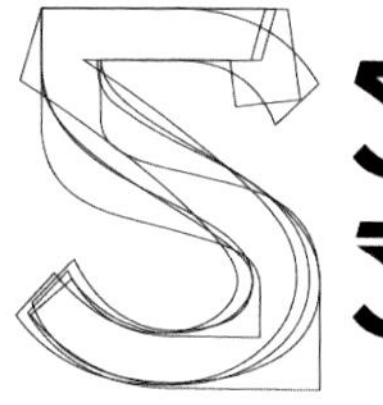

the case of public speech the confidence is crucial. From the outside, it feels as if the long collective co-creation as well as the historical burden have obscured these letters of clear aesthetic message. Given a chance to work on the design of this book, I couldn't resist but to try opening a conversation about the way written voices of football fans now and in the future could possibly look.

Ultras Liberi letters have an extreme physicality. They are not meant to be typed by fingertips softly touching a keyboard, but physically painted, sprayed, scratched, carved, and stenciled using not only hands, but the whole body. For the letters to appear in digital images, first they have to be physically marked *on* the real world. This important detail brings Ultras Liberi back to the calligraphic roots of all letters and becomes the central concept of the new version.

The flat tops of the characters and straight-curved line connections are the visual basis of the classical as well as the updated version of Ultras Liberi. The new elements are the wider and more symmetrical proportions — as in **A**, **F**, **D**, **J**, **S** and **U** . The redesign of this typeface needed to be easy to remember, so that anyone could recreate it. For that I introduce an important idea — each letter has to be written strictly in one continuous line. This will give the typeface a very specific, recognizable aesthetics, even if the proportions or details of the letters are not precise. With this primary guiding rule, the aesthetics of this updated version brand it as 'ultras'.

From the functional point of view, it is a display font, which is meant not for lengthy paragraphs but to be read in quick, bold typographic

punches. When observed from close distance, the new version
sports some additional subtle details making the characters
appear more dynamic and alive. I hoped that slight dynamism
would direct the typeface away from the monolithic extreme
political ideas and back towards football.

What is more, the diagonal cuts at the end of the new version's
horizontal tops unify letters into a "team" while the classical
version's broken serifs have divided it into separate individuals.
By removing those out-of-place serifs (on C, E, F, G, L, R, S, T,
Z as well as H and I) we can officially put the new Ultras Liberi
into the san-serif category.

Some of the new characters deserve a separate introduction. The
most important letter E, as a tribute to the classical version has
kept its unusual curved lower part. But in order not to become
an exception, this curve has been mirrored in B, C, J and S.

Another important letter, A, has brought relevant influences
from probably the most famous Ⓐ in history and became symmetrical compared with the old A. The connecting curves repeat
in H, M, W and Y. Furthermore, the new version has extended
the spectrum of Latin characters giving fans in different countries a right to write words like ŻALGIRIS, and ALINGSÅS,
BŁĘKITNI and MEZŐKÖVESDI in style.

Coming back to the functionality of Ultras Liberi, the new version has an important additional feature, a STENCIL VERSION
that allows the fans to make big banners, flags and posters easier
and cheaper. The STENCIL CHARACTERS can be printed on
several A4 sheets and traced on bigger card or plastic boards in
order to make long-lasting tools for painting big format words.
The letters are divided into smaller pieces in order to form more
bridges and make stencils stronger and longer lasting. The new
version, just like the CLASSICAL ULTRAS LIBERI, is made of only
capital characters, which allows access to the additional stencil
version by simply using Shift on the keyboard.

I saw Ultras Liberi as a kind of folk art design project, and its
open-source, free-access nature inspired me to suggest a possible
variation. In the beginning, I started with a much less ambitious
plan to clean up the existing letters that were used in the title
design of this book. But with time, I started to see its deeper
potential and decided to share my efforts with fans and provide it
to everyone for free. In order for it to appear next to the classical
version in search engines, it is named ULTRAS LIBERI SANS.

Berlin, June 2021

SELECTED LITERATURE

Adorno, Theodor W. 1973. *The Jargon of Authenticity.* Evanston, IL: Northwestern University Press.

Adorno, Theodor W. 2002. "Reconciliation under Duress." In *Aesthetics and Politics*, edited by Ernst Bloch, Georg Lukacs, Bertolt Brecht, Walter Benjamin and Theodor Adorno, 151–176. London: Verso.

Adorno, Theodor W. 2005. *Minima Moralia — Reflections from Damaged Life.* London: Verso.

Benjamin, Walter. 1977. *Understanding Brecht.* London: NLB.

Benjamin, Walter. 2007. *Illuminations.* New York: Schocken Books.

Brecht, Bertolt. 2016. *Me-ti — Book of Interventions in the Flow of Things.* London: Bloomsbury.

Caselli, Mauro; Falco, Paolo; Mattera, Gianpiero. 2021. *When the Mob Goes Silent: Uncovering the Effects of Racial Harassment through a Natural Experiment.* DEM Working Papers 1/2/21. Trento, Italy: University of Trento, Department of Economics and Management.

Chalfant, Henry, and James Prigoff. 1987. *Spraycan Art.* London: Thames and Hudson.

Cooper, Martha; Henry Chalfant. 1984. *Subway Art.* New York: Henry Holt and Company.

Čolović, Ivan. 1996. "Futbal, huligani i rat." In *Srpska strana rata — Trauma i katarza u istorijskom pamćenju,* edited by Nebojša Popov, 419—44. Belgrade: Republika.

Crommelin, Claude. 2016. *New Street Art.* Woodbridge, UK: Antique Collectors Club Dist.

Daichendt, G. James. 2017. *The Urban Canvas — Street Art Around the World.* San Francisco: Weldon Owen Inc.

Deleuze, Gilles. 1997. *Cinema 1 — The Movement-Image.* Minneapolis: University of Minnesota Press.

Deleuze, Gilles; Félix Guattari. 2005. *A Thousand Plateaus — Capitalism and Schizophrenia.* Minneapolis: University of Minnesota Press.

Djordjević, Ivan. 2015. *Antropolog medju navijačima.* Belgrade: Biblioteka XX vek.

Dobovšek, Tim. 2019. *Med miti in porazi — Zgodovina nogometa na Slovenskem 1900–1991.* Ljubljana: Tipografija.

Ghodsee, Kristen. 2017. *Red Hangover. Legacies of Twentieth Century Communism.* Durham, NC: Duke University Press.

Gueorguieva, Valentina; Goncharova, Galina; Karakusheva, Slavka. 2021. "'A Home for Our Children': The Bulgarian (Dis)illusion with Democratic Society Thirty Years Later." In *Europe Thirty Years after 1989 — Transformations of Values, Memory, and Identity,* edited by Tomas Kavaliauskas, 140-172. Leiden, Boston: Brill Rodopi.

Hadjinicolaou, Nicos. 1978. *Art History and Class Struggle.* London: Pluto Press.

Hardt, Michael, and Antonio Negri. 2004. *Multitude — War and Democracy in the Age of Empire*. New York: Penguin Press.

Jakovljević, Nebojša. 2018. *Fudbalska takmičenja južnih Slovena 1873-1941*. Subotica, Serbia: Visoka škola strukovnih studija za obrazovanje vaspitača i trenera.

Kuhn, Gabriel. 2011. *Soccer vs. the State — Tackling Football and Radical Politics*. Oakland, CA: PM Press.

Lalić Dražen. 2011. *Torcida: pogled iznutra*. Zagreb: Profil.

Lewisohn, Cedar. 2011. *Abstract Graffiti*. London: Merrell Publishers.

Macdonald, Nancy. 2001. *The Graffiti Subculture — Youth, Masculinity and Identity in London and New York*. London: Palgrave Macmillan.

MacMaster, Neil. 2001. *Racism in Europe 1870–2000*. Houndmills, Basingstoke, Hampshire and New York: Palgrave.

Montague, James. 2020. *1312: Among the Ultras: A Journey with the World's Most Extreme Fans*. London: Penguin Random House.

Mouffe, Chantal. 2000. *The Democratic Paradox*. London: Verso.

Nicolau, Felix. 2016. *Only Connect. A Passage from Modernism to Postmodernism*. Bucharest: Editura frACTalia.

O'Connor, Robert. 2021. *Blood and Circuses — A Football Journey Through Europe's Rebel Republics*. London: Biteback Publishing.

Perry, Marvin; Schweitzer, Frederick M. (eds.). 2008. *Antisemitic Myths — A Historical and Contemporary Anthology.* Bloomington and Indianapolis: Indiana University Press.

Plesch, Véronique. 2015. "Beyond Art History: Graffiti on Frescoes." In *Understanding Graffiti — Multidisciplinary Studies from Prehistory to the Present*, edited by Troy Lovata and Elizabeth Olton, 47–57. London: Routledge.

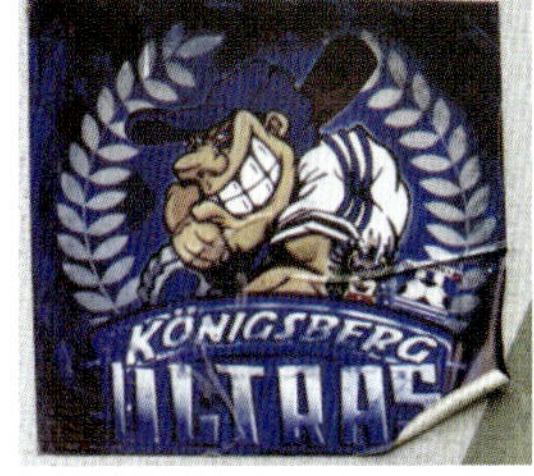

Poliakov, Leon. 1999. *Il mito ariano — Le radici del razzismo e dei nazionalismi.* Rome: Editori Riuniti.

Rancière, Jacques. 2004. *The Politics of Aesthetics.* London: Continuum.

Rancière, Jacques. 2010. *Dissensus — On Politics and Aesthetics.* London: Continuum.

Reynolds, Robert. 1975. *Magic Symbols — A Photographic Study on Graffiti.* Portland, OR: Graphic Arts Center Publishing Co.

Sindbæk, Tea. 2010. "Football Commentators as Historians: Uses of History and Serbian Club Football, 1990–2005." *Kultura polis (Novi Sad)* 7 (13–14): 535–547.

Sindbæk, Tea. 2013. "A Croatian champion with a Croatian name: national identity and uses of history in Croatian football culture — the case of Dinamo Zagreb." *Sport in Society* 16 (8): 1009–24.

Smith, Martin; Smith, Viv; Ward, Patrick. 2010. *The EDL (English Defence League) Unmasked.* Oxford, UK: Information Press Ltd.

Sulima, Roch. 2005. *Antropologija svakodnevnice.* Belgrade: Biblioteka XX vek.

Thornton, Phil. 2012. *Casuals — Football, Fighting and Fashion: The Story of a Terrace Cult.* Preston, UK: Milo Books Ltd.

Ugrešić, Dubravka. 2008. *Muzej bezuvjetne predaje.* Belgrade: Fabrika knjiga.

Verdery, Katherine. 1996. *What Was Socialism, and What Comes Next?.* Princeton, NJ: Princeton University Press.

Vermeulen, Timotheus; Van den Akker, Robin. 2010. "Notes on Metamodernism." *Journal of Aesthetics and Culture* (2): n.p.

Vrcan, Srđan. 2003. *Nogomet — politika — nasilje. Ogledi iz sociologije nogometa.* Zagreb: Naklada Jesenski i Turk, Hrvatsko sociološko društvo.

Wolff, Janet. 1994. *The Social Production of Art.* London: Macmillan, Redwood City, CA: Stanford University Press.

Zaimakis, Yiannis. 2018. "Football fan culture and politics in modern Greece: the process of fandom radicalization during the austerity era." *Soccer & Society,* 19:2, 252–270.

Zirin, Dave. 2005. *What's My Name, Fool? Sports and Resistance in the United States.* Chicago: Haymarket Books.

Žižek, Slavoj. 1987. *Jezik, ideologija, Slovenci.* Ljubljana: Delavska enotnost.

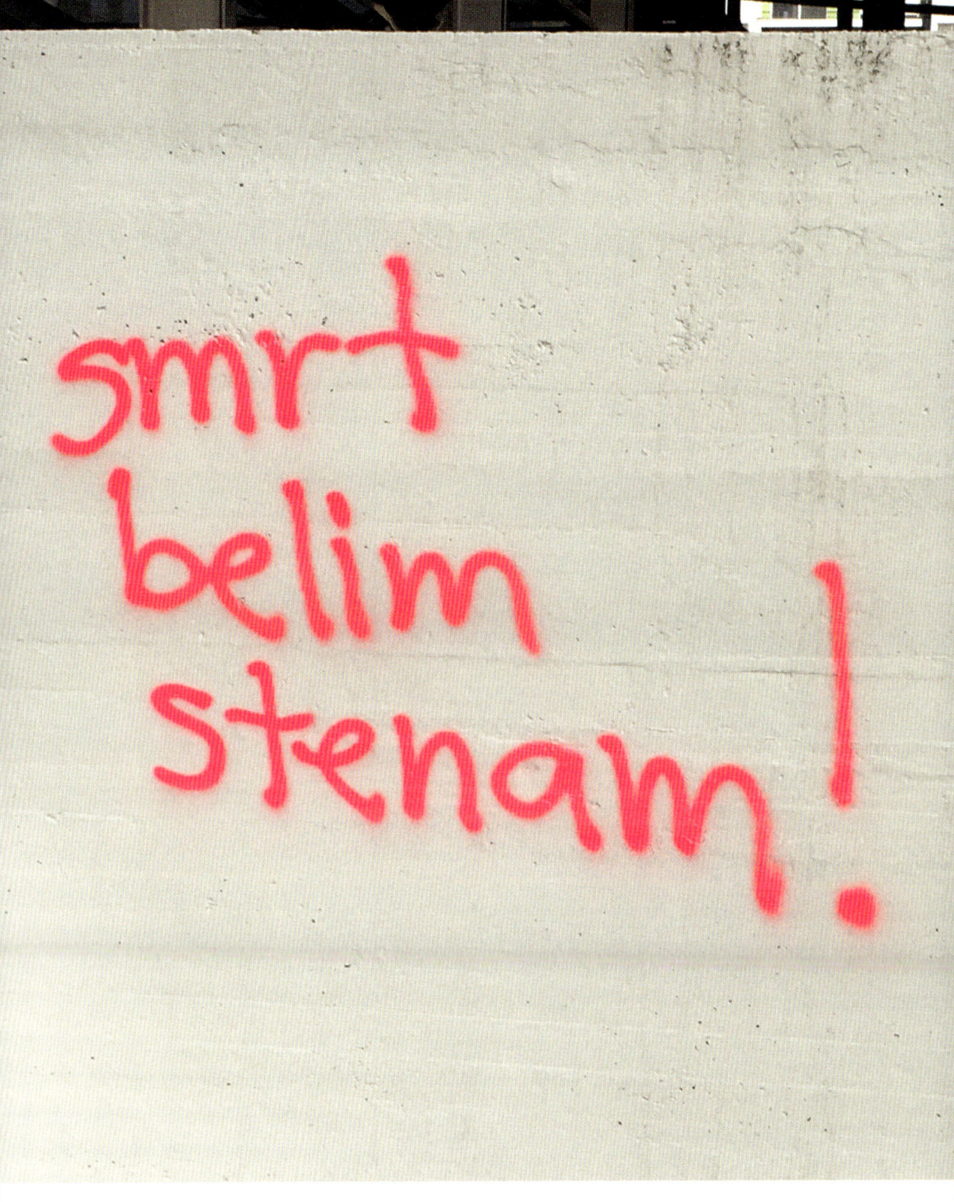

Prior page: *Königsberg Ultras*; by fans of FC Baltika Kaliningrad, Russia; sticker; Prague, Czech Republic; 2016.

Opposite: *Bad Humans Produce Style*; sticker; New York, USA; 2019.

Above: *Smrt belim stenam!* (*Death to white walls!*); graffiti; Ljubljana, Slovenia; 2021.

THANKS

My sincere appreciation and profound gratitude goes to everyone who inspired, supported or helped me in my adventures trying to document, analyze and understand the fascinating and intriguing world of graffiti and street art. I also want to acknowledge the creative potential and persistent efforts of all the anonymous writers, ultra fans, graffiti writers and street artists everywhere my research curiosity and my camera led me, and for their commitment to their work.

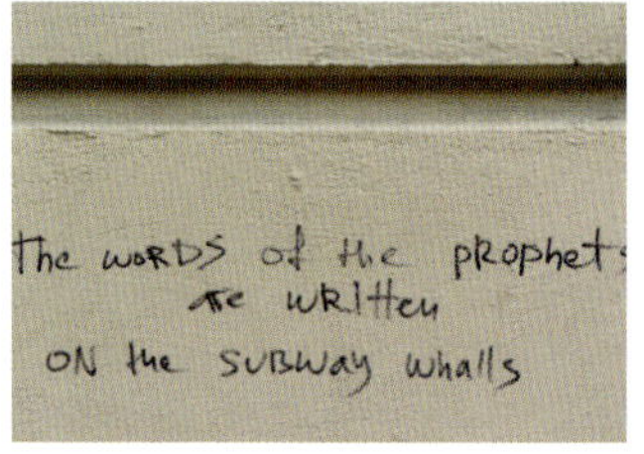

I also warmly thank the publisher of DoppelHouse Press, Carrie Paterson for her initiative and for all of her incentive and prompt editorial work, and to book designer Tauras Stalnionis for his sensitivity and visual empathy for the topic. We never met in person, but we collaborated together as if we had known each other for ages. It was a privilege for me to work with them.

I dedicate this book to my parents Silva and Slavko, who taught me, without big words, but through their own lived experiences and by their own examples, the basics of everything really important for me: solidarity, social justice, antifascism, and sensibility for the edges.

The words of the prophets are written on the subway whalls; inscription; St. Petersburg, Russia; 2016.

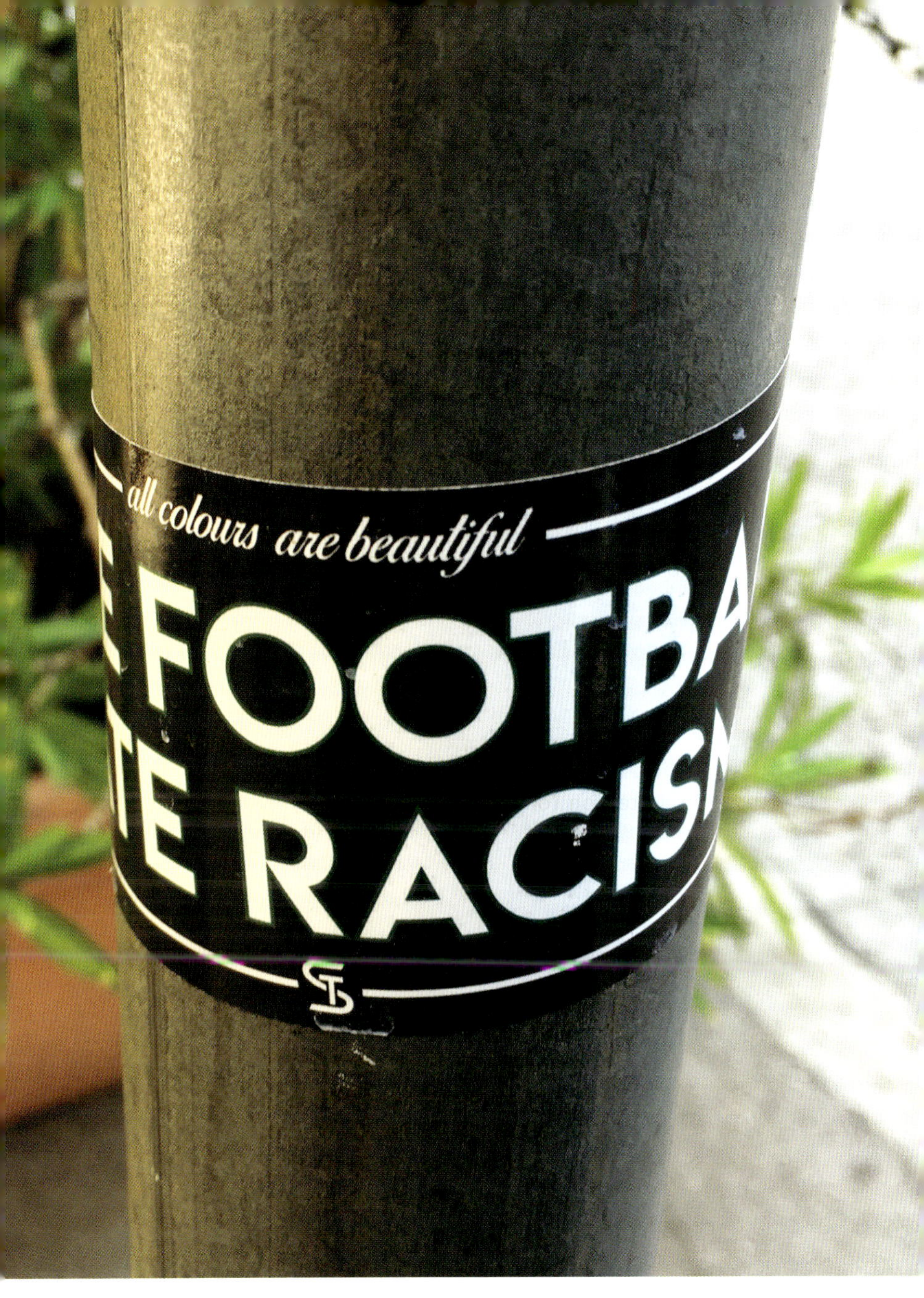

Love football, hate racism — All colours are beautiful; by unidentified ultras; sticker; Trieste, Italy; 2018.

ABOUT THE AUTHOR

Dr. Mitja Velikonja is a Professor for Cultural Studies and head of the Center for Cultural and Religious Studies at University of Ljubljana, Slovenia. The main areas of his research include contemporary Central-European and Balkan political ideologies, subcultures and graffiti culture, collective memory and post-socialist nostalgia. His monographs include *Rock'n'Retro — New Yugoslavism in Contemporary Slovenian Music* (Sophia, Ljubljana, 2013), *Titostalgia — A Study of Nostalgia for Josip Broz* (Peace Institute, Ljubljana, 2008), *Eurosis — A Critique of the New Eurocentrism* (Peace Institute, Ljubljana, 2005) and *Religious Separation and Political Intolerance in Bosnia-Herzegovina* (TAMU Press, 2003). He is co-author of the book *Celestial Yugoslavia: Interaction of Political Mythologies and Popular Culture* (XX vek, Belgrade, 2012), and co-editor and co-author of the books *Post-Yugoslavia — New Cultural and Political Perspectives* (Palgrave, 2014) and *Yugoslavia from a Historical Perspective* (HCHR, Belgrade, 2017).

He was a full-time visiting professor at Jagiellonian University in Krakow (2002 and 2003), at Columbia University in New York (2009 and 2014), at University of Rijeka (2015), at New York Institute in St. Petersburg (2015 and 2016), at Yale University (2020), Fulbright visiting researcher in Philadelphia (2004/2005), and visiting researcher at The Netherlands Institute of Advanced Studies (2012) and at the Remarque Institute of the New York University (2018).

For his achievements he has received four national and one international award (Erasmus EuroMedia Award by the European Society for Education and Communication, 2008). His last monograph *Post-Socialist Political Graffiti in the Balkans and Central Europe* (Routledge, 2020) was translated into Serbian and will also be translated into Slovenian, Macedonian and Albanian, and was awarded and honored as one of the most important scientific achievements of University of Ljubljana for the year 2020.

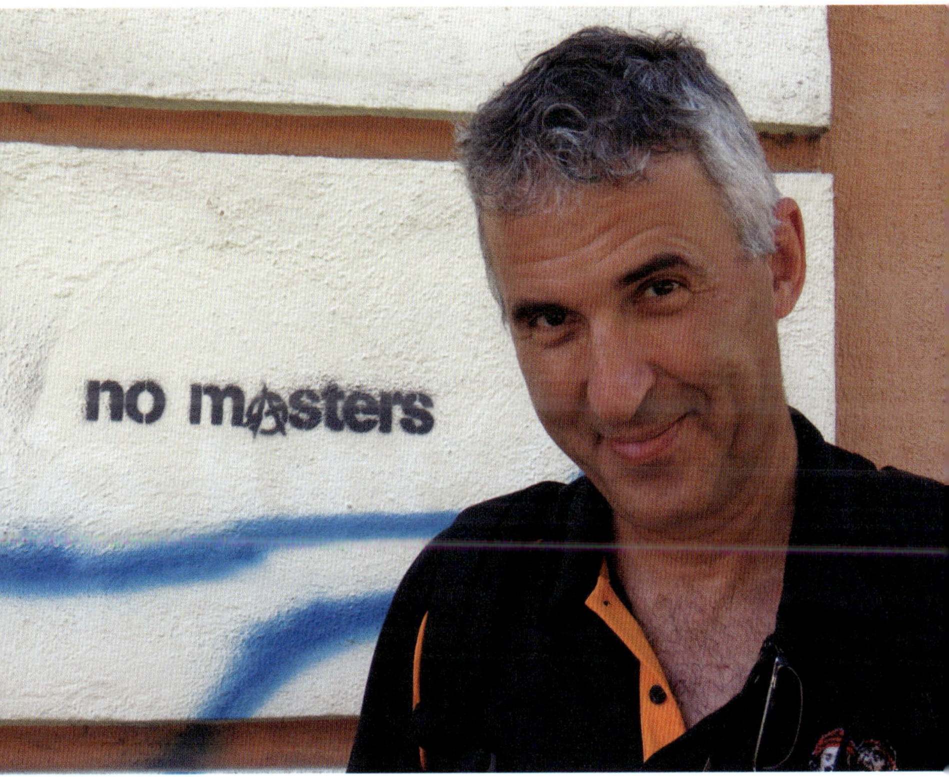

Above: The author doing fieldwork; 2017.

Following page left: *Sotto cultura Ultras (Ultras subculture)*; by unidentified ultras; sticker; Sibiu, Romania; 2017.

Following page right: *Ultras zone — Fakes piss off!*; by unidentified ultras; sticker; Piran/Pirano, Slovenia; 2020.

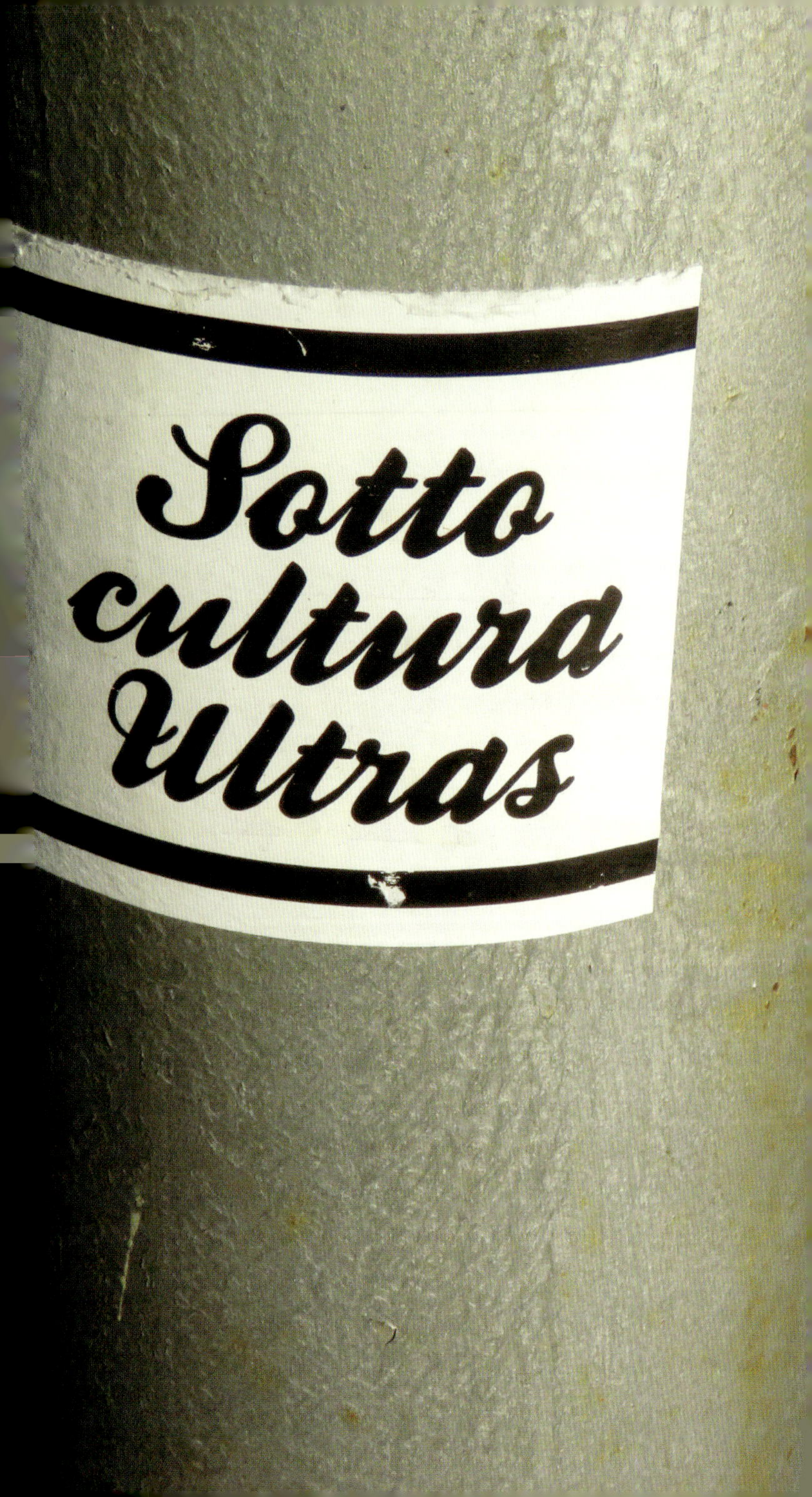

Sotto
cultura
Ultras

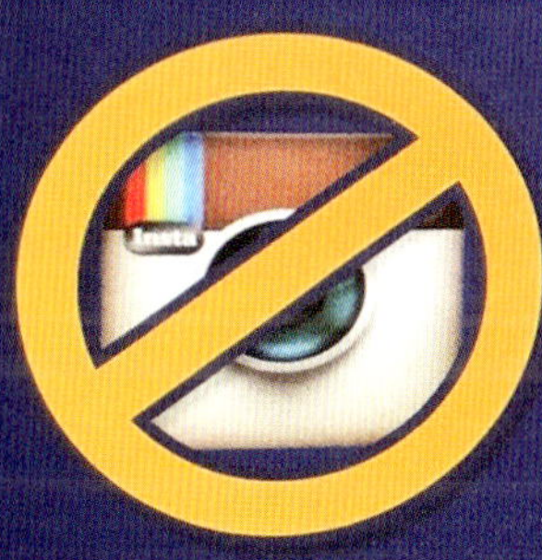
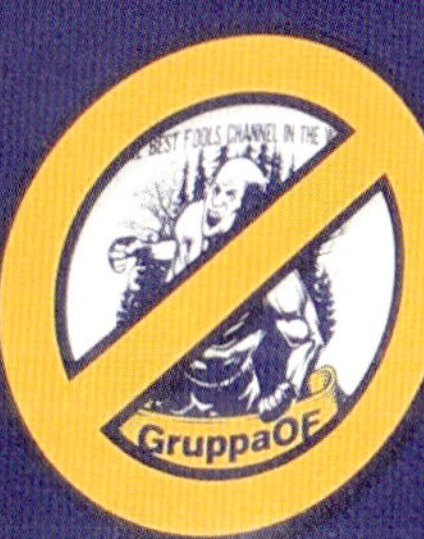
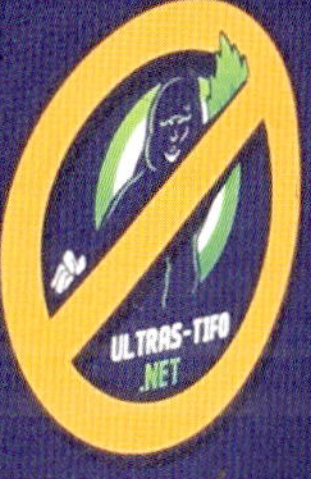

ULTRAS ★ ZONE
FAKES PISS OFF!
GruppaOF
ULTRAS-TIFO
.NET